Producing Dance

A Collaborative Art

Robin Kish
Wilson Mendieta
Jennifer Backhaus
Marc Jordan Ameel
Samantha Waugh
Kerri Canedy
Todd Canedy

Library of Congress Cataloging-in-Publication Data

Names: Kish, Robin, author. | Mendieta, Wilson, 1973- author. | Backhaus,
  Jennifer, 1971- author. | Ameel, Marc J., 1977- author. | Waugh,
  Samantha, 1996- author. | Canedy, Kerri, 1975- author. | Canedy, Todd
  P., 1969- author.
Title: Producing dance : a collaborative art / Robin Kish, Wilson
  Mendieta, Jennifer Backhaus, Marc Jordan Ameel, Samantha Waugh, Kerri
  Canedy, Todd Canedy.
Description: First Edition. | Champaign, IL : Human Kinetics, [2024] |
  Includes bibliographical references and index.
Identifiers: LCCN 2022035867 (print) | LCCN 2022035868 (ebook) | ISBN
  9781718207868 (Paperback) | ISBN 9781718207875 (epub) | ISBN
  9781718207882 (pdf)
Subjects: LCSH: Dance--Production and direction.
Classification: LCC GV1782 .K58 2024 (print) | LCC GV1782 (ebook) | DDC
  792.8/2--dc23/eng/20220825
LC record available at https://lccn.loc.gov/2022035867
LC ebook record available at https://lccn.loc.gov/2022035868

ISBN: 978-1-7182-0786-8 (print)

Copyright © 2024 by Human Kinetics, Inc.

Human Kinetics supports copyright. Copyright fuels scientific and artistic endeavor, encourages authors to create new works, and promotes free speech. Thank you for buying an authorized edition of this work and for complying with copyright laws by not reproducing, scanning, or distributing any part of it in any form without written permission from the publisher. You are supporting authors and allowing Human Kinetics to continue to publish works that increase the knowledge, enhance the performance, and improve the lives of people all over the world.

The online learning content that accompanies this product is delivered on HK*Propel*, **HKPropel.HumanKinetics.com**. You agree that you will not use HK*Propel* if you do not accept the site's Privacy Policy and Terms and Conditions, which detail approved uses of the online content.

To report suspected copyright infringement of content published by Human Kinetics, contact us at **permissions@hkusa.com**. To request permission to legally reuse content published by Human Kinetics, please refer to the information at **https://US.Human Kinetics.com/pages/permissions-information**.

The web addresses cited in this text were current as of July 2022, unless otherwise noted.

Acquisitions Editor: Bethany J. Bentley; **Developmental Editor:** Jacqueline Eaton Blakley; **Managing Editor:** Anna Lan Seaman; **Copyeditor:** Michelle Horn; **Proofreader:** Leigh Keylock; **Permissions Manager:** Laurel Mitchell; **Graphic Designer:** Dawn Sills; **Cover Designer:** Keri Evans; **Cover Design Specialist:** Susan Rothermel Allen; **Photograph (cover):** Jerri Li, Backhausdance (2019) performing *Scene Unseen* choreographed by Dwight Rhoden; **Photographs (interior):** © Human Kinetics, unless otherwise noted; **Photo Asset Manager:** Laura Fitch; **Photo Production Manager:** Jason Allen; **Senior Art Manager:** Kelly Hendren; **Illustrations:** © Human Kinetics, unless otherwise noted; **Production:** Walsworth

Printed in the United States of America   10 9 8 7 6 5 4 3 2 1

The paper in this book was manufactured using responsible forestry methods.

Human Kinetics
1607 N. Market Street
Champaign, IL 61820
USA

United States and International
Website: **US.HumanKinetics.com**
Email: info@hkusa.com
Phone: 1-800-747-4457

Canada
Website: **Canada.HumanKinetics.com**
Email: info@hkcanada.com

E8371

Contents

Preface vii

Acknowledgments xi

Part I Vision: Balancing Artistic Content and Production Realities

1 Vision and Collaboration in Dance Performance 3

Early Dance Performances and Vision 4

Performance Spaces 5

Design Elements 6

Summary 12

2 Artistic Vision 13

Inspiration and Purpose Tied to Artistic Vision 14

Audience 16

Performance Spaces 17

Research 21

Creative Brief 22

Summary 27

3 Logistical Considerations 29

SWOT Analysis 30

SWOT Application 34

Financial Structure 35

Collaborative Organizational Structures 38

Arts Administration 40

Summary 47

4 Getting Started 49

Venues 50

Funding 51

Visibility 55

Summary 60

Part II Process: Clarity Through Creation, Collaboration, and Conversations

5 Collaborators
63

Organization of Roles 64
Dance Collaborators 65
Production Collaborators 68
Defining a Collaborative Language 79
Production Meetings 80
Summary 82

6 Creation in the Studio
83

Auditions 84
Rehearsals 89
Summary 92

7 Stage, Scenery, Props, and Lighting
93

Stages 94
Scenery and Props 98
Lighting 101
Summary 108

8 Sound, Digital Media, Costumes, and Makeup
109

Sound 110
Digital Media 115
Costume and Makeup 117
Summary 123

Part III Integration: Blending Vision and Process

9 Production Timeline
127

Production Calendar 128
Milestones 129
Production Process 131
Pulling the Timelines Together 135
Creating a Gantt Chart 136
Production Meetings 139
Summary 141

10 Production Scope and Audience Experience
143

Production Scope 144
Audience Experience 149
Summary 153

11 Integrating Elements Onstage 155

Stage Considerations   156
Scenery and Props   158
Lighting   161
Sound   165
Digital Media   166
Costumes   166
Summary   168

Part IV   Culmination: Performance and Beyond

12 Production Week 171

Timeline   173
Cue-to-Cue Rehearsal   173
Technical (Tech) Rehearsal   176
Dress Rehearsal   180
Expecting the Unexpected   180
Summary   181

13 Performance 183

Front of House   184
Backstage Crew   186
Performers   187
Strike   189
Summary   191

14 Postmortem 193

Technical Production Perspective   194
Choreographer and Artistic Perspectives   197
Mediators   198
Feedback   199
Now What?   200

Glossary   203
Bibliography   209
Index   213
About the Authors   219

Preface

A performance that successfully brings an artistic vision to life can inspire, excite, and emotionally touch an audience. This fleeting event is the product of weeks, months, and sometimes years of work by a group of dedicated creators. Though the idea for a performance may stem from just one person, it will almost always be brought to life by a team of experts: choreographers, dancers, and design and production specialists. Each expert will approach the production with their own field at the forefront of their minds. Because of this, collaboration and communication are the keys to any successful production. By recognizing the common goals across disciplines and acknowledging misunderstandings, *Producing Dance* provides a realistic approach to effectively navigate the creative process from start to finish.

As a reader, you may be one of the multiple collaborators involved in producing dance or the person wearing many hats in the creative process. You may be the artistic visionary: dancer, choreographer, and artistic director. You also may be one of many design and production collaborators creating lighting, sets, costumes, and sound or someone leading the administrative or onsite production team. Regardless of your role, you are vital to the dance production field, and this book recognizes the value of the wide range of voices involved in a performance. By centering around collaboration, this text gives artists the tools they need to build a dance production that not only accomplishes its artistic goal but also fully realizes each voice.

Producing Dance is a comprehensive toolbox to draw from while creating any type of dance production. Like other dance production texts, it covers the essential production components. However, this book provides an even deeper understanding by focusing on how these elements relate to each other and to the core vision of a project. It leads a creator sequentially through every layer of a dance production: from the initial vision, through the collaborative process, into the weeds of integrating the vision and process, and finally to the comprehensive sequence of what happens just before and during the actual performance. Along the way, it gives the reader a behind-the-scenes look at pitfalls and successes, and it provides firsthand knowledge from different production collaborators. By the end of this book, you will have discovered the many options available to you in a production setting and be able to choose which tool is needed at the appropriate time.

Taking a creation from an idea to a fully produced performance is a daunting task, and this book shows how the production elements uniquely serve the vision. If you don't have a clear understanding of all production aspects, your brilliant choreographic idea could fall short when brought to stage because you didn't have the focus on the design and production elements that serve the vision best. Additionally, when misunderstandings, competing ideas, or other problems arise from a lack of communication, the final product suffers. By working sequentially through the full scope of a dance production, identifying the tools that will serve your own vision most successfully, and keeping collaboration at the heart of it, you will be able to keep the realistic multifaceted flow of a production in mind while still making the gigantic task of producing dance feel manageable.

The information is presented in the following four parts:

> Part I, Vision: Balancing Artistic Content and Production Realities

> Part II, Process: Clarity Through Creation, Collaboration, and Conversations

> Part III, Integration: Blending Vision and Process

> Part IV, Culmination: Performance and Beyond

In part I we begin by exploring how artistic vision and purpose have driven performances throughout history (chapter 1). In chapters 2, 3, and 4 we consider how a creator can intentionally craft their own vision while considering and reconciling the artistic and logistic parts of that vision. Part II dives into the collaborative process. We meet the dance and production collaborators that can be involved in a production (chapter 5) and explore the basics of creation in the studio (chapter 6) and creation with the production team (chapters 7 and 8). In part III we learn how to integrate our vision with the creative process by creating a production timeline (chapter 9), aligning production scope and audience experience with a vision (chapter 10), and blending production elements with a vision onstage (chapter 11). Finally, in part IV we address the performance itself and learn how a production week (chapter 12), performance (chapter 13), and postmortem (chapter 14) can integrate production elements with the intended artistic vision and create a successful production.

The chapters within each part include examples of successful collaborations, anecdotal tips for communicating, and templates supporting the entire process.

Although the final performance may be the ultimate goal when creating a dance production, the work that goes into creating this performance on the front end is much more extensive and complex than the performance itself. In figure 1 you can see an overview of this process that makes the frontloading of work evident. If you work hard on the front end of the process while you create your vision and lead the process of collaboration and integration, the performance will fall into place and be seamless, easy, and enjoyable. With this book as your guide, each step of the production process is made clear, and your vision will come to life while being supported by the great collaborations you develop along the way.

Students who have purchased this text have access to extra online resources for learning through HK*Propel*. As you work through the book's chapters you will be cued to visit HK*Propel* to complete assignments that challenge you to apply the chapter's content and to try on perspectives of multiple roles in a production. In addition to assignments, the student resource includes vocabulary flash card exercises and templates and samples of working dance production documents. Instructors adopting the text have access to a test bank with questions testing content from every chapter, a presentation package with PowerPoint guides to lecturing on each chapter, and an instructor guide with additional projects, questions, and resources. The instructor and student resources enrich the learning process with content designed by the textbook's authors, all of whom have worked in dance production and dance teaching for many years.

Dance is a living art form, from the moving parts of an artistic and logistic vision to the active collaboration that integrates production components successfully, to the dynamic performance itself and growth beyond. This approach makes this book a necessary addition to the library of any collaborator working in the field of dance production. This book and supplemental materials are meant to be a constant guide to support the collaborative process, keep the project on track, solve problems when things go sideways, and facilitate your team's journey toward a performance that fully reflects its artistic vision.

Preface ix

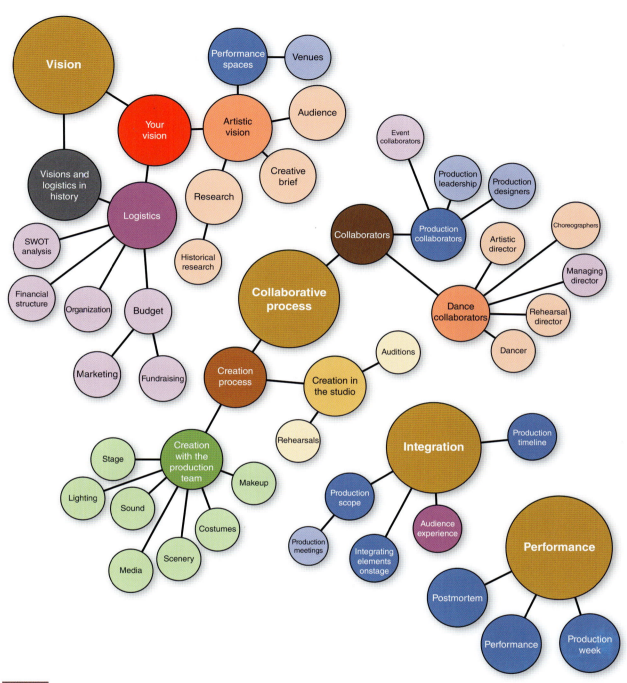

Figure 1 The work of creating a performance begins with vision and requires collaborative and integrative work throughout.

Acknowledgments

In March of 2020 when the COVID-19 pandemic shut the world down, we had choices to make about what to do with our time. As educators working in the arts, our production schedules had been completely thrown off, and we were all being asked to pivot overnight. As choreographers, company directors, theatre managers, and designers, we found that collaboration now more than ever was at the heart of our artistic practice. We took advantage of video meeting platforms and our flipped schedules to come together to discuss the one aspect of our artistic lives most affected by the pandemic: producing dance. Thus the idea for this collaborative project was born. Two years later, as we prepare to release this product and reflect on the journey, we realize we could not have reached this point without the support of our family and friends.

Keith, Cameron, and Riley Kish, thank you for supporting me and keeping me going through yet another project. Cameron, I am grateful for your photography and artistic vision.

—Robin Kish

Steven Sofia, thank you for your unconditional love and support. You are an inspiration!

—Wilson Mendieta

Mike Kerr, thank you for your unwavering support, love, and passion for the art form of dance. To all the Backhausdance team, thank you for your support, collaboration, and artistry as we continue to create and present dances together.

—Jennifer Backhaus

The most important things my mentors have taught me are about relationships, the foundation of collaboration: Joan Colson showed me joy and peace; Steve Gonella, kindness; Walter Wolfe, goodness; John and Lisa Bishop, gentleness; Chuck Meecham, patience; Jonathan Reed, self-control; Woody and Joy Ameel, faithfulness; and first, God showed me Love.

—Marc Ameel

Thank you to Ethan Gregory, Sophia Lang, my family, and my entire support system for your constant encouragement and support for my work and well-being. I'd also like to thank and dedicate my work to Pamela Nowak for your constant inspiration, influence, and loving support and enthusiasm in every endeavor.

—Samantha Waugh

Jane Hyde Ling, Ted Canedy, Linda and Donn Underwood, and Parker, Jackson, and Taylor Canedy: our family is everything, and we love you for your never-ending support. Thank you to my mentor and friend Craig (CB) Brown.

—Kerri and Todd Canedy

Thank you also to Chapman University, SUNY Potsdam, St. Lawrence University, Human Kinetics, and our editors. When you have a great team of collaborators and a support system, anything is possible.

Part I

Vision: Balancing Artistic Content and Production Realities

The creation process starts with a vision, the seed of the performance. Throughout history, artists' creative visions have evolved and paved the way for the complexity of our visions today. As a creator, it's your job to make sure your vision is clear both on the artistic side, making sure the ideas behind it are full, and on the logistic side, ensuring the tools are in place to make it happen. These two work together to drive both the reason and the ability to produce a show.

The chapters in part I explore the ways the vision informs the production of a creative work. Chapter 1 provides insight into the historical creation of dance productions and collaborations and shows how the expansion and development of visions over time have advanced our ability to bring complex visions to life in productions today. In chapter 2, we learn how to articulate the seed of our artistic vision and identify the audience, venue, and performance mode that serves it best. Once the artistic goal is established and clearly communicated, chapter 3 shows how to evaluate the strengths and weaknesses of the vision, its organizational structure, and its financial capabilities to ensure that the vision is brought to life with the most potential for success. After the artistic goals and logistic necessities have been identified, it's time to refine your realistic vision. Chapter 4 takes you through vital action items like booking a venue, fundraising, and marketing to ensure the logistic reality of your project can match your artistic goals. This chapter also explains the details and value of production meetings, necessary collaborative components of any production. Effective collaboration will ultimately allow the creator and production team to move forward with a clear action plan.

Vision and Collaboration in Dance Performance

1

Key Terms

collaboration
dance
designer
deux ex machina
orchestra
periaktoi
production
proscenium
skene
theatre
theatron

LEARNING OBJECTIVES

After reading this chapter, you will be able to do the following:

- Identify how dance and production elements support each other in producing dance
- Appreciate the intrinsic need for collaboration throughout history to support the performing arts
- Understand the historical reasons for using makeup, lighting, costumes, and performance space to clarify and support each performance
- Recognize how producing dance has evolved to challenge audience expectations, create new opportunities for choreographers, and provoke the imagination of designers and production teams

Dance is a form of communication and art that involves the human body in movement. Improvising, choreographing, comparing and contrasting, refining, interpreting, practicing, rehearsing, and sometimes performing are ways the moving body can be expressive. **Production** is the act of using technical elements such as costumes, lighting, music, physical and virtual space, publicity, and audience engagement to amplify the unique talents of the performing artists. Producing dance requires integrating production elements and artistic components. That integration occurring through **collaboration** is what makes a performance powerful.

Collaboration describes the process of two or more people working together to create something. Without collaboration in dance production, a choreographer's idea and work is likely to remain in the studio and never be witnessed by an outside audience. Through the creative process, choreographers collaborate with other production and design professionals and will find their work taking new and exciting directions. Throughout history, collaborations have spawned some of the most powerful cultural dance forms and iconic professional dance works. An artistic performance that lacks collaboration and an intentional use of production elements may be missing context or tone and fall short of its communicative potential.

Dance production books typically jump directly into the details of venue, lighting, and costumes and ignore the rich cultural roots and evolution of bringing dance to an audience. This book begins by exploring the history of how dancers, choreographers, and **designers** have collaborated to produce dances for audiences. The forms of collaboration and vision have evolved through the years, but the fundamental need to share an artistic vision with an audience has remained the same. So how are we able to do what we do? What came before? Who and what created the path that leads us to being able to create an entire text dedicated to producing dance?

Dance and production have always been linked—sometimes loosely and sometimes inextricably. Cultures worldwide have brought dance and production elements together to serve common needs. Whether it be using elaborate makeup and costumes to signify a character, having torches or candlelight to illuminate performers in the evening, or creating a sacred performing space where the audience or community knew magic was about to occur, these elements consistently enhanced the artistic purpose of each performance. From storytelling to sacred and social purposes, dance as a cultural experience has been an important part of human existence. We'll explore examples throughout history of the beauty that emerges from these experiences when dance and production collaborate.

Early Dance Performances and Vision

The impulse to dance may have existed as far back as early primates, before *Homo sapiens* became a species, when dance was used to communicate and bond socially (Frederick 2019). Before the power of speech or any written forms of communication, our ancestors used movement and actions to portray thoughts, feelings, and emotions; convey danger; and express early spiritual beliefs. Each of these motives is still present in dance and performance, and the performance forms and styles that came from them continue to be important culturally and communicatively. Many historians studying the

A dancer entertains a princess at court.

evolution of early human civilizations agree that dance forms, whether they be social, spiritual, recreational, or festive, played a key developmental role in these societies (Dils and Albright 2001).

Dance is an important method of communication. The natural human desire for storytelling, religious or secular, is always present. Some stories and exchanges evolved over time and became the first staged performances. Often, the performing group or cultural leaders chose performance spaces with an intentional audience or social aim in mind. For example, in Bali, temples, also called *pura*, had three courtyards where three different types of dance were performed. Production elements such as props, scenery, costumes, and music became tools to help tell a story, enhance a character, honor religious teachings, and so much more.

Lighting became necessary to view the performers at night and inevitably began affecting the tone of the performance. In other words, production elements developed from the performance requirements and continued to grow as the art form evolved. As the fundamental need to communicate through movement and performance expanded and began specializing, production elements became defining components of different styles, eras, and genres of dance and performance. Each element brought something unique, and the performative act and production elements worked together to bring the purpose and power of each dance form to life.

Performance Spaces

Additional styles and reasons for dance emerged, and performance spaces reflected the purpose of the specific dance or theatre design. Performers found homes in a range of both informal or nontraditional spaces and more formal spaces like temples, courts, theatres, and social events. When faith or religion was at the center of a dance, this origin would present itself in the often holy or spiritual spaces it occupied. For example, in India, where the extensive list of specialized traditional Indian dance centers around its purpose as a sacred expression of faith, dancers performed in temples, for festive occasions, and during seasonal harvests. These were all spaces and moments when it was important to honor their faith, and they did so by using dance.

In ancient Greece, performances mainly took place in outdoor open-air theatres. The Greeks used the stories to educate the lower class, so these performances were purposeful displays. They built theatres on tall hillsides because the slope allowed more of the audience to clearly view the performance. They called this viewing place the **theatron**, and it was centered around a circular performance space. This model became the basis for many theatres throughout history and is the source of many names for production terminology (Gillette 2019; Carver 2018):

› The term **orchestra** comes from where the storytelling happened and literally translates to "dancing people."
› The **skene** was a wall, backdrop, or building behind the orchestra that was originally used for performers to change masks and costumes. This area would eventually become part of the drama as the backdrop or scenery that the performance was done in front of and is where we get the terms *scenery* and *scenic*.
› The term **theatre** came to mean all of the theatron, orchestra, and skene and is still used today.

Later, in Europe during the Renaissance, plays and dramatic arts still took place in presentational theatre venues, but dance transitioned into more of a social space, such as in the court of Louis XIV of

France. The ballets presented in early 16th-century courts were different from the presentational stage form we see today. Court ballets were performed by and for the nobility. With the creation of the proscenium theatre at the end of the 16th century, the separation between the performers and audiences began to be prominent in theatrical dance. A **proscenium** is a wall or arch in a theatre that separates the performance space from the audience space (see figure 1.1). As dance moved into the proscenium theatres, the need and desire for collaboration among theatrical designers and dance artisans grew.

In America during the late 19th and early 20th centuries, dance went from being an accompaniment for stage plays and operas to earning a featured place on the stage. Dance was becoming the headliner of a performance, and entire spaces were being built to best showcase the art of dance. In 1942, the Ted Shawn Theatre at Jacob's Pillow opened its doors as the first performance space in America designed specifically for dance. Then in 1964, the David H. Koch Theatre opened, which is the home of New York City Ballet.

Dance performances take place in buildings specially designed for productions; however, the only true necessity for performing dance is a live performer and an audience, not necessarily a building. Performance spaces have traditionally fallen into four basic categories: proscenium theatres, thrust theatres, arena theatres, and found spaces. As technology has evolved in recent decades, dance can be produced in any space, then recorded and distributed to the audience using virtual platforms.

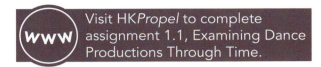
Visit HK*Propel* to complete assignment 1.1, Examining Dance Productions Through Time.

Design Elements

Scenery, props, costumes, lighting, makeup, masks, and other technical elements were key in telling the choreographers' stories. As these design elements became more necessary and intricate, dance artists started to work with and rely on theatrical designers and fellow artists to help tell their stories.

Scenery

Dance and theatrical presentations require collaboration among scenic designers and a crew of many people to create the world in which the production comes to life. Scenery as a design element in theatre and dance has evolved over time. At the beginning of storytelling, cave walls and cave drawings were used to help accentuate the stories (Carver 2018). As noted earlier, in Greek theatre, the story took place on stages in an amphitheater using a skene to frame the action of the story. The two major scenic contributions from Greek theatre are the **periaktoi**, revolving triangular columns also called *vertical scenery*, and **deux ex machina**, which was a machine built to allow performers to fly above the stage. The Romans were responsible for bringing live performances indoors and using more elaborate technical scenery backstage. In the same way, Japanese traditional Kabuki theatre used dynamic stage sets such as revolving platforms and trapdoors allowing for the prompt changing of a scene or the appearance or disappearance of actors (Carver 2018).

These devices and mechanisms, while rooted in the past, are still used today. The major contemporary shift has been in digital and visual technologies, such as projections and LED use. Many modern performances such as Cirque du Soleil, touring musical artists, and ballet companies use scenery to provide a visual spectacle and help drive the narrative of the performance.

Collaboration between choreographers and designers enriches the experience for artists and audiences. Choreographer Martha Graham and scenic designer Isamu Noguchi collaborated on numerous pieces, such as *Appalachian Spring* (1944)

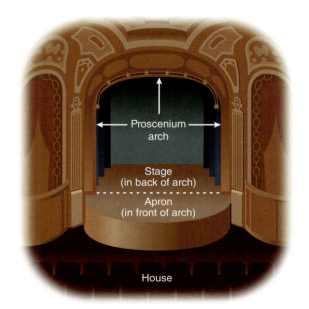
Figure 1.1 The proscenium stage.

Kabuki theatre.

and *Cave of the Heart* (1947). Noguchi had famously stated that, "I felt I was an extension of Martha and she was an extension of me" (Campbell 2020). The Ballet Russes is one of the best modern examples of this type of collaboration, as are postmodern artists Merce Cunningham, John Cage, and Robert Rauschenberg.

Lighting

Lighting is used to illuminate and accentuate the action in dance performances. It serves a practical need to show the story and action, but it is also an artistic component that complements the performance. Many indigenous dances are performed around a large fire. This is both a practical and ritual necessity. The fire allows the performers to be seen, so these dances and rituals can continue all night (Murphy 2007). Performances in public theatre spaces like a theatron in ancient Greece were held outdoors and during the day by necessity, ensuring performers could be seen, although the moon and stars could lend some light to nighttime performances.

Lighting has changed as technology has evolved. Indoor theatrical spaces were expanded as cities developed and cultural practices moved inside. This created a necessity for artificial lighting sources such as candles, whale oil drums, candelabras, and oil lamps, among others. The candles and lamps were purely functional at this point and used to illuminate the performers. The first successful use of gas lighting was in London's Lyceum Theatre in 1803. Gas lighting was a lot cheaper than candles or oil lamps, and it was more easily contained, which reduced the chances of fire from a lit candle or a candelabra. Using open flames caused many fires that destroyed ancient indoor performing structures. Also, gas lighting could be manipulated, making it dimmer or brighter. Gas lighting systems could be controlled from areas other than directly on the stage, such as from a backstage area. This is when we see that the audience lighting could be dimmed so that all the light was onstage and focused on the performance. This new lighting technology brings the early origins of light design (Gillette 2019).

Over time, lighting technology improved, and so did the versatility of light design. The invention of electricity led to incandescent lamps in the 1870s. At this point, the use of gas was phased out and removed from theatres almost immediately. The

Loie Fuller–inspired collaboration of lights and costume.

incandescent lamps were much safer because for the first time there was no need for an open flame of any type. This marked the beginning of the modern era of stage lighting.

One pioneer of theatrical lighting techniques was dancer, choreographer, and inventor Loie Fuller. She combined lighting and costumes for dramatic effect using modern technologies in the early 20th century. Fuller's costumes displayed the different colors she created in the light. By understanding how an artist can manipulate lighting to tell a story, Fuller was able to evoke wonder in her audience. Artists today continue to be inspired by the unique visual images the combination of costumes and lighting can create.

Using light effectively to shape and highlight costumes and bodies in motion helps support the choreographer's vision of the dance. Lighting designers and choreographers continue to collaborate, creating breathtaking visual effects. David Parson's work "Caught," choreographed in 1982, captivated audiences. A strobing light on the dancer seemed to make the dancer float or fly across the stage (Kourlas 2014).

Lighting and lighting design are continuing to evolve. New technologies such as LED and projections are helping shape the future of storytelling through the medium of dance. Dance productions today can use a range of lighting options, from simple light designs to full moving light extravaganzas.

Music and Sound

Dance and music have historically worked together to communicate, help tell stories, and create and sustain community. In many West African cultures, for example, drum circles bring communities together with a sense of equity demonstrated through the idea that a circle has neither a head nor a tail. These customs have been passed down for centuries, both in Africa and elsewhere. Many of these West African traditions have evolved through the African diaspora. In North America, these traditions have been a crucial component in developing jazz music and dance. An illustration of how dance and music continue to work together can be seen in the rela-

Cab Calloway at the Cotton Club with dancers.

tionship between jazz musicians and tap dancers. During the early part of the 20th century in the Harlem neighborhood of New York City, the Harlem Renaissance was an artistic and cultural phenomenon. Many celebrated musicians—including Duke Ellington and Cab Calloway—played music while dancers such as Bill "Bojangles" Robinson participated in elaborate, staged shows at venues like the Cotton Club (Guarino and Oliver eds 2015).

Once music could be recorded, a shift away from live accompaniment took place. Dance no longer had to rely on live music for performances, and access to many different types of sound and music opened vast possibilities for choreography. While canned or recorded music is now the norm for many dance productions, there is still something very inspiring about having live musicians playing while dancers are performing—that will never change.

Costumes

In early dance environments, the scenery or sets were minimal, using only framing to mark the edges of a stage and basic coverings along the back of the space to allow characters to enter and exit. Due to the limited scenery, the costumes and simple props dominated the performances. Costumes in classical dances of India were lavish and beautiful, with everything having a purpose and meaning. Each form, from kathakali to Chhau dance, had very specific costuming. This provided consistency and made characters and stories recognizable. Defining gender roles was also a costuming device and helped guide the audience as to what was happening in the performance. In cultures where men portrayed all roles, including the female characters, it was important for the spectators to see feminine figures and socially relevant presentation of the female characters. In Japanese Kabuki dance, portraying a female was called *Onnagata* and the male actors took great care to portray a female character.

A highly decorative costume, either by color, material quality, or even embellishments, could represent a character's status, gender, or wealth. Characters in simple dress would typically be

A crowd in India watches a Chhau dance.

identified as the peasants or the lower class in a performance. For example, in Medieval times, the lower-class peasants wore their own plain daily clothing made of wool and duller, darker colors. The costumes for the upper class were vivid and made of silk and other expensive materials. In Africa, Indonesia, and China, costuming has been used to portray the stories and traditions told in the dance and have deep cultural significance. Indigenous American dances rely heavily on their regalia to represent their traditions and stories. Headdresses and jewelry are essential in communicating and representing tribal identity, and parts of the regalia can be passed down through the generations and are a cherished component of each dance.

Costumes used in dance today can vary dramatically based on the style, performance venue, and purpose of the dance. Competition dancers can have hundreds of rhinestones sewn onto every inch of a costume to create a flashy presentation. Contemporary and modern choreographers may choose simpler looks to highlight the shape of the body or the mood of a dance. Ballet costumes can range from traditional tutus to simple tights and a leotard. As dance genres such as tap and hip-hop emerged, dancers used costuming to represent their cultural roots or to symbolize their cultural identities.

Broadway shows such as *The Lion King*, with costumes designed by Julie Taymor and choreography by Garth Fagan, are excellent examples of costumes and puppetry helping bring powerful stories to life onstage. The costume designs in *Hamilton* were a fresh take on period pieces, allowing artistic vision to support the impact of the production. Paul Tazewell, the costume designer for *Hamilton*, best described the art of collaboration and integration of new and old concepts:

> *As for any other production, my process always starts with reading the play enough times to ingest what's there. Then it's asking, how is the story being told? How can I support the telling of story? So much of that is a sit-down conversation. Then I go to different kinds of imagery. If I'm doing something set in a specific year about specific people, I'll go*

online and research. But something can be set in a period, and I'll be told to abstract it and mash it up. That's what Hamilton is. It's an exploration, a journey. We needed to decide the most compelling way of presenting this visually. These are people we've lived with most of our lives, the founders of this country. How are we going to make it new and exciting? It was important for the audience to feel a youthful vigor (Tell 2016).

The final costume design must be justified through diligent research and open communication and ultimately must support the style and overall concept of the dance production.

Visit HK*Propel* to complete assignment 1.2, Production Elements Across Dance Forms.

Makeup and Masks

From the beginning, dance and theatre were used to tell stories. Performers needed a way to distinguish their character from themselves and the other characters onstage. Therefore, design elements such as makeup, masks, wigs, and headpieces became increasingly important as performances drew larger audiences and were performed at night. The more elaborate the makeup or masks, the clearer the characters were to the audience, who might be viewing from far away with only fire or stars for light.

In many cultures, makeup covered the performer's face to convey the exaggerated character. Kabuki theatre, a Japanese theatre form rich in vibrant characters, features extremely exaggerated movements and facial features. The facial features are highlighted by unique color schemes that signify villains and heroes. The movement helps tell the story, but the exaggerated makeup and wigs help visually distinguish characters and demeanor. In many dance forms makeup, costumes, and masks help define the gender roles being represented.

Masks function similarly to makeup but can further disguise characters, allowing different performers to take on the same role. In ancient Greece and during the Renaissance, masks covered the performer's face and had exaggerated features and expressions to help reveal the character's gender, social class, age, and even mood. This can be seen in commedia dell'arte, which was prominent in Europe from the 16th to 18th centuries.

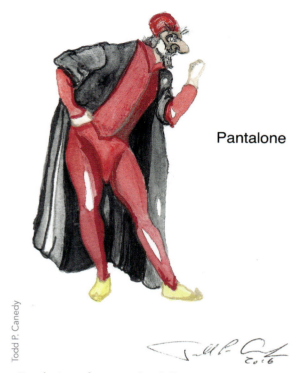

Rendering of commedia dell'arte.

With the support of modern lighting, performers have more options for how they use makeup and masks. The dancer can choose to wear black lipstick or hot pink, have a slicked-back bun or wear the hair down, or have exaggerated makeup or an understated look—all will have bearing on what the artist is trying to portray. It is important to remember that traditional cultures didn't make random color or design choices; there was a purpose.

In Japanese Noh, men are the performers playing all the roles, whether it be male, female, monster, or god. The masks, wigs, and robes indicate these characters to the audience. Everything will always come back to the reason for using a mask and what it represents to the individual artist or culture.

In today's eclectic dance world, performing groups like the hip-hop crew Jabbawockeez use masks to remove all ethnic and social barriers when they perform. Masks, wigs, and makeup are a vital design element and can be used in many different ways, from subtle and understated to exaggerated and flamboyant (Mallare 2008).

The dance group Jabbawockeez uses masks to remove visual barriers related to ethnicity.

Summary

Understanding how the elements of dance and technical theatre have inspired collaboration for thousands of years for different venues, cultures, purposes, and budgets is important for a young artist. With a clear purpose and a collaborative team, you can be creative in developing your vision, think beyond what you know, and discover unique ways to tell your story. By understanding what each artist does and learning how to speak each other's language, the choreographer and the technical theatre artist can both find new avenues of exploration and collaboration. Collaboration allows each art form to expand and thrive. By letting ourselves as the creators of dance be open to the new ideas and concepts that other art forms bring, we can surprise ourselves and reach new heights.

Artistic Vision

2

Key Terms

artistic vision
creative brief
evocative research
site-specific performance
theatre-in-the-round
thrust stage

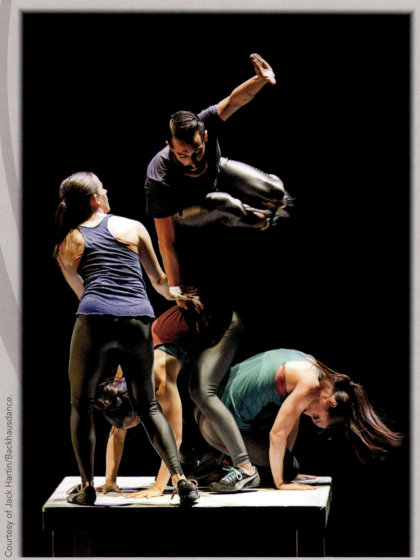

Courtesy of Jack Hartin/Backhausdance.

LEARNING OBJECTIVES

After reading this chapter, you will be able to do the following:

- Identify the elements involved in creating a thorough artistic vision
- Recognize the effect that audience, performance space, and operational structures have on artistic choices
- Identify the idea, purpose, audience, performance space options, and operational structure to create a project
- Analyze different performance spaces and describe the different effects a performance space has on an audience's experience
- Communicate an artistic vision clearly with collaborators
- Present clear and comprehensive historical and evocative research on the artistic vision
- Produce a creative brief detailing the artistic vision

At the heart of any production is the **artistic vision**, the creative conceptualization of the work you want to bring to life. It answers the question, Why is the work being made? Whether the work is an evening-length show, a festival submission, or an individual work, the clearer and more intentional the artistic vision, the more potential it has for growth and success.

Impactful dance that is both relevant and spectacular should be conceived within a greater context. An effective artistic vision communicates, to a specific audience, a cogent argument for the performance purpose within its aesthetic and technical frames—this is called *production value.* The argument may be considered in the structure of storytelling for the following elements:

› Character—the dancer
› Setting—the time and place
› Plot—the story and movement, or choreography
› Theme—the lesson for the audience

And the spectacle may be considered in the production structure for these elements:

› Audience and venue
› Scenery and props
› Lighting and sound
› Costume and makeup

The argument should inform the spectacle, and the spectacle should support the argument. In this way, producing dance is a successful collaborative art. Context informs all aspects of a clear and comprehensible artistic vision, which is a requisite for any dance performance. You are the creator, and the vision is the design template.

The creative choices you and your collaborative team make for the work—such as the number of dancers, the movement vocabulary, costume design, spatial direction, emotional context, and lighting design, to name a few—are all informed by contextual elements. If each choice is made with the vision in mind, every part of the work serves a purpose.

You have to be able to not only create and curate your vision with specificity but also communicate it with clarity. Articulating your vision with a creative brief supported by both historical and evocative research conveys a clear picture and allows everyone on the creative team to contribute their creative experiences and expertise. When everyone is on the same page, the creative process can thrive.

Inspiration and Purpose Tied to Artistic Vision

The artistic vision drives the entire production, and every choice that's made should reflect this intention. As an artist, you become inspired to create, tell a story, and make an impact in your community, and once the initial inspiration hits you, it can dominate your every thought. At the beginning of the creation process, the decisions about the content, location, and other components of a project become important.

To make informed decisions about these areas with the artistic vision in mind, consider the initial idea, purpose of the work, audience, and performance mode. For example, at the beginning, you might notice that the idea for a piece addressing gender norms needs to be produced differently for an elementary school audience than it would for a university audience. Or you might notice that your site-specific outdoor piece will require different production equipment than one on a traditional stage. Anticipating these elements at the beginning will help make the artistic choices intentional as you continue creating with your collaborators. When the intentional artistic choices are influenced by an in-depth consideration of the elements involved, you collaborate with the creative team. The artistic work and the elements that influence it also work together, both supporting and being supported.

Inspirational Spark (Idea)

The initial inspiration for the work, or what we'll call the *idea*, is the seed that needs to be nurtured for the artistic vision to thrive. What made you want to create the work? What is at the core of what you're trying to express? The answer to these questions will kindle the rest of your artistic process and orient it around a core idea.

If you have the urge to create but haven't yet found that seed for a production, you may not know where to start. Inspiration can come from any number of places, including the following:

› A piece of music, art, or literature
› A social issue or cause
› An intellectual concept
› A personal or emotional experience
› An exploration of movement
› An environment
› A mood, tone, or emotion
› A new piece of technology you want to use
› A desire to parody or emulate a respected predecessor
› A collaborator you want to work with
› A specific venue you are excited to work in

When you've found something that is important to you—that you have a clear focus on while still making room to explore where the creative process may take you—you've found your idea. A clear idea is the first step toward a successful artistic vision. Having a foundation to support your artistic vision allows it to grow, evolve, and unfold while still being fed by and aligned with its core intention.

While the initial inspiration motivates the process, it is only the start of a fully realized artistic vision. It gives the process direction, but it doesn't dictate every decision made within it. Sometimes when an artist is passionate about an idea, the guiding role of an idea is forgotten as the artist tries to control every aspect of the process. Blind to the context in which the work will be placed, this artist can get stuck in a limited view of what their work could be.

Allowing your inspiration to evolve with the help of the new perspectives from your collaborative team broadens the work's scope, making it more informed, more evocative, and richer than you could have imagined. If you find yourself holding on tightly to an idea you'd like to control from start to finish, first acknowledge the parts of this idea that are most important to you. Maybe it's the feeling you want to convey, the movement style you want to work within, or the societal need that you want to address. Then remember that there are many ways to achieve this goal.

Journaling about these ideas or bouncing them off a respected colleague can allow you to clarify your intention without holding tightly to every production detail. Once you have your core idea, bringing it to the production team will allow them to add to it. Gaining new perspectives from your collaborative team instead of deciding everything before you work with them gives you more options for approaching your core ideas and ultimately allows those concepts to reach a wider audience.

Visit HK*Propel* to complete assignment 2.1, The Inspirational Spark.

Purpose

The idea may plant the seed for the content, but the *purpose* of the performance drives that content forward. Why is this performance being created? The work may be for a fundraiser, a university concert, an educational assembly, or something completely different. Whatever it is, every purpose takes the content in a different direction. For example, if the project is meant to educate, you might need to approach the work with more concrete expression than if it's meant to showcase technical prowess or

The initial spark of inspiration is the starting point of a fully realized artistic vision.

portray an abstract emotion. If an artist creates a project without a purpose in mind and tries to fit it into a purpose retroactively, areas of the project will not be as well suited to the purpose as they could have been. In other words, instead of trying to fit a square peg into a round hole, acknowledging the purpose early in a creation process allows a creator to notice the need to fill a round space and create a round peg to meet that need. When the intention and approach align with purpose, the final work becomes curated for its function.

To find the purpose of your performance, ask yourself these questions:

> Who is the audience?
> Is this performance part of a larger body or season of shows?
> Am I or is someone else hoping for some financial gain from this?
> Am I contractually obligated to create this piece?
> Is this performance meant to highlight or bring awareness to a social issue or cause?
> Is this performance meant to honor or pay tribute to another artist?
> Is this performance meant to educate?
> Is there any other reason the performance is being produced, other than to create?

Though productions *can* be produced solely for the joy of creation, often there is another element like the previous list to consider, and that element will necessarily inform the choices a choreographer, lighting designer, costume designer, and other collaborators make during production. If choices made along the way are made with the purpose in mind, the piece will be able to fulfill its intention completely.

Audience

Once you have the idea to create the piece and the purpose to drive it, it's time to consider the audience. An **audience**, at its core, is a group of people who attend, watch, or experience a performance. They are the people who will see your work. Each audience will be different for each performance, even for shows that have run for years. As you begin to create the work, you must clarify what the experience will be for the audience. In some ways, considering your audience is another way to evaluate your purpose. The people experiencing your work guide why it's being created, and who the audience is will help determine the creative choices you make. For example, if a choreographer knows from the beginning that they need to create an interactive dance for a museum opening, they would approach the work differently than if it was for a world premiere for the public.

There are various elements to think about when considering your own audience, including the projected demographic and the scale. The audience demographic defines the section of a population your audience might represent. This includes their ages, socioeconomic status, education levels, interests, and more. Knowing or at least anticipating this demographic will help you evaluate what content will effectively engage or influence your audience.

The scale, or how large your audience will be, can also help determine some choices. A larger audience, for instance, often means many will be seated far away. If a choreographer takes that into account when making spatial choices or a lighting designer considers it while creating the lighting, the performance will be much more effective for a larger portion of the audience.

An audience chooses to go to a performance for a reason, and they have expectations for what they're about to see and experience. These expectations help shape how your work is perceived, so it's important to consider them as you're creating your work. For example, on a professional stage for a performance like Alvin Ailey's *Revelations*, an informed audience of dance patrons would have high expectations for what the work should look like because it is canon in modern dance ("Revelations," 2021). Similarly, for a ballet production of *The Nutcracker*, the audience would expect a certain quality: an incredible tree effect and a prima ballerina cast as the Sugar Plum Fairy.

In contrast, an audience of middle schoolers may not have context for historically significant dance works and would probably be more forgiving of your junior presentation of an otherwise highly criticized work. When you present a new work to an audience, you are free from precedent, and the only people who recognize mistakes are you and your company. The audience will live in blissful ignorance—at least for a little while.

Once you have a clear picture of your audience, you can use what you know about them to define the choices and direction of your work. For example, you might use elements like their ages, interests, and education levels to decide the subject matter and themes for your piece. You might use other elements like scale and socioeconomic status to decide what type of venue and ticket prices would best suit your performance. Whatever the choices are, keeping audience characteristics in mind will help you and your collaborative team make decisions that will benefit the perception of your work. A performance is not a performance without an audience, so knowing them and considering their perspectives is one of your best tools for success.

INVITING OTHERS TO SHARE YOUR VISION

The initial creator and the team interact to enhance and develop the original vision. It can be hard for the creator to step back and listen to others and see how suggestions and discussion can continue to hone the initial idea. There is no "I" in "team," so if you want to truly collaborate as the initial creator, you must allow for open discussion and welcome every artistic voice. Then you can integrate those voices as they align to advance the same vision.

Think about how you address the group and present your ideas. Avoid using the words "I want" and instead focus on what the piece, work, or vision aims to do. Instead of "I want to challenge gender norms by . . ." try "The piece aims to challenge gender norms by . . ." This takes some of the ego out of the creation when working collaboratively with others and allows the work more space to grow and evolve.

Performance Spaces

While considering the idea, purpose, and audience of the performance, you will also have to start thinking about how and where the work will be presented, if it hasn't already been defined for you by someone like your producer, university department, board, artistic director, or someone similar. Will you present it live, virtually, recorded, or any variation of these? Where will you present it? When making these decisions, it's important to consider the scale and budget of the performance as well as audience direction. These choices will have a large impact on what mode will serve your project best. As logistic considerations, these details will be more fully explored in later chapters, but in general, the size and price of the venue or location and the production value quality you will receive will depend on your budget and the projected size of your audience.

When choosing how to present your work, you'll also need to consider how close or far the audience is from the performers and where you want their eyes directed. In a theatre, for instance, the audience is stationary, and their gaze is in a fixed direction. In a film, the audience is stationary, but the camera directs their eye. For a site-specific work, the audience may be able to move around and are informed by external elements like the time of day or location. Will the work be served by being seen at a distance in a large proscenium theatre or up close and from many angles, like an in-the-round theatre? If you want the audience to be able to choose what parts they see and want to place the work in a real-world location, maybe a site-specific venue would be best. On the other hand, if you want to control the distance of the audience at different parts of the work, maybe a film or a livestream performance is best for your vision. If you are extremely tech savvy or interested in pushing boundaries, you could even collaborate with a virtual reality or augmented reality expert to create a totally immersive experience where the audience could be part of the performance itself.

It takes a careful analysis of your existing vision to decide where your work will be presented. Each option presents its own benefits, limitations, and features to consider.

Theatres

The theatre might be an obvious consideration when deciding where to present. It's not the only option, though. A theatre has its own limitations to consider. In a theatre, the audience is stationary and positioned to view the performance from a fixed place. The audience may be large or small, depending on the size of the theatre, and they can be either close or far, depending on their seat locations. The theatre gives a creator lots of control over the environment in which the work is presented. With the right technical collaborators and capabilities, it can take a work out of reality and into its own world.

When thinking of a theatre, the image that comes to mind is likely one of a proscenium stage. The proscenium is the structural arch that separates the audience from the stage (see figure 2.1a). A theatre with one of these arches is called a *proscenium theatre*. These theatres can be small and intimate, but large proscenium theatres can fit thousands of people. The difference between these theatres and the distance of the audience will determine if the audience can see facial expressions or just spatial patterns. Knowing the venue will inform the artistic choices you'll make.

Though they may be common, proscenium stages are not the only types. A theatre with a **thrust stage** has the audience seated on three sides (see figure 2.1b), as if the stage has been "thrust" into the space. This might be used to allow the audience to get a closer or more dimensional look at a performance

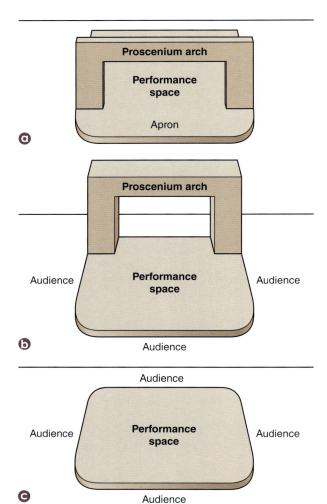

Figure 2.1 Three major traditional theatre styles: *(a)* proscenium theatre, *(b)* thrust stage, and *(c)* theatre-in-the-round.

but still allow it to have a general "front" and allow the performers to enter and exit the stage easily.

A **theatre-in-the-round** accommodates an audience seated on all sides of the stage (see figure 2.1c). This means that the work will be viewed from every angle, and there is no defined "front" of the stage. If you are creating a work for an in-the-round stage, it will change how you approach entrances and exits, how you stage to avoid blind spots for the audience, and where your performers are projecting their energy.

These are just three types of theatres, and there are many other options available to stage a performance. Sometimes the stage is in a gym with an audience on two opposing sides. Sometimes the stage is on a float and is rolling down a street. Sometimes the stage is on a hill in a public park.

The space you put your performance in can greatly affect how the audience views and perceives your production.

Nontraditional Spaces

There are more options for a performance space than just the theatre. Unlike a theatre performance, a **site-specific performance** places the work directly into the real world and is created to exist in a certain space, usually outside of a typical performance space. Almost any location could be turned into a performance space—even an old home or building could serve as the place for an immersive art experience.

By using your imagination and opening your mind to new opportunities, you might be able to find a new, beautiful, and intriguing space to present your work to an array of audiences. Often, a site-specific work means the audience has more agency in how they view the performance. They can move around, choose what parts they watch, get closer to or farther away from their focus, or choose to not participate at all. This ability to choose what they're watching and when they watch it can make for an immersive experience that involves the audience as much as the performers. Instead of simply sitting in a theatre and watching whatever is put in front of them, an audience can create a unique experience by choosing a vantage point, direction, and timing while watching a site-specific performance.

Regardless of how nontraditional the space is, as the curator of the performance, it's up to you to consider following:

› How will this space affect the audience's potential to view the work, both in terms of proximity and context?
› How does it change the feel of the piece?
› What logistic capabilities are needed to make it happen?

Some nontraditional spaces, especially those not created for performance, may bring some unexpected hiccups that make performance difficult, such as floor quality or spatial dimensions for an audience. The earlier you take those into account, the easier it will be to accommodate those challenges. In chapter 9, we will cover what production options you have to create your intended effect on the audience as they make choices viewing a site-specific performance and how to overcome any potential difficulties.

Festivals

Another way to present a performance is by submitting it to a festival. This often takes place in a theatre, but variations like film festivals might happen in a different place. In a festival setting, many works are submitted and performed, one after another. This means your work will be presented next to many others that may be very different. In this case, the show as a whole may not have the flow or curation that an individual presentation may have, so your work must be able to stand alone in its own context. You also may have limited technical options when presenting in a large setting like this, and that will affect your ability to collaborate with a technical team while creating the work. Though you may not have the production value of a stand-alone production, a festival often grants you exposure, builds your audience, and gives your work a chance to be seen by a wider range of people. Investigate the requirements of any festival before entering your work. Some events require you to pay a submission fee even if you are not selected to perform, and others require you to sell a set number of tickets if your piece is accepted. Some festivals select winners at the end of the evening—you can win anything from cash to a produced concert. Weighing the cost of rehearsal, costumes, production elements, and submission fees against the tangible or in-kind rewards of participating will help identify whether the opportunity is worth it.

Film

Dance on film presents a work in a very different way than a theatre or live performance does. In a theatre performance, the audience has freedom to take in different aspects of the dance and views the dance live in a set environment. In a film performance, the camera allows the creator to showcase a specific point of view in a work and direct the eye of the audience. The creator also loses control of where and when the audience views the film because they can view it in any location and as often as they want. Furthermore, the level of detail that can be captured in close proximity with a high-definition camera these days has changed the amount of detail the audience can see. Lighting, too, is very different for film productions and can be affected by postproduction and editing processes. Therefore, it is important that the lighting designer know how to light for film when that is the delivery method. When creating a work for film, notice if you're directing the audience's eye to anything specific or

This production is being produced in a theatre for *film* distribution. Observe the contrast of color between the lighting as it appears in person onstage and what the camera captures as displayed on the monitor in the lower right of the photograph. The image on camera is muted and cooler.

to important details in the frame. In this mode, collaboration with a cinematographer or video editor with an educated perspective on how to capture and portray those important details effectively will enhance your film.

DANCE ON FILM

Check out these examples of dance produced on film over the years:

- *Singin' in the Rain*, Gene Kelly, 1952
- *Mary Poppins*, Julie Andrews, Dick Van Dyke, and animated penguins, 1964
- *Saturday Night Fever*, John Travolta and Karen Lynn Gorney, 1977
- *Thriller*, Michael Jackson, 1983
- *Swing Kids*, Robert Sean Leonard and Tushka Bergen, 1993
- *Step Up* franchise, Channing Tatum and Jenna Dewan, 2006
- *Black Swan*, Natalie Portman, 2010
- *West Side Story*, Ansel Elgort and Rachel Zegler, 2021

Streaming

When the COVID-19 pandemic shut down live performances in the United States in early 2020, livestreamed performances became necessary. As in-person venues closed, the arts world rose to the challenge of bringing live art to audiences remotely. Though challenging at first, there were unexpected benefits to livestreaming. In this mode, the creators have lots of control over how the audience views the performance in terms of proximity and focus, and the audience still participates and watches in real time, even though it may be remote. Streaming allows you to find an audience for your work beyond your immediate geographical location. Dancers could train in livestreamed classes from expert instructors all over the world, and companies could provide classes to dancers who may never have had access to training with them. The wide reach allowed some theatres to engage more people than ever in performances, and the potential to continue using livestreamed performances even after the pandemic became a very real and beneficial opportunity for many arts organizations (Komatsu 2020).

While YouTube and other creator-driven online video streaming services had already been increasing in popularity for artists of all genres, the COVID-19 pandemic sparked an influx of content uploads and made people reexamine their approach to an otherwise very traditional performing arts process. Directors and choreographers began conceptualizing their performances through the eye of the lens rather than the portal of the proscenium. Because outdoor environments were more protective against COVID than indoor environments were, streamed performances were often staged outside, and dancers were compelled to adapt to the unpredictable great outdoors. Weather, sunrise and sunset, and the path of travel became more important than dressing rooms and stage directions!

The abilities to stream on the social media platforms that emerged became an easy way for the arts to continue providing performances to audiences all over the world. Platforms like YouTube, Facebook Live, Instagram Live, and Zoom are available as a free or low-cost platform to present work. Free versions are great to start with but tend to have limitations on time, file types or sizes, and the ability to reach larger audiences. Research the online platforms to see the cost for additional services that can increase your advertising reach, especially the number of viewers on a streaming platform. If you are producing online content, quality matters over quantity. While the streaming service may have limited fees, your production and editing costs will increase as you improve your online content. Streaming or virtual content creation can quickly become a full-time job.

Though an audience may miss the details and tangible energy of an in-person performance, virtual and livestreamed performances provide an incredible control of the performance environment and the ability to influence and affect a global audience. Especially in their increasing popularity, this type of performance is an interesting way to produce a moving performance to an audience that's scattered and not necessarily in the same place as the performer.

Research

To effectively bring the vision to life, the artist must do a lot of research and communicate the vision to the team. Research helps an artist clarify the vision for themselves and creates context for the team, helping the collaboration process. Each collaborative team member handles a different element of the project. For decisions to support the purpose and concept of the vision even across disciplines, it is important for every collaborator to have a thorough understanding of the artistic vision for the project. By articulating the larger context of your vision into a creative brief, you communicate to your team in a way that is comprehensive but not limiting. You may have an in-depth understanding in your own head about what your work is, but if you can't communicate that understanding, the rest of your team won't be on the same page, and the vision won't come to full fruition.

The first step to communicating your vision is giving it context. You need a solid idea of where your vision sits in the context of existing work, situational tone, and personal experiences, and you determine that through research. There are two main types of research: (1) *historical research*, where you will obtain accurate information about the content of your idea, place your work in historical context, and identify how it relates to existing work; and (2) *evocative research*, which helps you establish a general tone and broad aesthetic understanding for your vision in a less concrete way. These two forms of research are different, but together, they are important to articulating a comprehensive vision.

Historical Research

Historical research involves examining both the subject and historical context of your work. This involves examining the accuracy of both the subject and historical context of your work, especially if it is nonfictional or inspired by real events and people. This is a vital step in approaching research for your work to ensure you are informed and can portray a concept accurately. It is also important to review the concept's artistic historical context and related works as well as any existing content, asking the following questions:

› What has been created in the past on this subject?

› Who has made other art or writings about it?

› What was their purpose in creating it?

› What other art forms can you connect to?

› What discussions are happening on this issue today?

Knowing where other works about the same subject came from will inform how you place your work in the landscape of what already exists around that theme. It also might give you more intellectual content around the subject to consider as you create the work.

You also have to consider what your choice in movement vocabulary says about or adds to your work. Ask the following questions:

› What movement vocabulary are you interested in using?
› Why did you choose it?
› What movement influences or people do you need to look into if you're using that vocabulary?

If you're the choreographer, knowing these answers will not only inspire you in creating the movement but also bring it more information and depth than you might have had otherwise.

Remember, whether this vision came to you spontaneously or was inspired by something you saw or heard, the existing historical pieces of art and movement vocabulary that relate to it are relevant and important to examine. Without this research, your work could be uninformed and even could offend or be ill-timed, regardless of your intention. Taking the time to find out how your vision relates to those of others in the past and present not only informs it but also places it in time as its own part of history.

Evocative Research

Evocative research is a compilation of elements like images, video, text, colors, and more that help define the general aesthetic, tone, and feeling of a work. These items have inspired you, spoken to you, or seem to match the mood of the work or movement. For example, a painting may epitomize the environment you're looking for, an abstract image or texture may point directly to an emotion you're trying to convey, and a quote or literary passage may hint at a specific environment you want your work to live in. The beauty of this type of research is that rather than being specific about the outcome, the broader you can be, the more successful connections you can make.

Creating a collage for what has inspired or influenced you as you created your vision is a good way to put your evocative research in one place. You can do this physically, by printing images, cutting clippings from magazines, collecting fabric swatches, and so on, or digitally, by combining images, colors, and even sounds to create this abstract composition. Consider things like the colors that speak to you and images or art pieces that inspire you; expand from there as you find more material. Once you've put it all together and look at the whole image, a broad feeling and aesthetic begin to emerge.

Later, when you draw from this visual bank to create the creative brief that you bring to the collaborative team, these more abstract elements will show your collaborators the environment you see for your work so they comprehend the complexity of your vision. Creating a collection of inspiration means the connections become clear without letting the content details limit the possibilities of your project.

Creative Brief

Once you have completed your research, key parts of it should be consolidated into your creative brief. A **creative brief** is used to clearly convey the core of an idea to your collaborators (Blakeman 2019). This clarity comes *after* your research. Your research provides a broad range of context for your unique vision, and the creative brief summarizes the vision. The creative brief should give your collaborators a clear view of the environment you intend to create. Throughout the process, your larger collection of research will still be valuable because you may offer more specific research to each collaborator, but the initial creative brief is just that: brief. It serves as a clear, concise tool for you and your collaborators to continue to return to and be grounded in, ensuring every part of the production works in alignment with the same core idea. Generally speaking, it will cover the topics shown in figure 2.2.

The creative brief is an evolving document. The framework does not have to be completely filled

Figure 2.2 Topical areas of a creative brief.

Artistic Vision   **23**

(a and b) Courtesy of Cameron Kish; *(c)* Mina De La O/DigitalVision/Getty Images; *(d)* Vizerskaya/E+/Getty Images

These are examples of images that might be useful to share with a team as products of evocative research. *(a)* An image of a lone tree against a colorful sunset might evoke strong emotions ranging from loneliness to strength. *(b)* Perspectives showing how humans view the world through different lenses can lead to the investigation of relationships with others or our environment. *(c)* Structural image of design and space demonstrating the flow of and interaction of the performers. *(d)* Faces and emotions showing the dimensions of human personalities.

out when initially presented to the collaborators. The parts that are important and clear to the creator might be defined when brought to the group, but some parts may be unknown at the beginning of the process, and that's OK. As the production team collaborates, the vision may expand, and any "holes" in the creative brief are filled with the perspectives and expertise of the team. This way, every production element is deliberate and works toward the intended vision.

The creative brief may look a little different depending on when collaborators are brought into the process. In an immersive collaborative process, where the production team works with the creator from the very beginning, the creative brief would be introduced at the beginning of the process, during the first design meeting. It provides collaborators with more abstract adjectives, metaphors, and imagery to describe the artistic vision of the project.

A creative brief can be developed for an individual piece or for an entire event. When developing a creative brief for an event that brings multiple artists together—such as a festival—the brief may be introduced to the collaborators closer to the end of the process. More defined parameters and clear intentions for your production collaborators are provided because they are involved only in the final presentation of the process. The more clarity the brief provides, the better the production elements will align with the vision and create a cohesive performance consistent with the initial intention.

Communicating your artistic vision in the creative brief does not mean the artist tells the team exactly what should happen in the production—it is not "the dancers will wear tight black unitards and be lit with harsh red light." Instead, context is provided by answering broader, more abstract questions. When discussing lighting, for instance, the creator offers the context—what emotions, moods, or tones the piece represents—and then the lighting designer uses their expertise to express what color, angle, and intensity of light can portray the intended tone.

The creative brief gives collaborators a comprehensive snapshot of the artist's vision and creates a solid foundation for that vision to grow and evolve as the collaborative process continues.

To convey the creative brief to the team, a digital presentation like a slideshow, a comprehensive document, or a spreadsheet is necessary. A program such as Google Slides or PowerPoint allows the text and visual representations of the project to be integrated so the team can more clearly see the vision, and these documents can be easily shared in live presentations digitally and with printed PDFs. Having the document accessible to all team members on a shared cloud site (i.e., Google Drive, Dropbox, Microsoft Teams) creates a central location for reference. With all the information in one place, collaborators can consistently refer to and update it as the vision evolves. This helps keep all parties aligned on the project.

In the creative brief presentation, include general information, the concept, thematic environment, structure, lighting and aesthetics, music and sound, costumes, and visual and evocative research.

General Information

All collaborators will need to consider some general practical elements when first approaching a project. For instance, you may already know who the choreographer is, where the performance will take place, the approximate length of the work, how many dancers will be used, and so on. If these elements are already determined, they are important for every collaborator to know as soon as possible as they begin the early stages of their own tasks. For example, a costume designer will prepare differently for a cast of 20 than for a soloist, regardless of concept and tone. Defining these elements early will ensure that every member of the team approaches their craft from the same foundation.

Concept

After the general information is considered, the creator should communicate the concept and intention of the work. One way to do that is by creating an elevator pitch, a brief synopsis of your idea that you could get across clearly on a brief elevator ride with a stranger. Without going into too much detail or going off on a tangent, can you articulate your vision in one or two sentences in a way that would make sense to someone else not involved with your work? Creating this kind of succinct but comprehensive statement is a skill that will help you communicate effectively with your team throughout the entire process. If there's a working title to your piece, you can also include it here to give your team a more complete picture of your intention.

Thematic Environment

The thematic environment includes the emotional aesthetic or mood, what the dancers and performance space represent, and supportive elements. Production elements like lighting, sound design, and costume design will define the performer's environment, so it's important that collaborators are clear on what those choices should communicate. Answering these questions will allow your team to begin to see the type of tone, aesthetic, and themes that your work hopes to address. Consider the following questions:

› What type of mood does the environment represent?

- › Is the dance somber and heavy, possibly addressing a sensitive topic?
- › Is your dance meant to be a high-energy closer to the entire concert?
- › Who are the dancers, or what do they represent?
  - › For example, are they people from a specific time period, or are they playing specific characters?
  - › Are your dancers representing abstract ideas?
- › Where does your piece fall on the scale from narrative to abstract movement?
  - › Maybe your piece is meant to follow an existing or fictional storyline.
  - › Does it exist solely to represent an abstract experience like falling in love?
- › What movement aesthetic will the dancers be moving in?
  - › Aside from the obvious (e.g., ballet, jazz, soft contemporary), consider being more specific when describing your movement aesthetic.
  - › Using movement metaphors like the idea of waves, highways, pathways, and so on is helpful to defining how the movement connects to your idea.
- › Are there any props or scenery you anticipate working with?
  - › Why would those items be important to the work?
  - › What do these items represent in the literal or abstract piece?

The last thing to consider is how you would describe your environment. Can you describe the thematic environment of your piece with just five adjectives? A description with five adjectives is a tool that can be used throughout your creative brief. As you choose your descriptors, remember that it's not only the adjectives themselves that help define the work but also the intersections between them. For example, if you have an environment that is *comedic*, quirky, satirical, angular, and exaggerated, it will read very differently than one that is *creepy*, quirky, satirical, angular, and exaggerated. One different adjective and the relationships between each of the five words shift, completely changing the direction of your vision. Being clear with your descriptors can help specify an environment without confining it to specific production needs.

Structure

Collaborators need to be aware of how the creator plans to approach the structure of the piece. A piece could follow a traditional form such as ABA (opening section, middle section, repeat of opening section), or perhaps it's a collage of different moments around the same theme, or it might follow a narrative storyline. The form it takes will require different approaches from each of the collaborators. The structure itself is not the only thing that needs to be conveyed to collaborators. It's also important to consider the following questions:

- › How is the form operating to reinforce the concept?
- › What changes over the course of the structure?
  - › Does tone change?
  - › Do movement and music change?
- › What happens from the beginning to the end of the work?
- › How is one section different from the next?
- › How do you plan to transition from one idea to another?

Lighting and Aesthetic

The intricacies of lighting will vary depending on your venue and mode of performance, but the light on your work serves a function. Lighting can dictate what the audience sees and doesn't see and influences the lens through which they see it. If you are outdoors in a site-specific piece during the day, the bright sunlight will inevitably influence your work in a way that is different from being in a theatre with only dim sidelight on the dancers. As a creator, it is important to consider the following questions:

- › How does light function in your piece? Does it illuminate or conceal different parts of the work? Or does it provide emotional tone?
- › What tone or environment does your work live in? What is the tone or environment of each section of your piece?
- › What emotions, moods, or tones will your work transition through?
- › What do the dancers represent? Are they characters whose faces and facial expressions need to be visible, or are they abstract concepts whose body shape and lines are more important to notice?

Creative use of lighting in a parking garage.

Clearly, lighting discussions will intersect with other elements discussed in your creative brief. Knowing how the tone of your piece changes over the course of its structure, for instance, informs decisions about how the light should progress throughout the course of the piece. Further, knowing the descriptors for the thematic environment will help give the lighting designer an idea of how to create the lighting environment for your work.

Music and Sound

Music or sound is often a part of a dance production. At the beginning, a creator may have chosen music, may be waiting to work with a composer or sound designer to create the score, or may choose to go without music at all. In any case, this part of the creative brief will help define how sound or lack of it will function in the work and how it aligns with the rest of the vision. Consider questions such as the following:

> How is the score giving information or relating to the other production elements in this work?
> What will the instrumentation or tone of the music be?
> How will the movement relate to the music? For instance, will soft, delicate movements mirror the subdued, intricate music, or will the movement contrast the music completely?
> Are the dancers creating sound in the performance either via spoken text or breath work?
> Is the sound coming from tap shoes on the floor, slapping or stomping of limbs?

Once again, it will also be helpful to find five adjectives that describe your music. As you go through this descriptive process, you might notice how the adjectives describing music relate to each other and to the adjectives you used to describe the environment.

Costumes

The costumes will help define the characters onstage. In many ways, this relates to the question you answered in the Thematic Environment section: Who are the dancers, or what do they represent?

A costume designer will clothe a dancer meant to represent an abstract feeling differently than they would a character in a period piece from the 18th century. Consider other questions as well, like the following:

› How are the costumes functioning in the piece? Is it to portray a character, show shapes and lines of dancers, or both?
› How will the costumes characterize the dancers?
› How will the costumes operate in the piece with movement?
  › Does the costume need to allow floor work or partnering?
  › What kind of flow do you want the material to respond to movement with?

Another helpful element to include is an assortment of inspirational images or resources. These are not intended to dictate exactly what the creator wants the costume designer to produce. Instead, they should help inspire the costume designer. As you draw from the evocative research you gathered initially, what are some images or styles that seem to match the general theme or aesthetic of your work? Whether they be images of clothing or just of colors, pieces of art, or descriptions of feelings, these items will help a costume designer gather the necessary context to create costumes that are both functional for the movement and characterization of the dancers.

Visual and Evocative Research

Throughout the creative brief, or in its own section at the end, include some of the key evocative research from your initial research collection. It might be visual research for a specific element, like a costume from a specific period; a photograph of what light looks like when it comes through smoke; or abstract pieces of art, textures, items, colors, and even sounds or videos. The more imagery you have, the more specific your environment can become. The evocative section allows your collaborators to *see* and *feel* the environment you hope to create, not just read about it.

One of the most valuable parts of the creative brief is its abstract nature. When you answer these broad questions and provide evocative images and metaphors to communicate with the team, that range of information gives the whole production team context and helps each collaborator create as complete a picture as possible of your vision in their head. When they add their own perspectives to the picture, it generates even more context and helps create a product that is full of substance and depth. Because of this, presenting the team with this brief will give the collaborators a more complete understanding of the vision and help you further define the vision yourself.

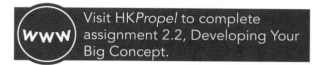

Summary

Your artistic vision is the core of the production. Articulating this vision to others and making logistical production choices that accurately represent your intention are key to making sure this vision stays at the heart of the performance.

To bring this artistic vision to life, the context of the performance—elements like the purpose, audience, and performance space—must be carefully considered and curated to reflect your vision. The purpose, or reason for creating the performance, should inform the production choices made along the way so the piece will fulfill its intention completely. The predicted audience should be evaluated to make sure the content of your vision aligns with your intent for the people coming to view it. Finally, the performance space you choose should align with the physical and financial scale as well as the intended presentation of your vision to reflect your intention as fully as possible.

To ensure all these decisions are made with the fullness of your vision in mind, the vision needs to be communicated to your production team through a creative brief, a document or presentation used to outline the strategy and context of your creative project. This brief will include general information, your intended concept, thematic environment, structure, lighting and aesthetics, music and sound, costumes, and visual and evocative research. This information will give your production team thorough context for your intention and vision as a choreographer, ensuring that every production decision is made with the creative intention in mind and that your production logistically represents your artistic vision, the core of the performance.

3

Logistical Considerations

Key Terms

addenda
amendments
budget
contract
co-presentation
copyright
deductible
employee
expense
fiscal receiver
grand rights
independent contractor
letter of agreement
liability
market
memorandum of understanding (MOU)
premium
presented
reel
revenue
self-producing
SWOT analysis
sync rights
workers' compensation

LEARNING OBJECTIVES

After reading this chapter, you will be able to do the following:

❯ Recognize the logistical considerations tied to the artistic vision
❯ Execute an effective SWOT analysis
❯ Understand the levels of collaborative organizations and your role in them
❯ Distinguish between an employee and an independent contractor
❯ Acknowledge important aspects to look for in a contract as a producer or as an individual artist
❯ Identify what type of liability protection you may need for a project
❯ Create a clear budget for your project

Once the artistic vision is clear, it is time to analyze logistics to ensure that the vision is brought to life with the most potential for growth. Though it may not be as fun as artistic creation, analyzing logistical considerations will help identify what is possible and beneficial for your project as well as what is unnecessary. Knowing the limitations early will guide you toward opportunities for expansion and growth and away from threats to your chances of success. A thoughtful and thorough analysis enables you to structure your team and address the logistical aspects of producing dance, find the balance between the visionary artist and the logistical realities, and maximize your potential for success.

The production resources readily available to you will depend on your current situation as a student, a creator early in their career, or an experienced choreographer, designer, or production collaborator. A student in an institutional setting needs to understand the complexities of a production and the roles and responsibilities of all the players. For students, many production elements may be taken for granted or handled at an administrative level out of your control; however, understanding all production facets will increase your appreciation for all the moving parts and prepare you for producing your own work. Once outside the support of your institution, as a young professional it is your responsibility to have a comprehensive grasp of the world of dance production. In this chapter, you will be introduced to some of the more practical factors that go into a production.

SWOT Analysis

As the foundation for a production begins to come together in the form of concept or idea, it's import-ant to put the vision to the test by doing an in-depth analysis of its realistic potential. A thorough analysis will assess positive and negative components both within and outside of the project. One way to do this is with a SWOT analysis. SWOT stands for strengths, weaknesses, opportunities, and threats, and a **SWOT analysis** is a strategic planning tool used to assess the internal (strengths and weaknesses) and external (opportunities and threats) factors of organizations (Teoli, Sanvictores, and An 2021).

Although organizations and companies typically use a SWOT analysis, it can be beneficial for individuals as well. It can be argued that successful artists have been doing all along what a SWOT analysis aims to do—they are aware of what they bring to the table and can recognize the opportunities on the other side of it. Therefore, it would be beneficial for artists to grasp fully how this planning tool can support their artistic endeavors and career development.

Leaders use a SWOT analysis for the following:

› Implementing successful strategic planning
› Navigating competitive markets
› Launching new initiatives
› Enhancing what companies excel at
› Recognizing areas that may need to be improved
› Taking advantage of industry trends
› Reducing areas of vulnerability

In its classic structure, the components of SWOT are laid out in a matrix comparing the internal and external helpful and harmful elements of a project (see figure 3.1). The top row has the elements originating internally—the things you can control—and the bottom has the elements out of your control—external sources. The left column contains helpful

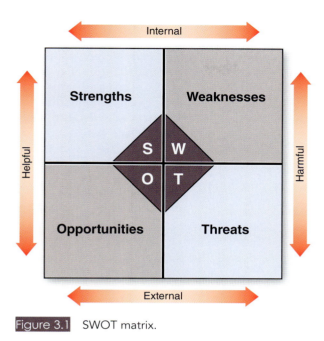

Figure 3.1 SWOT matrix.

components, and the right contains harmful. In this layout, *strengths* are helpful internal elements such as beneficial skills or knowledge of internal origin. *Weaknesses* are harmful internal elements such as the problems, obstacles, or vulnerabilities coming from within the team or project. *Opportunities* are helpful external elements: things outside your project that can benefit your creation. Finally, *threats* are the harmful external components to consider, like unfavorable trends in the market. Though the defined structure of a SWOT matrix is not the only method to approach an analysis of a vision, the components of its structure are present in any analysis that allows the artist to see both the internal and external potential and possible pitfalls.

Strengths

The first elements to acknowledge are the tools you already have. These include the following:

› Intrinsic knowledge and experience
› Internal assets and resources
› Alignment to a clear mission statement (or an idea)
› Honed skills and qualifications

What physical and experiential resources do you have at your disposal already? What experiences, knowledge, and capabilities do you have that will serve the project? Maybe your work involves live musicians, and because you played the violin when you were younger, you are able to read sheet music, notice musical nuances, and use classical terminology to better communicate with your musicians. If you already have a collaborative team, what strengths do they bring to the table? Maybe your lighting designer has a history working with the most current projection technology—this might be beneficial to your new piece, which uses projection mapping.

Remember, your strengths are also the actions that you can control that benefit your project. Your initial idea and commitment to its essence are within your control, so that can be a strength to your project. Your inspiration and drive will be unmatched in your own endeavors, so lean into your passion and find strength in your convictions. Similarly, the research you conduct while developing your vision statement and the clarity in communicating it can be another strength for your work. The effort you put into gathering these resources is under your control, and collecting and communicating thorough research will allow you to be well prepared for approaching donors, investors, business partners, and patrons. The more intelligent you become on a subject, the more strength you will have in supporting your work both in conversation and funding.

Other strengths include things that are simply integral or "a given" about your project. These may be unchangeable, but when approached and considered carefully, they could serve as productive strengths. Maybe it's your operational structure. For example, if you are working as a nonprofit, you might have access to more grants than an independent creator would. Maybe it's an institution or organization you're working within. As a student, you might have a venue chosen for you already, an allotted costume or set budget, or guidance and counsel from trusted professors and established creators. Any elements that may seem standard to whatever realm you're working in may benefit you in some way.

All these strengths—the tools and knowledge available to you, the effort you put in, or the integral elements of your structure—are there to help you. Though some may seem obvious or small, each strength is an asset at the core of your ability to produce the project and available immediately as you begin creating. With an in-depth analysis, you might find more strengths and capabilities that you didn't see before. Acknowledging them, obvious or not, and putting them all in one place allows you to address them, giving your work the best chance of success.

Weaknesses

The foils to your strengths will be your weaknesses. They include the following:

> › Resources, knowledge, and experience you and your collaborative team *do not* possess
> › Vulnerabilities
> › Needed assets

Just as you may possess knowledge that could help your process, there may be some knowledge, experience, or resources that you lack going into your creation. Conceptually, if you're creating a piece about a cause you care about but haven't experienced it firsthand, you may be lacking some crucial experiential knowledge. As you begin the creation process, it might benefit you to bring in a collaborator who possesses this knowledge. It's also important to acknowledge if you or your collaborative team lacks any practical or technical knowledge or experience. If you're hoping to create a work that uses multiple new technologies, but your collaborative team has never worked with these technologies, this might be a weakness you need to address.

Actions under your control should be considered for weaknesses as well. Even though your commitment and research could be a strength for the work, it could just as easily be a weakness if you are unprepared. You have control over your own preparation, and it's important to make sure you are dedicating your time to a clear and intentional production so that your effort benefits your project rather than damages it. Your communication of these ideas is the same. It could be a strength if you are communicating with clarity but a weakness if you aren't conveying the core vision effectively. People generally support great ideas, and if yours is misunderstood or unclear, your collaborators may not be interested in your vision or present it clearly. Without a cohesive presentation of your vision, your production is inevitably weakened.

Your operational structure or other unchangeable elements to your performance can benefit your approach to the work, but other integral or operational aspects may hinder it. The same elements of being a student that may be strengths for one work might be a weakness for another. For example, you may find yourself struggling for funding as an independent creator or limited by your donors as a nonprofit organization. As a student, if you have a venue chosen for you that doesn't allow the full scope of your intended vision so it needs to be addressed or altered but you lack the skill to do so, that inability to adjust becomes a weakness.

Some weaknesses can be easily remedied; others are more difficult and may require a strength or opportunity to offset them. Gaps in your knowledge and experience or assets you're missing might be helped by hiring people with the knowledge or experience you are lacking to consult on your project. This may come with an added financial cost, but it could help reduce the blow of existing limitations on your vision. Weaknesses that are more difficult to change should be offset by acknowledging your strengths to balance and reduce the number of avoidable weaknesses on your chart. Sometimes you can find a helpful strength in yourself, and sometimes an opportunity to work with someone or a strength they bring to the collaborative team provides the strength that will offset or reduce the power of a weakness.

It might feel easy to ignore some of your weaknesses, especially the difficult ones, assuming that focusing on what you do have will help you work around what you don't. But taking action and strengthening your setbacks rather than ignoring them allows you to get a fuller picture of what's at your disposal and a more realistic depiction of your ability to produce the performance. Acknowledging this right off the bat will give you a sense of what you're up against and what your vision's realistic potential is.

Opportunities

Your opportunities represent where your vision could grow. These are the external components out of your control that have the potential to serve your vision. What can help your vision be the best it can be? When you take the time to notice these and take advantage of them, your work has a better chance of thriving. These opportunities may include the following:

> › An awareness of competitors
> › Potential partnerships with external organizations, events, or causes
> › Favorable trends in the market you are presenting in
> › The external niche you can align your artistic choices with

One of your biggest opportunities are the people coming to see your piece. An intended audience, or **market**, for your production is the group of people your creation is aimed toward and the environment in which it sits. For most dance productions, the market tends be individuals of varying ages who are interested in and exposed to the arts community, but this can be expanded with the specifications of your unique vision. When considering your artistic vision, you took into account the audience for your piece as you made artistic decisions. Now, use that group to notice what niche market could be available. Considering the market also involves the thinking about what else exists around you already. This is where you dive back into your vision research. Ask the following questions:

› What makes your project different or important to a specific group of people?

› What are the current events or social movements going on that might relate to your work?

› Is there a lot of work being made about this specific concept?

Knowing what exists around your work will allow you to better notice where it fits into the community and where it will thrive. These components of your market tie back to your audience and your purpose explored in chapter 2. By intentionally aligning your purpose with the opportunities your intended audience presents, you give your work an opportunity to grow and reach more of the people you want to reach. If you choose a purpose that doesn't align with your market or intended audience, that purpose could become a threat to your work's survival.

Along with addressing and *assessing* the market you're bringing your work into, it's also beneficial to consider partnering or starting conversations with organizations or movements you find in this market. Noticing entities in your community that align with different aspects of your purpose, whether it be conceptually or financially, may help you find potential alliances for your project. Maybe a piece addressing climate change could be served by a partnership with an environmental group. Partnerships like this are mutually beneficial and allow you to reach more people in the community who may not have arts access but are interested in your subject matter. It also allows your partnering organization to reach those who may not know much about the subject matter they're supporting, but have an interest in the arts.

Other external elements like your venue or mode of performance can provide specific opportunities to further benefit your performance. However, a venue or mode that doesn't serve your vision may serve as a threat instead of an opportunity, so choose wisely! An *appropriate* space with the resources *you* need is an opportunity. It doesn't need to be perfect. It just needs to be the best option for *you*, *your* production, and *your* audience.

Threats

When you consider market trends, potential partnerships, and other opportunities that may benefit your vision, there may be unfavorable elements you need to consider as well. These are your threats. Threats are the items outside your control that affect your process negatively. They may include the following:

› Necessary permits

› A trend of lack of external financial support

› Audience or market perceptions that don't align with your artistic vision

A big threat to many productions has to do with financial support and capability. There are always some financial elements within your control, but often, unless you are completely self-produced and self-funded, as a creator you are working as a nonprofit or with other organizations that aid you financially. If a project is depending on grants or other means of financial support beyond your control, that could be a threat because the decisions to grant financial backing are not up to you. Even if you're self-produced or financially supported by another entity, there is still a limit to the financial *capacity* you have for a single production. If the project continues and more threats and weaknesses emerge that need to be addressed, there may be adjustments to costs that are unreachable. If your financial need outweighs your innate capability to a point that is out of your control, that is a threat to your ability to finish the production.

Just as an intended audience or market can serve as an opportunity for your work, the same audience and their perceptions could also be a threat. If your work is recurring, or you are a creator who has a reputation, audience perception is extremely important as you consider how to avoid negative reactions. Negative audience perceptions of an initial performance (bad reviews) can hurt the rest of the run, and depending on how deep these perceptions penetrate, they may affect future works you produce. Of course, any reaction from the audience is out of your control and unexpected, but doing a thorough and considerate analysis of your intended audience ahead of production can minimize any negative reaction to your work after it's created.

Just like any other aspect of life, unforeseen events can threaten your work. From a small event, like being denied a necessary permit for a site-specific venue or finding out a specific talent you were expecting doesn't sign on to the project, to larger events like injuries, emergencies, disasters, and pandemics, an unexpected bump in the road will inevitably cause a creator to have to adapt as they create. Of course, these threats are not usually predictable, but acknowledging their possibility ahead of time at least gives you a semblance of preparation if any do happen. If you have an inkling that an unforeseen event may affect your performance, even better, because you can be prepared with a plan to adapt before the event even occurs.

SWOT Application

It's one thing to notice the individual strengths, weaknesses, opportunities, and threats in your vision separately. The *intersections* of these elements determine the success of your work. Once you've filled in each section of your matrix, take a step back and start to notice patterns and possible alignments between them.

Aligning an existing strength with an opportunity grows *potential* for your vision. Maybe your lighting designer's strength in pixel mapping could be paired with your opportunity to choose a venue with a high-quality LED array and lighting rig, creating potential for your vision. One without the other may be valuable, but the potential is made stronger by noticing their alignment and acting on both of them.

On the other hand, an existing weakness that aligns with a threat can create a *risk* to your vision. The best a creator can do to offset these risks is to minimize their impact. Though threats cannot be changed, the risk they create can be minimized by strengthening weaknesses or countering them with an existing strength or opportunity. These strengths can help offset risks by making them smaller, but they do not completely eradicate them. Noticing the risk by finding the connection between the weakness and the threat is the first step to minimizing it.

This is an evolving matrix. As more information emerges, you will add to or remove from the matrix, and you'll notice connections shifting. As your vision becomes clearer, your goal is to hang on to and align as many potentials as you can while

YOUR SWOT MATRIX

Imagine you're an independent choreographer creating a piece for a festival, and you've decided to submit a piece casting some of your friends who are professional dancers. You might include the following questions to help you fill in your SWOT matrix.

Internal Research

> Do I have experience making the type of work I would like to submit to the festival?
> What knowledge do I have about the submitting process to the festival and the type of work they prioritize?
> Do I have enough internal resources (including money and time) to create, rehearse, and submit the work by the deadline?
> Will I be able to pay the dancers? If not, do I have a network of dancers that may be interested in volunteering for this project?
> Do I know a costume designer who can work with me on the concept of my piece?
> Do I or any of my assistants have knowledge and experience writing grants?

External Research

> Does the festival consider new, up-and-coming choreographers like me, or do they prioritize choreographers who have substantial choreographic experience?
> If my work is chosen, will the producers or organizers fund the travel expenses for me and the dancers?
> What grant options are there to help fund my project?
> Who are the choreographers that typically submit to this festival, and what advantages do they have over my company?
> Will I have enough time before the submission to secure the rights to the music I want to use for this project?

minimizing as many risks as possible. Take a look at figure 3.2 to see a sample of a SWOT analysis matrix.

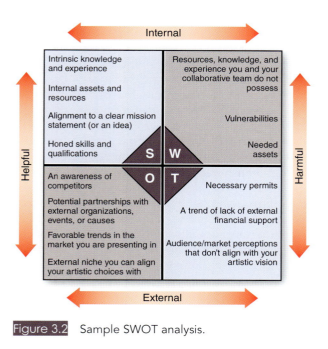

Figure 3.2 Sample SWOT analysis.

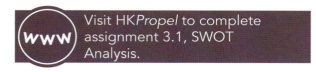

Visit HK*Propel* to complete assignment 3.1, SWOT Analysis.

Financial Structure

The financial structure your future performance operates under allows you to plan a realistic budget within your limits. The operational form your work falls under may serve the vision in a specific way. You may work as a freelance artist, part of a nonprofit organization, or part of a for-profit entity, and each brings its own financial benefits and risks. Where your work is situated is important, and your role as a creator or collaborator changes based on its financial structure. Understanding different structures will help you recognize how to best serve it financially and artistically.

Independent Artists

Many creators begin their careers working with their friends in a shared apartment, dreaming of fame and fortune. This is where they develop their first artistic vision, create the work, and identify the means to make the performance happen. As the sole person responsible for the work, an independent artist, sometimes referred to as a *freelance artist*, needs to generate the resources necessary to support their production. Some of those resources are financial, but nonmonetary resources also become incredibly valuable to an independent artist. While in college, you can develop a network of creative voices, with everyone sharing a common goal of expanding their skills and résumés to gain some attention for their art. Independent artists with minimal funds may find that trading with others or donating time and technical skills early in their career can be mutually beneficial. A friend's father may have a repair shop that is the perfect set for a period musical theatre piece. A budding costume designer may donate their time to make costumes (and only charge for supplies) to build their portfolio. Independent artists "make it happen" by finding creative ways to raise money, barter, secure rehearsal and performance spaces, and procure necessary resources. These are some of the most creative and collaborative people when they have a clear vision.

An independent artist can also get temporary work, commonly referred to as a *gig*, often as a choreographer or dancer. A one-time opportunity is called a *one-off*; the artist is contracted to do one project and will not expect to be included in another project after completion. Many jobs are one-offs, and while they don't officially lead to another booking, they establish an artist's reputation, for better or worse. If you demonstrate skill, professionalism, and collegiality, the collaborators with whom you work will often recommend you to others. This is how the networking cycle works to your benefit. Conversely, if you display negative tendencies, you can be sure that your colleagues will let others know. It's a small world out there, and your reputation precedes and follows you wherever you go.

An independent artist with a good reputation may earn paid contract work with the same company or companies repeatedly, often at the same time. Independent contractors can set their own schedule and accept as many or as few projects as they wish. However, they are almost always hustling for their next gig. Independent contractors are not an employee of any company but sign an agreement (a contract) with a company to provide a service (i.e., talent, choreography, design) for a predetermined period of time in exchange for a fixed rate or set fee.

BE AWARE OF TAXES

Independent contractors must be personally responsible for their business affairs, including the paying of taxes. Unlike an employee–employer relationship, wherein the employer withholds money from the employee's paycheck throughout the year in order to send tax payments on the employee's behalf, the independent contractor receives payment in full for services rendered and is solely responsible for paying all taxes due on that money. Taxes may be required by the federal, state, and local governments.

The company paying the contract fee will send the contractor artist a 1099 tax document at the end of the year if the amount earned was at least $600. Depending on the taxable income for the year, holding back a percentage of each check in a savings account is a good idea. The IRS and most states charge penalties for underpayment if the taxpayer doesn't pay any taxes until filing their annual 1040 return, so consider sending quarterly estimated tax payments. It's always a good idea to consult with an accountant to set up the structure that's best for you.

Independent artists can also produce their own work for submission into dance festivals, film festivals, social media outlets, and talent agents. These works can also be used as material for a talent **reel** to increase one's online presence and can be used as choreography samples when applying for residencies. If hired for a choreography residency, you will be asked to set works on other dancers or companies.

Independent artists should read any employment offer, contract, festival agreement, or business document very carefully. You need to know to what exactly you are agreeing. You might be responsible for most or all the production elements discussed in this book. You may also want to ensure that any original intellectual property (IP) you create (i.e., the choreography of a dance or design of a costume) remains yours. Many companies will state that anything created for their company will belong to them once the contractor submits the work and is paid. But this does not have to be the case, and ownership can be negotiated. If you think the work may have future revenue potential, be assertive in pursuing retention of your IP. As with tax issues, with business decisions it is a good idea to consult a professional—in this case, an intellectual property lawyer.

It can take some time to build your repertoire and start some buzz around your work. While you are producing your own work, it is helpful to be a part of the arts community in your area, support other artists' shows, and offer to collaborate when appropriate. No one builds a career by themselves; it takes a community. If you and your dancers attend a local artist's show and provide support, they will be more likely to reciprocate.

Some independent contractors do gigs throughout their entire career, and they move from one project to another, year after year, season after season. You will have to define the type of work that best suits you, your personality, and your work style. Some choreographers work only in film and television, while others prefer to work only with staged productions. And some move between the commercial and concert industries, including working with residency shows in Las Vegas or in niche markets like cruise lines, or even pursue Broadway and musical theatre.

Nonprofit Organizations

Many dance and other artistic companies are established to educate the public on artistic endeavors, including "art history or helping to set up spaces where community artists can display their work," and commonly operate as nonprofit organizations (Indeed 2020). These entities are built to benefit the public in a particular way rather than focus on financial gain for themselves or their owners, and they operate under a specific set of rules and expectations. Many dance companies and festivals, and some freelance choreographers, are part of nonprofit organizations.

A nonprofit business is one that has applied for and been granted this status by the government. This means that the business has proven or demonstrated that their core business activity is charitable or helps the community in some way. The IRS (2022) defines *charitable organizations* thusly:

> *Organizations organized and operated exclusively for religious, charitable, scientific, testing for public safety, literary, educational, or other specified purposes and that meet certain other requirements are tax exempt under Internal Revenue Code Section 501(c)(3).*

Nonprofit organizations may make a profit, but the profit is not distributed to the founders or other private individuals. Instead, it goes back into the organization to support its mission and objectives. Nonprofits also attract donations from various sources, including individuals and businesses

(Indeed 2021). Remember that being a nonprofit organization or working for one does not mean that the organization doesn't make money. On the contrary, nonprofits can work with large budgets. For a nonprofit, though, the money that the company earns simply goes back into making art and benefiting the community rather than in the pocket of an individual. Because nonprofits are run by a board of directors, not an individual, no one person owns the organization, so no one person benefits from it. Instead, a collaborative and communal structure—the board of directors—makes decisions together and operates as the responsible party for all fiduciary, compliance, and best-practice decision making.

One of the most essential elements of running a nonprofit is fundraising. Grants can be acquired from foundations and governmental agencies. Donations may be gathered from the community the nonprofit serves, and these donations may be single gifts or part of an ongoing gift-giving campaign such as a monthly subscription. Corporations reap some benefit from donating to charitable organizations and can provide funding through a direct contribution or by partnering with a nonprofit to increase awareness in hopes of greater donations from the public. Posthumous gifts called *bequests* may be given to a nonprofit as instructed in a person's last will and testament.

The nonprofit world in the arts has a specific landscape. It is driven by social consciousness and artistic voice and is, due to its purpose in serving the public, especially grounded in community. Some nonprofit funds come from grants and community programs. However, a large portion of nonprofit revenue comes from donations, both small and large. The donors get the benefit of deducting the donation amount from their taxable income, but their primary motivator is typically seeing the impact of their contribution to a community-serving nonprofit. Independent donations build a network of supportive people around an organization, creating a community who believes in the purpose and vision of the creator.

Nonprofits rely on volunteers to do much of the work but can also have paid employees and independent contractors who provide regular services and conduct day-to-day operations. The salaries of the workers vary, but people who work for these organizations are generally passionate about the mission of the organization and are willing to pass up higher-paying jobs for the personal satisfaction of working for a nonprofit. The primary legal stipulation regarding payroll at a nonprofit is that salaries must not exceed what is "reasonable" for any given role (Indeed 2020).

If you want to create a nonprofit organization, you have to apply to the state and federal government, and applying does not guarantee approval. You must be very clear about your public benefit. Just stating you are an artist will not satisfy the agencies that make the final decision. You will need to clearly define your mission, how you will benefit the community, and your goals. You will need a board of directors because no one directly owns the company. Selecting a board of directors is important because you will need people who are invested in your vision, are willing to work as hard as you are, and bring expertise to the table. There may also be state regulations regarding the board makeup that you must to adhere to. Spend time vetting board members—a bad board member can derail an entire organization.

Organizations like the National Council of Nonprofits exist to help "newly formed nonprofits that need to raise money during the start-up phase, before they are recognized as tax-exempt by the IRS" (n.d.). You can apply to an organization as an artist, and they may choose to accept you. If they accept you, their nonprofit umbrella will house you underneath it by serving as a fiscal sponsor. People can donate to you through this sponsor nonprofit so that donors get their tax write-off. The umbrella nonprofit takes a fee from each donation. This setup can also be beneficial because you often can't apply for certain grants if you're not a nonprofit or part of a nonprofit.

NONPROFIT VERSUS FOR-PROFIT

Let's look at some examples to illustrate nonprofit and for-profit entities. Say a small local dance company has a roster of eight dancers, creates and performs one or two concerts a year, and offers community classes at a local studio. This company can bring in money from ticket sales and class fees, but this income will not be enough to pay for the dancers and cover the rehearsal space and production elements needed for the production and classes. If the company is organized as a nonprofit, it can then fundraise (through various methods) to balance its budget at the end of the year. Conversely, in a for-profit business, the primary goal is to make money for the owner. This means that the business will have an owner who will be working to make sure that the business is profitable. The owner has full authority to do what they want with the money and can take the profit for themselves or pay it to investors or stockholders.

For-Profit Organization

For-profit organizations make and sell products or services with the goal to make money. They are owned by a person or persons who make all decisions and pay income taxes. For-profit entities in the arts world, where investors or shareholders in an organization *do* expect some return of investment, usually involve more commercial work. Entities like a union house (a theatre or venue that hires only workers who are members of a labor union), theme park, TV commercial, dance convention, resident show like Cirque du Soleil, Broadway production, or other industry film or video project can all be for-profit. For-profit entities are usually governed by unions and local laws that ensure employees are treated well and not exploited.

In a for-profit entity, funds can often come from investors and shareholders in the organization or from ticket buyers, fees, and advertising. Regardless of where it comes from, the goal is to get a return on investment. Some festivals or clubs use this for-profit model, and have created a system where a creator submits choreography to be showcased and either pays a large fee for the production of the piece or sells a set number of tickets for the show themselves. In this situation, the organization gains entertainment for their establishment, and choreographers gain a place to produce their work, but at a cost. Developing a for-profit business model is beyond the scope of this book, but it can be an option for choreographers wanting to move into producing their own events. If you are interested, research developing a business plan, securing investors, and understanding state and regional laws and tax codes. You are becoming a business owner and may spend more time on the business side than the artistic side in your industry.

STARVING ARTISTS

Artists deserve to be paid for their work. The phrase "starving artist" is an old sentiment, and new generations of entrepreneurial artists can begin to shift this perception. For-profit and nonprofit organizations can connect to support each other. It is important for you to define what the goals for your organization are and then determine which structure seems to be the best fit. Take the time to research and look at other artists you admire and see what types of structure they have developed.

Collaborative Organizational Structures

As a student or young artist, much of the work you do occurs through collaboration with friends. This may mean there is a trading of services or a mutual pooling of resources for a common goal. Many great companies and partnerships started in this organic way and eventually developed a business plan and formal structure. Everyone would like to be paid for their talents in some way, and understanding some of the complexities of either being the hired artist or hiring the team to work toward your vision is helpful as you grow your career and vision for the future.

Whether you are the choreographer, designer, technical director, or part of the production staff, all collaborative artists have gaps in knowledge. The previous two chapters have helped identify these gaps as well as your areas of strength and weakness. Now, as your collaborative team starts to form, you can find collaborators that fill the "holes" of your weaknesses, emphasize your strengths, and add necessary value to your project. When the right collaborators assemble, the hypothetical vision you've planned for becomes tangible and is made whole. This "whole" vision can be formed in more than one way, though. The number and roles of these collaborators may vary based on the size and scope of the project. It may simply be you and a couple friends doing the jobs of what might be 12 collaborators in a larger organization, or it might be a well-organized large-scale nonprofit where each technical aspect has its own designer. In any case, having the big picture in mind is the key. In a collaborative production, players come from different perspectives, disciplines, and directions to support a singular vision and bring it to life as fully and as completely as possible. The vision is the heart of the collaborative body of players.

Every collaborative project and team may look different. Sample dance production organizational flowcharts are shown in figures 3.3 (independent choreographer), 3.4 (freelance artists), and 3.5 (dance company). These collaborations can be arranged in several ways depending on how many hats each collaborator must wear, as is common in the arts world. In some cases, for example, the choreographer may also be the artistic director, costume designer, facilities manager, and marketing director. Whatever the case and whatever the scale, the whole team works together to support

Logistical Considerations   **39**

the creative vision, so it's important to choose players who will dedicate themselves to that purpose.

 Visit HK*Propel* to complete assignment 3.2, Creating an Organizational Structure.

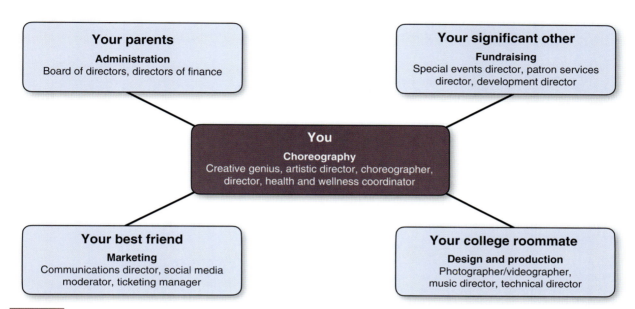

Figure 3.3   Sample organizational chart for independent choreographer.

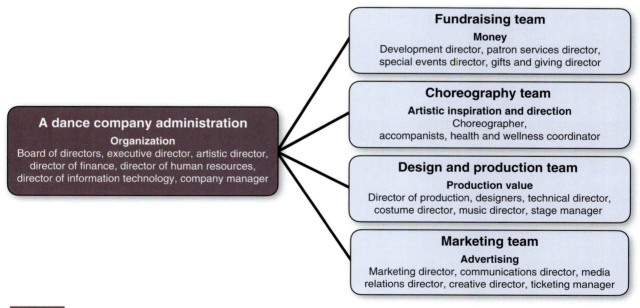

Figure 3.4   Sample organizational chart for freelance artists.

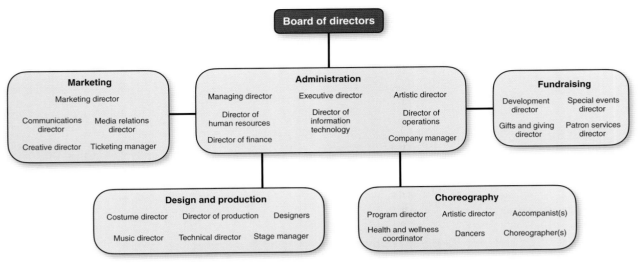

Figure 3.5 Sample organizational chart for dance company.

Arts Administration

Regardless of which professional pathway you choose, at some point you will be responsible for administrative tasks. You will need a working knowledge of the organization's operations, and in the beginning, you will wear many hats as you develop a business structure. The areas you need support in will become apparent to you. If you thrive in the creation process but not in the administrative side, find someone to collaborate with. If it is your company or your vision, you can hire someone to help you with the administrative work. Some administrative activities can be delegated to an assistant or a company member, but other jobs will need someone who has experience in arts administration.

You will need people—maybe lots of people—to bring an artistic vision to life. The people you collaborate with are your human capital. These are the most important people in your pursuit of a production because you are responsible in some way for or to them. Whether you are the creator hiring others or an employee or independent contractor yourself, it's important to know how the pieces fit together so you can collaborate with the best people for the job.

This section gives you an overview of some key administrative topics: modes of producing, workers, contracts, insurance and liabilities, music rights, and budget. At some point in your career, you are likely to encounter these in your working environments. They can be tricky, and depending on your city, state, or country, there may be different regulations, forms, and rules. Understanding the roles for these components will empower you to navigate these systems or at the very least be informed enough to ask questions.

Modes of Producing

There are different modes of presenting a work at a venue: You can self-produce, be presented by an organization, or have a co-presentation. You might not have a choice about which mode is used for your work.

Self-producing is when you create your own work and produce all of it yourself. It means that any risk (financial or otherwise) will fall on you and you alone. You are responsible for creating, marketing, ticket sales, and everything in between. You hold all the risk and all the reward. You will book and pay for the space or venue, provide the funds to pay any collaborators, and take on any other necessary responsibilities to produce the performance. Early in your creative career, you may self-produce most of your works. It's a way to begin to get your work out into the world, and even though it may seem daunting to carry the risk yourself, it does mean you have complete control over your collaborators and artistic choices.

If an organization asks you to create for them, you are being **presented** by an organization. For an artist, it can be exciting to be presented. In this model, the creator gets paid a fee to make their art while the venue is responsible for most marketing, ticket sales, crew, and everything else. Though the artist has some responsibilities for providing marketing materials like information and images in a timely manner and will do their own marketing to their general audience, the main thing they are required to do is to essentially show up and do a great job. In this model, the presenting organization—the theatre, performing arts center, arts society, or foundation—contributes to the funding for the project and takes most of the risk. You can be presented in commercial venues, and creating for a university or festival setting would also fall under being presented. Remember, though, the financial contribution you receive may not cover your expenses, so it doesn't guarantee full financial support.

Sometimes, both the venue and the creator will take on risk. This is called **co-presentation**, and can take many forms. Both parties assume some of the risk and returns from the performance. This could mean you get paid a smaller fee with a bonus if a set amount of tickets are sold, or maybe you're not paid a fee but split the box office revenue with the venue, or maybe you share the accolades for a spectacular event that draws people to the venue for future events and provides some media buzz for your own work. Whatever it is, the risk and interest in selling tickets is taken on by both the artist and the venue. Wonderful collaborations can come out of this model where everyone is invested in the success of a project.

Each strategy has strengths and weaknesses and can be found in the freelance, commercial, concert, film, and musical theatre production realms. In each mode, regardless of the risks taken, designers, choreographers, dancers, and production teams all need to be on the same page and have clear understandings of roles and responsibilities for each party, driven by how the work is going to proceed to a performance.

Personnel

In any production or organization, whether you're the producer taking on people to work for you or an artist managing your jobs, the logistics of hiring or being hired can be complicated to navigate. Earlier in this chapter, we discussed financial structures and how you might establish yourself as an artist. As an arts administrator, you might have the responsibility of hiring the dance, design, and production team. It's important to consider whether you will hire an employee or an independent contractor. There are different laws and regulations for each that need to be considered and followed.

Every state has its own set of labor laws for employees, and there are federal laws related to worker protections, such as minimum wage require-

ments. Each jurisdiction, county, or city imposes its own statutes, including, perhaps, an even higher minimum wage for employees. When you are hiring the production team, consult your local labor laws to determine whether you should hire an independent contractor or an employee. You can hire people for part-time, temporary, limited-term, and full-time work. Each classification carries a certain set of rules and regulations as well as benefits:

> *A short-term position is a temporary job that can last from one day to about one month. You are assigned specific duties, and then you are finished after the allotted time is up. A long-term position is often considered to last beyond six weeks, or if you work more than 1,000 hours in a 12-month period. These jobs can involve more responsibilities and a consistent schedule, depending on the nature of the work. A part-time job can be either short-term or long-term. Part-time employees work less than 40 hours a week, but a full-time employee typically works 40 hours per week every week, and often receives benefits (ZipRecruiter n.d.).*

If you can pay someone on a regular basis, hiring an employee is advantageous because they can have a sense of buy-in to the company and production. They act on behalf of the company, and their actions and performance reflect the standards the company establishes. A contractor acts on their own behalf, and delivers a product, whether it be a design plot or choreography. In the production, products being created are also called **deliverables**. Once the deliverables have been received and payment has been made, the relationship with an independent contractor is over. You can contract with that person again, but in the meantime, they have no legal affiliation with your company or any moral or ethical responsibility to you or the production.

If you are a worker, you may choose to pursue regular employment, contract or gig work, or a combination of both as you develop your career. There is no right or wrong approach, but each person should consider their personal needs and how to meet those needs each month or year to determine the best path forward.

In the arts, it is not uncommon to hear the story of a dancer who works as a barista by day and dances for experience by night. The cliché is that an artist will work for a low hourly wage all day and either volunteer or get paid a small performance fee to have the privilege to dance at night. Consider what jobs you could get in the dance or broader performing arts industry by day! Break the cliché and get a job in an educational setting or a theme park or tourism organization. Working within the industry as a stagehand, office intern, or social media representative keeps you connected—and your network is the most valuable resource you have other than your dance and production skills.

Contracts

A **contract,** or an agreement, between two or more parties is a way for the parties to agree on how to do business together in a written and legally binding document. When entering an agreement, your mindset should be that the contract is for mutual benefit and fair treatment under the law yet protects your interests. As a choreographer, dancer, or designer, you may be the one being hired for a gig, or you may be the one doing the hiring to support your vision. Understanding both sides of this equation will help you become a better negotiator and benefit both parties. Having legal support to develop a contract that works for you as the employer and to review any contracts you sign as a contractor will cost money but help you avoid mistakes and conflicts later. It will protect your best interests.

Most contracts for an employer are aimed at protecting the employer from liability and getting sued. The terms specify the deliverables and who is responsible for them. Everything else is geared toward making sure that the company is not liable for any legal mistakes by the contractor (like not paying taxes). Contractors typically carry their own liability insurance so the employer does not pay workers' compensation or cover an injury while on the job; this will be stipulated in the contract (Chapman, Lai, and Steinbock 1983).

The contract may define intellectual property (IP), including copyrights, trademarks, and patents, indicating who owns them before and after the contract period. In the arts, intellectual property may include the choreography, technical designs, or innovative production elements. "Intellectual property is generally characterized as non-physical property that is the product of original thought. Typically, rights do not surround the abstract non-physical entity; rather, intellectual property rights surround the control of physical manifestations or expressions of ideas. Intellectual property law protects a content-creator's interest in her ideas by assigning and enforcing legal rights to produce and control physical instantiations of those ideas" (Moore and Himma 2018).

Privacy, conflicts of interest, and confidentiality are common sections of contracts, especially in the performing arts, where the producer does not want the show spoiled by leaking or early sharing of information. Exit clauses allow the parties to part ways in a professional manner and can include information about arbitration, dispute resolution, and force majeure. Sometimes contextual clauses need to be included, such as language that prevents an employer from being sued over something like someone contracting an illness or injuring themselves on the job, a pandemic, or an especially risky work environment.

When you are the contractor or worker, you need to pay attention to what protects you. The first step is actually reading the contract! Most contracts are developed from templates that cover the typical legal issues associated with a particular endeavor. You cannot work without signing the contract, but you can respond to the employer with questions or concerns about any portion of the contract.

Almost everything is negotiable, so feel confident in raising questions and making changes. **Amendments** to contracts may come in the form of initialed strikeouts (and rewrites), **addenda** (additional material added to the contract), or a **memorandum of understanding (MOU)** (an agreement before the contract is finalized; it gets the terms written in a new form for a rewritten contract). Remember, both parties want to find an agreement, and that sometimes requires compromise or education. The contracting process should be a conversation, not a demand. This includes all the terms and fees. If an employer is firm on a point, you need to consider whether this point is worth negating the entire contract. If not, go for it. If the sticking point is too important to you, walk away. You're not required to do anything until you sign the contract.

Contracts vary depending on performance industry sector. The main differences tend to be in the complexity and specificity of the contracts. Contracts communicate what each side will be responsible for. The two sides can be defined as but not limited to the following:

› Employer (a dance company) and employee (a person)

› Theatre (location or space) and Guest Dance Company (a traveling group)

The more detailed the contract is, the easier it will be to see who is responsible for what. The best way to avoid conflict is through a clear definition of who is involved, what is being done, why it is done, and how it is done. Clear details lead to better contracts. Contracts include the following elements:

› *Who:* Defines the name and title of the person in each role
› *What:* Defines tasks or jobs that need to be accomplished (safely)
› *Why:* Decisions are dictated by rules and regulations: Details whether it will be union, OSHA or the dance company rules defining how to proceed, including where conflict, compromise, and agreement lie
› *How:* The protocol for that specific theatre or space, its dynamics, any timelines or restricted areas (such as warm-up times or rooms that can be used during the experience)

Typical elements of a contract or agreement may include the categories shown in figure 3.6.

Productions often run smoothly and are quite successful. Everyone goes home (or to the next town) satisfied and safe. However, if something goes wrong, such as something was not done or perhaps someone is injured, the violation and who is responsible for it needs to be clarified. A contract will be used to clarify this liability.

In the event of conflict, the people involved should be reminded about what they signed and agreed to. A simple misunderstanding can be resolved by consulting the contract itself. As an example, a dance company could arrive at the venue and discover the safety is not what they agreed to in the contract. If the dance company doesn't feel that their best interest is being looked after, the company could refuse to perform and cancel the gig. Read your contract carefully before making any decisions regarding a conflict. The contract is your defense against legal action from the other party on the contract.

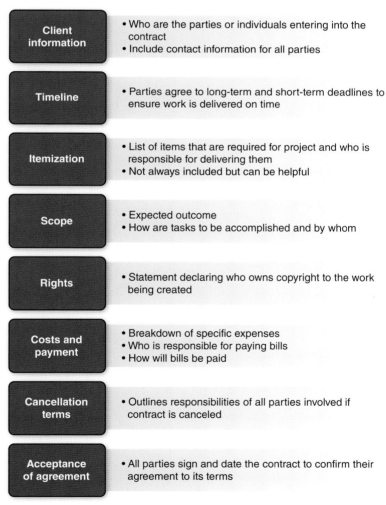

Figure 3.6 Elements of a contract.

In another scenario, the dance company may simply not live up to what they agreed to in the contract. The theatre company can use the contract to avoid paying the company.

A nontraditional or smaller or newer company may have a very informal or simple contract and contracting process. They may use a letter of agreement or a contract from a template within a popular computer application. A commercial contract will be dense and read like legalese, as in an academic contract. The type and extent of any contract will be influenced by two primary factors: the employer's legal advisor or department and the employer's litigation history (if they've been sued before, the contracts will be watertight).

This information might seem overwhelming, but you will grow into this process. Keep your first projects small and simple and expand as you increase your experience. Understanding the big picture may save you some missteps along the way. Review the list of elements in figure 3.6 to prepare yourself for what to expect when reading or writing a contract. If you are under the umbrella of an institution, you may not be aware of contracts. However, if you do freelance projects or hire freelancers, take the time to understand what you are signing or agreeing to. The essentials will likely be included in any contract, but company specifics may expand on essentials or provide additional details specific to the contractor or task. Because a contract could include other parties, a contract will acknowledge whether they are involved or allowed to be involved and to what extent.

Conditions refer to requirements that make or break the agreement, including things like requiring either party to hold insurance to authorize the contract or specifying how and why a party might legally exit the contract. *Liabilities* are things that could burden or harm either party; liability assigns responsibility to someone for wrongdoing or loss. *Protections* provide language to avoid or mitigate negative legal actions toward either party in the event of a disagreement or a greater breakdown of the working relationship between the parties involved.

A worker might be offered a **letter of agreement** (LOA) instead of a traditional contract. A letter of agreement is an offer of employment and includes the terms of employment and an acceptance of the offer in letter format. This may precede or be an offer of regular employment. A letter of agreement can be a binding contract if signed by both the contractor and employer. In the traditional sense, a contract is a more structured, templated (boilerplate) docu-ment that outlines in detail the specifications and nuances of an agreement. It is usually presented with many sections and subsections and has blanks to add production-specific terms and information. All contracts or agreements require signatures by both the employer and contractor, and sometimes they require a witness or notary.

If you do your homework, consult professional counsel, and partner with reputable people and companies, a contract can be a valuable tool among your production resources. Be willing to negotiate so a contract benefits both parties. Contracts exist to protect you—just read the fine print and know what you are getting into.

Insurance and Liability

Most people are familiar with health, renter's, or car insurance. The general idea is you regularly pay a fee called a **premium** to an insurance company, and if you encounter covered expenses, the insurance company will step in and assist with some costs, depending on your **deductible** and policy terms. The type of insurance you need to consider carrying as a professional will depend on your role. If you are only protecting yourself as a freelance dancer or choreographer, you may need personal general liability, which covers bodily injury and property damage claims. If you are renting a location or presenting work in a venue, your business will likely need to carry a liability policy. Before signing any contracts, see if you will need insurance to protect yourself and your dancers. Many gamble with their livelihoods and don't purchase insurance, but if something goes wrong and you are found responsible for the damages, this can have a devastating effect on your life for years. Having some liability insurance is a good business practice. Do your research and protect your assets.

If you are used to working with dancers, or are one yourself, chances are you have seen a twisted ankle or similar injury occur in the production process. **Liability** refers to who is responsible when an injury takes place. Professional liability policies and general liability policies can be held by an individual artist and a company. There are plenty of options for insurance policies out there. Choose a reputable company. You can review a company's reputation by researching them on the Better Business Bureau (BBB) website. Policies of $1 million to $2 million are most commonly required. Some jobs or venues may require you to have a liability insurance policy before allowing you to work or perform.

The costs vary by company and will change over time, so you will need to shop around. Though this is an out-of-pocket expense, it means you do not have to pay for medical bills, property damage, or even things like a libel suit, and the employer won't have to spend more money to finish the production if you cannot for some reason. Insurance has terms all its own, so consult with your sales representative to make sure you are getting coverage that satisfies your contract and your own willingness to accept risk.

TYPES OF INSURANCE FOR ARTISTS

Insurance can be purchased for a specific project or as general coverage during your career. It is common to combine insurance policies to help cover all the bases. Some options include:

> *Commercial property insurance* typically covers equipment used in creating your art. This could include electronics like cameras, lights, sound equipment, expensive costumes, or rented props. Any gear used to create your work and that would be difficult to replace due to the cost if damaged is covered.

> *General liability insurance* covers general liabilities or risks that may arise due to the event. This typically covers you if an audience member is hurt by tripping over cables on the ground in the theatre or if a light or piece of scenery falls and hurts a guest.

> *Errors and omissions insurance* tends to cover issues with the production not being produced correctly and to the extent specified by the contract. For example, the performance is filmed to be streamed later and someone forgets to turn on the camera, and the opportunity to capture the footage is gone.

In addition to general liability insurance mentioned previously (which is like other insurance policies for your car or health), **workers' compensation** is a benefit that covers employees who suffer illness or injury while working for a wage or salary. It can also cover disability, lost wages, and pay out a death benefit. If you are an employee (not a contractor), and you injure your toe while mopping the dance floor, the employer's worker's compensation insurance will cover your visit to the doctor. If you are a contractor, you may be asked (required) to carry this insurance in addition to or in place of general liability insurance. This would be especially true if you, as a contractor, employ hourly or salaried staff of your own.

Music Rights

If your performance includes music that is not original, whether it is played live or from a recording, you will need to obtain rights to use the music. Just because you can listen to a piece of music on the Internet does not mean you have the right to use the music. Much of the music available is protected by a **copyright**. A copyright represents the author's rights over the use, publishing, or selling of their work. You can use music considered to be in the public domain or royalty-free music if you want to avoid dealing with music rights. Public domain music was either created before copyright existed or it has been more than 70 years since the author's death. Royalty-free music is under a creative commons license and tends to include modern music, and it will not limit how you can use the music. It is common to pay an upfront fee for royalty-free music, but this fee typically is less expensive than trying to obtain rights for a copyrighted song.

Unless you select music that is in the public domain, you will need to sign a license agreement with either a composer or licensor of music rights. A license agreement will generally be drafted by the rights holder (the composer is the rights holder for a new work), and stipulates that you, the licensee, have the right to use the indicated music for a specific purpose (the performance), during a specific period (the term), and for a certain compensation (the fee). How that fee is calculated is up to the rights holder. It could be a standard flat fee or scaled based on many factors including the number of performances, the number of available tickets to the performance or performances, and the cost of those tickets.

If you choose to pursue rights to popular music, be prepared to spend a lot of time and potentially a lot of money on that selection. Music is "free" to listen to on the radio because that is how the music labels advertise their product. Music is not free, however, to use in a performance without compensating the owner of that music. Regardless of where your performance is held, the owner of the music has the right to charge you to use their property.

Broadcast Music, Inc. (BMI) and The American Society of Composers, Authors, and Publishers (ASCAP) are two of the largest licensing agencies in the world. They cannot help you license music for your production—thinking they can or will is a common misconception. These organizations provide business licenses to organizations that want to use music in a context that's not entertainment, where the sale of goods and services is not connected to using that music. Because you intend to host an audience for entertainment and perform a dramatic act with music, you need what are called *grand rights* and perhaps *sync rights* as well to be legally compliant.

Grand rights must be obtained from the rights holder or holders—yes, many works have multiple owners, and you must get the rights from all the owners to be compliant. You will need to research the music you want to use and contact the producer or label who recorded the music originally. This information can be found on the liner notes from physical media or in the description of digital media. Contact information can be found by doing an Internet search. Every piece of music is unique and has its own path to licensing. Be patient; this is a grueling process. The best way to get rights to music is to hire an attorney versed in music and copyright law.

You will also need **sync rights** if you plan to stream or broadcast your dance production. You need sync rights even if you want to put a short clip of your dance on your own website (with audio). These rights may be held by a separate rights holder than the grand rights, so make sure you consider your options early and carefully.

PUBLIC DOMAIN TIPS

Public domain law is quite complex, and you should seek legal counsel for an authoritative answer to specific cases. In the beginning, there are some basic tricks you can use to identify whether music is in the public domain or has a copyright. The key is to never assume.

› PDinfo.com is a great source to check if the music you want to use is in the public domain. This site lists all musical works in the public domain and is updated every year on January 1.

› YouTube is another great tool for finding music and discovering if a song has a copyright. When you check the video description, there will be a description of the music source, music rights, and music label. This can be a helpful starting place if you want to use a specific piece of music. Also pay attention to when you upload a project to YouTube because the program will give you a warning if the song is copyrighted and may even block your content.

One other option is a *work-made-for-hire agreement*, which you can sign with a composer who creates new music just for your dance, and you pay to own the music outright. You become the rights owner!

Budget

Generating an artistic vision doesn't cost anything, but bringing that vision to life in a production does cost. Where will you get the economic underpinning to realistically finance your endeavor in the material world? How do you know how much you'll need, or even where to start?

A **budget** balances the projected expenses and revenues associated with a project. This critical tool helps you plan how to pay for your project. Depending on the scale of a project, the size and scope of the budget will vary. Regardless of how big or small the budget, an **expense** is any service, resource, or component of your production that has a required cost. Examples include these items:

› Artist or collaborator fees

› Venue rental

› Music rights

› Payroll (paying yourself and your employees)

› Designers

› Materials for costumes, sets, and props

› Rental expenses

› Videographer and editor

› Food, housing, and transportation if travel is involved

› Social media, websites, marketing, and advertising materials

› Photographer

› All related business costs and fees

To offset these costs, a project needs **revenue**, which is the income or money received by the organization or entity. Revenue comes in two forms: earned income and contributed income. Earned income includes ticket sales, merchandise sales, masterclass fees, and any other product or service you provide for purchase. Contributed income includes donations, sponsorships, grants, and other resources given by an outside entity. In any arts production endeavor, you'll probably be dealing with both types of revenue.

The format and detail of any given budget can vary (a sample budget is shown in figure 3.7). There are numerous sample budgets online to show the various ways budgets can be set up, as well as

Income			
Ticket sales	Price	Amount sold	Total
Student	10	69	690
General	20	127	2540
Total tickets sold		196	3230
Merchandise	20	80	1600
Fundraising			0
Grants			500
Total income			**5330**

Expense	Fee	Amount	Total
Artistic director	1000	1	1000
Choreographer 1	500	1	500
Choreographer 2	500	1	500
Dancers (3 dances)	400	10	4000
Costume design	400	1	400
Costume materials dance 1	75	5	375
Costume materials dance 2	100	5	500
Costume materials rep	20	10	200
Lighting design	400	1	400
Stage manager	400	1	400
Technical director (venue)	25	12	300
Light board operator	15	12	180
Deck crew	15	12	180
Sound board operator	15	12	180
Merchandise expense	10	100	1000
Marketing/printing postcards	200	1	200
Online marketing	100	1	100
Programs	1.25	215	268.75
Graphic design	20	4	80
Insurance	250	1	250
Lighting materials	100	1	100
Miscellaneous	50	1	50
Venue rental day 1 (8 hours)	500	1	500
Venue rental day 2 (4 hours)	250	1	250
Rehearsal space fees		0	0
Ticketing fees	1	196	196
Merchant service fee	0.03	4830	144.9
Merchandise sales venue fee		0	0
Total expenses			**12254.65**

Net income			-6924.65

Figure 3.7 Sample production budget.

templates built into spreadsheet software and apps. Software programs are available for reasonable cost and can coach even a beginner through establishing a budget and managing money. Some of these programs and apps can even connect to banks and help manage debits and credits directly. If the financial portion of production is intimidating, it would be wise to consult with a financial advisor, hire an accountant, or take an accounting class and educate yourself in this critical skill.

When you begin a project, your budget is an educated guess. As the project continues, updating the budget with actual spending and revenue is extremely important to ensure all financial decisions are reflected. When the project is complete, you'll have the full record of actual expenses and income as well as an idea of how these compared with your predictions. This gives you not only a record of your financial decisions but also a valuable tool so you can reflect and review for your next production. This comparison will help you see what went well, what didn't go well, and help you discover how accurate your prediction was so that each time you undertake a new project, you can make clearer decisions. These records demonstrate your ability to manage your project successfully, which can be helpful when seeking funds for future productions.

Your budget reflects your priorities; where you put your money is what matters the most to you. In many ways, your budget can become your value statement. This can help you weigh decisions as you move through your process. Do you want to pay more money for costumes or lighting? How much will you pay for artistic labor versus the cost of venue rental and marketing? In any case, make choices based on what would be best in *this* specific performance, and make your budget a reflection of each process's specific values and intentions. The larger the scope of the production or the dream, the more costs may be incurred. Some choreographers believe it is essential to pay their dancers for rehearsals and performances. In a for-profit model, this will be easier because the cost of the tickets are higher to pay all the production costs. In a nonprofit model, payment for rehearsals and performances is sometimes harder to manage due to the constant need to fundraise.

Summary

At this point in the creation process, you are bringing your artistic vision to life by working with your team to flesh out the many production logistical details. To create a production plan, you have to analyze the strengths and weaknesses of the vision, the organizational structure, and the financial capabilities. This analysis helps determine your strengths and limitations as a production, and it gives you the most potential for success. As you conclude this chapter, you may feel as if you need business, advertising, legal, and financial degrees to continue with your artistic vision. This is not the case. Remember that your knowledge will grow with time and experience, and for the areas where you are not an expert, your collaborative team can support you. You may find a second passion in the details of the business of the arts yourself! In any case, always surround yourself with a great team of people who complement your own strengths and weaknesses. Your artistic vision is worth pursuing!

Getting Started

4

Key Terms
company
crowdfunding
grant
merchandise
personal ask
press release
production meeting
ticket sales

49

LEARNING OBJECTIVES

After reading this chapter, you will be able to do the following:

> Effectively contact and secure a venue for a performance
> Conceptualize a fundraiser for your project
> Analyze factors in your production to help create an effective marketing strategy
> Recognize the significance of production meetings and learn how to set the tone for the entire project

The previous chapters discussed a wide range of factors that take us far beyond the first inspiration to create. The information in a clearly and thoroughly articulated artistic vision is the foundation of all production choices moving forward. The information provided by tools such as the SWOT analysis and understanding the logistics of structural organization, work environments, and the budget supplies an artist with a tangible direction and a way to navigate the project.

After clarifying the artistic vision and logistical considerations, you can start bringing this vision to life. Getting started requires integrating these elements to create a comprehensive production. You'll need to create a plan that pairs artistic vision and the creative brief with logistical analysis to align creative strengths with material realities. Making this plan takes an understanding of where your work sits creatively conceptually, structurally, and financially in the market and artistically among the collaborators. It takes a strong collaborative team with the work's best interest in mind to create a performance full of considerate choices and thorough exploration.

In any production, these decisions need to fall within the laws of nature and within the resources available. This chapter will focus on finding a venue, planning for income and expenditures, and marketing to support the work. These tasks are critical from a logistical perspective and offer the opportunity to continue building your network and your reputation in the arts community. They will also deepen your connection with your audience.

Venues

The venue where a dance is performed is a key component. For a student this may be predetermined, but as you grow as an artist and take your work off campus, securing a space will become a major focus as you continue to develop your craft. Some spaces provide you with essential components such as light and scenery design and a production team. Others will be just shells, and it will be up to you to find your collaborative team.

When searching for a venue, be prepared to do some homework to determine whether a site is appropriate for the type of work you are doing. Be prepared to pay good money for a rental; the cost is relative to geography, venue size, amenities, and length of residence. The process is somewhat like looking for an apartment. When you want to contact a venue, look for a page for rentals or a link on the website. There will often be a name or department associated with venue rentals, and they should get back to you within a reasonable amount of time. (If they don't, you probably don't want to partner with them anyway.) These contacts are usually from the facilities, production, or business departments.

Once you tour a space, you can ask to speak to all these departments, and you probably should. Facilities can tell you specifics about amenities, logistics, safety, and much more. Production can tell you about the capabilities and limitations of the space in terms of your spectacle. And the business contact can work with you on the contract, including the expenses associated with using the venue.

Ask questions, even if you don't think it's important, because it probably is important. Every venue has its quirks, so there's a story for everything. Ask questions even if you know the answers! This can test your would-be business partners. It can keep them honest and show you how trustworthy they are. Ask about the cost, because when you go to the next venue, you can use the cost of one venue against the other to get them to compete for your business.

These items are considerations as well:

> Ask about accessibility for performers, staff, and audience. The government website

detailing the Americans with Disabilities Act is the primary source of information about accessibility (www.ada.gov).

> Check out the parking—bad parking can ruin a show, especially if it has an extended run.
> See the dressing rooms and amenities for the cast—this might be home-away-from-home for a while.
> Find out about the heating and air-conditioning—seriously.
> Ask about selling merchandise.
> Determine the nearby restaurants and bars.
> Ask about nearby hotels and other accommodations and transportation.
> Ask about ticketing and box office requirements.
> Determine the required staff.
> Find out about what security is needed.
> Evaluate the restrooms—ask to use it so you can see for yourself!
> Ask about anything and everything you can think of.

You also need to be prepared to answer questions. The venue will want to know who they are allowing in their space, so know yourself, the company, production, and the intended audience very well. Your venues may not be traditional theatre settings. If you are filming a music video, you could be in the desert or at the beach, a modern choreographer may create a work in a museum, and you may be producing a dance convention in hotel ballrooms or convention centers. Dance is adaptable to locations, and the options are endless; however, all the suggestions apply regardless of location.

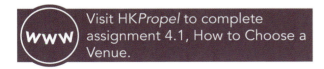

Visit HK*Propel* to complete assignment 4.1, How to Choose a Venue.

Funding

To move forward, create work, and expand the vision, the team will need funding. This section introduces you to possible funding streams and explains how they work.

After you've created your budget, you should have a sense of how much money you'll need to cover performance expenses. Ticket sales (*earned income*), while an important part of the production

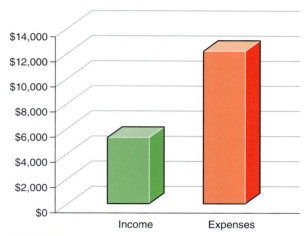

Figure 4.1 Without any fundraising, the revenue for this dance performance falls short of the expenses incurred.

budget, typically will not cover the cost of creating the content and presenting the performance (see figure 4.1). Therefore, fundraising is often needed to add *contributed income* to the revenue in your budget. As a creator, you will have to decide how much you need to fundraise based on the scale of your performance, and you'll have to create an appropriate and feasible method for raising those funds. Furthermore, freelance, nonprofit, and for-profit organizations have differences in how they are structured and can have limitations on fundraising. For a nonprofit organization or a freelancer, fundraising may be more necessary than a for-profit organization. In fact, for most arts nonprofits, the ratio of earned income to contributed income is about 50/50 (Renz 2003). For a freelancer that ratio may vary depending on the type of production and resources available to you. Part of an artist's mission is to create art that is accessible to a large audience, and that means making sure the ticket price stays within an affordable range.

Earned Income

Ticket sales are a major source of earned income. When setting the cost of the ticket, you should know your expenses for the performance and what type of ticket cost the market will bear. Will you offer early-bird discounts, student rush, senior discounts, preferred seating with higher costs, tiered seating costs, and so on? Each decision you make to either increase or decrease the cost of a ticket will affect your overall budget. For many events, the ticket sales will not be enough to cover all the costs involved in creating and producing the performance.

Note that some ticket-processing systems charge service fees that can quickly cut into your profit and need to be accounted for when making your projected budget. For example, if a ticketing service takes a 3 percent fee, a $10 ticket does not equal $10 in revenue. You will need to account for the expense side of about $1 per ticket. Anticipated sales are not a guarantee of how many seats you will sell to any given event. While we hope we will sell out every performance, this is not usually the case. So, if you budget expecting to sell out and forget to also take out the merchant service fee, you will be disappointed and have a budget that is not accurate.

Merchandise created for your event or **company** is another way to bring in earned income. You are selling products to your audience for a profit. This does take an initial investment because you have to have the merchandise made and anticipate the items your audience will want to purchase and take home with them. This can include posters, key chains, T-shirts, music, or recordings of the show. Having merchandise that can be sold at multiple events can be helpful so you don't end up with a garage full of T-shirts from a performance that is not being performed again. Knowing your brand and having high-quality items but low initial investment costs to increase your profit margin is something to think about. You will also need extra staffing to sell the merchandise and again merchant service fees to consider.

Contributed Income

Contributed income will come from people or organizations willing to support your work. Potential sources of contributed income include donations, events, competitions and festivals, and grants. The process of identifying donors and funding opportunities extends beyond finding financial supporters and ventures and goes into engaging board members, attracting volunteers, collaborating with other organizations, and so on. This all translates into contributions that affect the bottom line.

When creating strong relationships with donors, it is important to recognize that their support is more than just signing a check. Typically, if donors want to support the arts, they already recognize the importance art has on society. The goal then becomes about exciting them about *your* project, *your* voice, *your* art, and *your* ideas. It is about understanding their own missions and aligning them to yours. This sense of clarity can help you focus on donors who potentially could support you rather than exerting energy on those you need to convince about the power of the arts.

For example, if you are a university student who wants to take one of your works to an out-of-town festival, grant opportunities within the university (including student and alumni associations) that support student creative or research initiatives could be a great resource. Or perhaps you look for funding that supports your choreographic concept; if your work is about a specific topic (i.e., social justice) or explores a specific genre (i.e., the intersection of jazz and tango), you may be able to apply to grants that haven't funded dance in the past but align well with the concept of your work.

Donations

Whether large or small, individual donations can make up a significant portion of your revenue, especially if you're a nonprofit. In the arts, because contributed income plays such a large role in the revenue for organizations and productions, intentionality when appealing for philanthropic gifts and community contributions is incredibly valuable.

Asking people for money may not feel like an easy or exciting task, but a specific and effective **personal ask** allows you to fulfill your financial needs while forming more meaningful and lasting connections with your donors. Donors who feel invested in their contribution's impact are more likely to become lasting supporters of your work. If you are providing a service to the community or creating artistic works a donor can get behind, then you can ask each year for a donation to support your ability to move forward. Developing a donor list with different contribution levels and acknowledgments is a great way to begin to build a predictable yearly income. Communicating clearly, following through with your promises, and showing your donors how their money is being put to good use will help with future asks.

TAX-DEDUCTIBLE DONATIONS

Donations made to a nonprofit organization are tax-deductible by the donor, so you must provide them with a receipt. And it's important to acknowledge their gift and let them know how it will be acknowledged. Typical locations for gift acknowledgments are your website, the printed program for the performance, a personalized video posted on social media, and personal written notes to the donor.

Specificity is key to a good ask. People want to know their money is going to a meaningful cause. Your request should identify a specific need. For example, "Would you consider making a $500 donation to help fund a dancer's living costs on our upcoming tour?" This gives potential donors a clear idea of what their money will accomplish and gives you the ability to have a discussion about the financial commitment they feel comfortable making. If you are transparent with the donor about how their funds will be used, they can be more transparent with you about their ability to contribute.

With technology comes multiple opportunities to reach new audiences and new funding sources. **Crowdfunding** is "the practice of funding a project or venture by raising many small amounts of money from a large number of people, typically via the Internet" (Prive 2012). Crowdfunding websites like GoFundMe, Kickstarter, and Facebook fundraisers help people raise money for a specific cause or purpose.

The most obvious advantage of crowdfunding sites is that they give you the ability to reach a high number of potential donors, leveraging the power of your production team's combined social network strength and casting a wider net for potential donors. Instead of just reaching the 40 people invited to your in-person gala event, you can reach thousands by sharing a link to your online fundraiser on your social media. Another benefit is that as an artist you are not limited to connecting to people only in your immediate geographical location, allowing your work and presence to have a broader reach.

The downside to crowdfunding is the lack of personal investment. You may get donors and people who support your work, but they may not feel as attached to the company, organization, or artist as they would if they had come to an event and engaged with your work in some way. The fundraising platforms often take a small portion of your funds raised or might deny you the funds if you don't reach a goal, so they may not be as reliable as other methods, depending on the scale of your fundraising goal. Even so, if you need a low-cost, high-reach fundraising plan, online fundraising may be a great option for you. Once you know your business structure (nonprofit, for-profit, or freelance), you can look for crowdfunding platforms that work for your model. If you decide to try your hand at crowdfunding, do your research as it requires a large investment of time and energy if you want your campaign to be successful.

Events

Fundraising events come in many different forms, from intimate dinners to large gala events to creative ways to engage the community. Tailoring your fundraiser to fit your specific performance and vision will inevitably bring the strongest support from your audience.

Some of the best fundraising opportunities are those that engage the audience and get them involved in what you do. Events like open rehearsals, talks, and question-and-answer sessions give your audience a chance not only to *witness* what you do, but *engage* with it. When people experience the process for themselves, they see the tangible impact their support has on your organization. Bringing your audience into the process of creation can be a great way to show them how things happen and make them feel a part of it, and as a bonus for you, it is a cost-effective strategy because it takes advantage of opportunities already at your disposal.

PLAN FOR EVENT COSTS

Events cost money to put on: It takes money to make money. Set aside a section of your budget for this, and if you have resources, connections, or allies that you can use to help offset costs for the fundraiser, even better!

Fundraising is a multifaceted process sometimes requiring both conventional and unconventional thinking to manifest the required funds for any given production. Every event will be different, since each creative process is different. You might be able to get the right type of engagement for your project from an idea of an event highlighted in the sections that follow, but don't be afraid to think outside the box and create an event that works for you. The more specific the event is to your vision, the more likely people will relate to it and support it.

When we think of fundraising, often we think of fundraising events, galas, dinners, and more. The scale of events like these may vary largely based on the structure and size of your production. It could be a small dinner party hosted in a home, or it could be a large, themed gala hosted in the ballroom of an extravagant hotel. Regardless, fundraising events help build your community, allowing your patrons and supporters to engage with you and your vision and feel like they are part of something as they contribute to your production or organization. The best fundraisers are fun, so put the "fun" in fundraising and use your creativity to create an event your patrons will remember. Events can be self-managed, hosted, or participatory structures, depending on who is organizing and managing the event (see table 4.1).

Table 4.1 Fundraising Event Comparisons

	Pros	Cons	Example
Self-managed events	Throw a great party and encourage engagement with your mission	Expensive and time intensive	Annual gala and silent auction
Hosted events	Someone else does the work for you	Limited control of the event; smaller in scope	Board member hosts a cocktail party introducing your company to small group of community leaders
Participatory events	Active event and goal is to reach a large number of people	Generally makes less money per person and needs access to a larger population; less personal	Dance-a-thon, golf tournament, 5K

Self-Managed Event Any event that you create and manage yourself to raise money for your cause would be considered a self-managed fundraising event. These could be anything from small-scale fundraisers like a pre- or post-show gathering to a gala full of big donors. Regardless, a self-managed event requires the investment of your own money and resources.

Large events might require a ticket price, ensuring that attendees know the purpose of the evening is to raise money so they come prepared to give. These events are labor-intensive. Scheduling activities, managing donations, deciding on a menu, creating talking points, running auctions, coordinating volunteers, and more can be a big endeavor for a three-hour affair, but scaled correctly, this dedication can create a well-run event where patrons feel involved and engaged and can generate significant support for your project (Thorpe 2018).

Hosted Event Sometimes, a friend, dedicated donor, or invested supporter may offer to host an event for you to help support *your* artistic endeavor. Maybe it's a dinner party where your friend offers to invite some friends over to convince them to support your upcoming project. Events like these are a sort of an "endorsed" ask; it adds credibility to your project to have someone who believes in your vision so deeply that they will make an effort to convince others to support it as well. This type of event is beneficial to you as an independent artist because the host will generally cover the costs while you collect the proceeds from the event. To approach donors, be sure you can articulate the mission of the organization or the purpose of the project clearly and with passion and energy. Your commitment to the project is what makes people excited to become involved.

Participatory Event Some events involve letting the patrons participate in a cause to support your organization. Maybe you partner with a business or restaurant and get a portion of their revenue for a night. Maybe you host a dance-a-thon or organize a 5K in support of a cause or your organization. Participatory events usually involve more people and have a smaller ticket price. These events are more focused on the amount of people you bring in and less on the size of individual contributions. A large number of people with a small contribution is a significant addition to your revenue and can broaden your network of support to a wider audience. These participants are often physically engaged, making them feel more connected to your organization.

Competitions and Festivals

Choreography competitions and festivals can cost you money or reward you with money or future opportunities. Typically, competitions will require an entry fee to place your work in the organization's program. If you are paying someone else money to perform your choreography in a specific venue, take the time to weigh the pros and cons. Though you risk losing money with entry fees and possibly travel costs, increasing the exposure of your work is a plus. If the competition has a large following on social media, a successful showing may also allow you to leverage their viewership to increase your own. Festivals solicit for submissions that are then sorted through, and a select few are accepted. Some festivals award prize money or production support for the top works presented during the festival. This can help support future endeavors. Both competitions and festivals are available all around the world to enter your work in, but at the end of the day, you need to decide whether entering these events serves your bigger career goals. A great way to evaluate these opportunities is to go back to the SWOT analysis discussed previously in this book.

Grants

A **grant** is money or an in-kind service provided to an individual or company to support a specific project. Grants require extensive proposals and applications and have considerable requirements, conditions, and specifications to both confirm eligibility and receipt of the funds if you're awarded the grant. Large grants are often reserved exclusively for nonprofit organizations, but arts grants exist for the freelance artists as well, though you may have to do some research to find them. Start by looking for grants you qualify for, because many grant applications are denied when the grant writer does not read all the grant requirements. Ideally, you can find grants that align to your artistic mission. Grants can be found at the local, state, national, and international levels. Check with your local arts councils to see what may be available in your area. In the United States, the National Endowment for the Arts funds matching grants to nonprofit organizations every year. Grants are very competitive, and you may apply several times before receiving a grant. Once you have received smaller grants, this helps build your resume and can assist your chances in receiving larger grants.

Grants are often geared toward supporting a project with a specific purpose. It might be tempting to adapt your work to fit the grant purpose for a chance for the funds, but remember that you have to follow through with whatever you put forth in the grant. It's not enough to craft a proposal that fits the grant's purpose; the finished work must fit the purpose as well. It's more beneficial to find a grant that fits your vision instead of trying to alter your vision to fit the grant after the fact. Depending on how the grant's purpose aligns with your vision, this fundraising approach can be more work than it's worth.

Writing a grant proposal is an art in itself. There is a very specific way to approach it, and it's a curated skill, but it is extremely important and valued in the arts world. In fact, it's so specific and complex that you can get a master's degree in grant writing. If you enjoy writing, understand and enjoy the arts, and enjoy networking, this would be a valuable and marketable skillset to consider pursuing.

Grant writing takes time and attention to detail. If the successful completion of a project depends on receiving grant funding, you will need to have already researched funding cycles and time lines and have all your information ready to develop the grant application. You will need to be able to thoroughly articulate your vision, passion, and purpose in words. Sometimes you must show work samples, professional writing samples, letters demonstrating you or your organization's capacity, budgets, and financial reports. In addition, all grants have some kind of reporting requirements after the grant is complete. After the project, you will submit paperwork that details what you used the money for and the success and results of that event. Good record management while working with other people, organizations, donors, and investors, especially if you fall under a nonprofit financial structure, will help with grant applications. It's important to have these financial records to be able to show people before the project, as it's happening, and after it's finished to give them a clear picture of how their investment was used, whether it be time, money, or resources.

Visit HK*Propel* to complete assignment 4.2, Fundraising Events.

Visibility

Promoting your work is about making yourself visible to others, whether that's through marketing or social media or other avenues. Various venues and campaigns will benefit from different types of marketing materials. Marketing involves both print and digital media to reach donors and audiences. Regardless of the media type, you will need to create graphics, hold photo and video shoots, and have all the event information confirmed and ready to go before publishing any materials.

Your marketing materials will be more effective if you apply the principles of branding, which involves developing and consistently using a recognizable style or image. This may start with a logo, a color scheme, and any additional graphics. Clear graphics and photos that visually display the style and values of the company will make your work distinct and recognizable over time. Dance photography needs to be dynamic, capture the physicality and the tone of the work, and demonstrate the aesthetic of the performance or company. One clear impactful image is better than a variety of sloppy ones. Remember, your marketing materials will reflect on your professionalism.

The marketing materials need to come together long before the event. Marketing campaigns ini-

A single dynamic image can be very effective in marketing a dance production.

tially may come down to your budget and your target audience. The cost of creating, printing, and mailing flyers or save-the-date postcards can very quickly add up to hundreds of dollars. While it's always exciting to see your dancers in print, you may not be able to justify the costs. When funds are limited, posting on social media platforms such as Instagram and creating email lists is a simple way to distribute information to your target audiences. Having a website where you can direct your online traffic to provide more information helps limit the amount of content you need to provide in each post.

You will need quality content, eye-catching photos and video clips of your work for all your marketing and social media content. As you begin to build your company, keeping current information will facilitate communicating with all collaborators working on advertising, program copy, and any other company information. Keep updated dancer bios, director notes for programs, donor lists, and advertising information. All information on your social media needs to be current and relevant so interested donors and audience members have a sense you are creating new projects on a regular basis, and you can build anticipation for upcoming events.

The Four Ps of Marketing

Though ticket sales aren't always the main driving financial fuel for an arts performance, it is valuable to meaningfully engage with as large of an audience as possible and find ways to excite your patrons and connect them to your work. How can you market in an authentic, intriguing way to build this supportive community and bring people to your work? First, find the factors that influence your marketing strategies; then analyze how you will consider each factor and how they intersect while you develop these marketing strategies. And always remember that marketing comes back to articulating your project's unique identity in an honest and engaging way.

Authentic and fruitful marketing comes from knowing *what* you're marketing and using its unique characteristics as assets in its promotion. The four Ps of marketing, or the marketing mix, was popularized by Neil Borden and is a marketing tool used by all types of companies to identify key factors involved in marketing their goods and services to the public. They can just as easily be applied to an artistic production. Analyzing your artistic vision through this lens could help you gain a better understanding of what you're offering to your audience and help you create effective marketing strategies that will help make your production successful. In this model, the four factors that influence how you market your work are the *product* itself, its *price*, the product's *place* both in the market and physically, and the method of *promotion*.

Product

For a dance production, the "product" is the performance. At its core, what are you making? Consider the who, what, when, and why of your production. Who's dancing? What style is it? What is the subject matter? When is it happening? Why are you creating it? This will give you a basic sense of its identity. Then, consider what is interesting or unique about the intersection of these factors, the concept, purpose, or the vision itself. Identify what sets you apart from others. This distinct identity is what will draw an audience to see your production, rather than another performance.

At this point, you should have already spent time articulating your vision in your creative brief. Referring to this document as you consider how to best promote your production will remind you of its unique features and put them into a marketing perspective. Considering the identity of your product in terms of marketing also means considering how this identity will be described in words. You want to take what's in the brief and articulate it in a way that's not just understandable but engaging. Word choice is everything. How you articulate your production in words draws an audience in to see it in its fullness, so it's important to be both clear and authentic in its description.

Price

The next factor to consider is the price of your ticket. How does this price compare to other price points in comparable venues? What does this price say about your project? Your price inevitably affects how your customers view you. A low ticket price could imply a performance meant to be accessible to the public or a lower-budget production. A high price could suggest a high production value, a large investment in its creation, or a more luxurious audience experience.

If you're still deciding what the price of the ticket will be, it's important to consider that the price affects not only your profit but also how you are perceived. When choosing the cost for a ticket, external factors might require research. What other kinds of performances have been presented at this venue, and what was their price? What else is happening in the performance community around the same time as your production, and what is their price point? What audience are you marketing to and what can they afford?

You'll also want to analyze your specific production. In an arts setting, a creator will charge as much as they can that's realistic for their situation. This involves considering your level of expertise, how long you've been creating work, the performance's production value, and more. These factors influence the price, and the price frames how you promote it. You would never market an expensive show in a huge theatre with extensive technical capability in the same way you would a low-priced showcase in an empty warehouse. In this way, noting the unique characteristics of your production can help you discover what ticket price may be most effective.

Place

When considering the place of your performance, think about what's interesting about that specific place or venue. Noticing what the place does for the uniqueness of your work will give you valuable points to address in your marketing materials. For example, a proscenium theatre that holds 750 seats in an urban area and presents dance regularly, an experimental warehouse venue in a downtown arts district, or a site-specific work created in a coastal botanical garden will all draw different types of audiences.

The concept of place addresses the venue of your performance as well as where you are marketing your product. For dance productions, this "where" often has some sort of geographic limit due to the in-person nature of performances. However, with the virtual world expanding and livestreamed performances becoming more common, in some cases your audience can be anywhere. For this reason, and because of increasing marketing on the Internet, geographic location is just as important as being on the Internet or the choice of marketing platform. In both cases, consider where your ideal customer would be and what social media platforms, geographical locations, and markets they will occupy. This will help you articulate valuable location elements in your marketing materials and discover the best potential marketing locations.

Promotion

At its core, promotion is all about how your audience finds you. Just as you would consider *where* your ideal customer is, consider *how* you would like a patron to come across your performance and what you want them to take away from that interaction.

An important aspect to remember about promoting dance is how well it lends itself to visual materials. Images, videos, and graphics are integral to dance promotion because of the visual nature of the art form. A radio commercial for an upcoming dance production would have a hard time matching the effect of a beautiful promotional video or poster. Because a visual image is worth a thousand words, these images should accurately represent what you will present.

What makes a "good" image? For successful visual marketing in dance, it's important to use dynamic images that align with your vision. Maybe a blurry photo of a dancer in motion captures the abstract and fleeting nature of the piece you're presenting. Maybe a clear shot of a dancer flying mid-leap is perfect for expressing the excitement and technical prowess of your work. In any successful dance image, make sure you are using the body to tell a story about your work, that the technique is the quality you expect of your dancers, and—most of all—that you are proud of what it looks like.

It may benefit you to also invest in an experienced graphic designer or invest time yourself into learning how to use graphic design software proficiently. Because dance productions rely so heavily on visual marketing, the whole image, not just the dancer on it, is important to the effect on the viewer. The graphic design of a poster changes the mood and tone of the image on it. The last thing you want is for the image you chose so carefully and intentionally to be ruined by the surrounding graphics. Instead, it's important the essence of your performance should be clearly translated into graphic design, even if that takes a small investment.

There are many avenues at your disposal to promote your performance, including these elements:

› Your website
› Targeted email lists
› Social media posts
› Hard copy marketing materials (postcards, posters, etc.)
› Billboards (think Shen Yun)
› Discounts
› Promotional videos

With the influx of advertisements daily, people often need to see things multiple times to consider engaging. This means it might benefit you to use more than one mode for marketing your work. With so many options, it's best to think what combination of these marketing elements will best serve your project. Do you need posters and billboards for a one-night show that's a week away and only open for a private audience? Probably not. But a social media post, email blast, and personal ask to the group that's invited may get a higher rate of turnout or ticket sales.

Whatever marketing structure you decide on, it is important to remember that this is another item to budget for. Physical marketing materials cost money to design and print, and targeted social media ads can help you reach that niche market but will take money to make them happen. Budgeting for these expenses or seeking other opportunities to obtain these elements is absolutely necessary. Just like your fundraising budget, it is helpful to have a separate detailed budget sheet for marketing expenses only and have it feed into your main budget.

Marketing Plans

Considering all these factors, you can create a marketing plan that highlights the unique identity of your project and builds your community by attracting an audience excited about that identity. Integrating each of the four Ps into a cohesive and comprehensive marketing strategy that is both true

For successful visual marketing in dance, use dynamic images that align with your vision.

to your vision and clear to the audience is the first step. From there, you can bring your production to life by presenting it to the public in press releases, and, most important, by speaking personally about your vision.

A marketing plan is a list or calendar showing all of the activities and events you are planning to advertise your show and generate sales, along with dates and deadlines associated with the activities. The plan should include activities such as the following, along with their respective deadlines:

› Photo shoot and photo selection
› Graphic design for marketing image (This image will represent the production and will contain important details about the performance, so it should be consistent across all platforms, press releases, websites, social media content, and print marketing materials.)
› Press release
› Website updates
› Promotional video (filming date, editing deadline, draft reviews, and final deadline)
› Ticket sales begin
› Detailed schedule for email campaign (listing content and day of release)
  › Initial email announces ticket release date; emails continue with increasing frequency until the performance concludes
  › Ask the ticketing service for a list of email addresses of patrons attending so you can email them after the performance thanking them for attendance
› Detailed schedule for social media promotions (listing platform, content, and day of release)
  › Content can include interviews with people involved in production, rehearsal snippets, live video streams during rehearsals, etc.
  › Consider linking email content and social media content to reinforce messaging across multiple platforms
› Print materials (posters, postcards, and programs)
› Merchandise creation, ordering, and sales (presale, during performance, and postperformance)

Maintaining a clear calendar with all of the events, dates, and deadlines is crucial to keeping the marketing running smoothly. Assigning who is responsible for each deadline or item is also a good idea and keeps everyone on track.

It's important to remember to account for marketing costs in your project's budget. How much will the photographer charge for the photo shoot? How many hours will the graphic designer need to create a strong promotional image for the performance? Are you using a free or paid platform for your email campaign? How much will printing posters and programs cost? These are some examples of marketing costs you might need to plan for. When you create your budget you will be estimating these costs, but as the production gets under way and estimates become expenses, remember to update the budget accordingly so you can see how marketing decisions are affecting the overall production budget.

Keeping your budget and marketing plan up to date helps you make good decisions about how to tweak your approach to certain demographics during the sales process. For example, if you are a month out from the performance and your ticket sales are lagging, perhaps a targeted email to past ticket buyers with some sizzling information about a choreographer or dancer might generate more interest that results in ticket sales. Perhaps a bit of exciting movement might be just the thing to remind dancers and other artists to purchase tickets. Or if you notice that the student ticket sales are low, increasing social media posts and paying for ads might be needed to increase visibility. Encouraging members of the cast to post on their social media accounts might collectively help boost the ticket sales as well. Table 4.2 shows a three-week snippet from a sample marketing plan.

Press Release

A **press release** is an incredibly important tool for getting the word out about your performance. Press releases are targeted and concise and bring attention to your production as a unique and newsworthy performance. They are released to targeted members of the media, in hopes of getting picked up by a journalist for news coverage and free publicity. In a press release, wording and verbiage is incredibly important. Any time you're creating an event, you want to use powerful images and the unique strengths of your event to get free advertising. A captivating image with a beautifully written press release will often get picked up and run as a news story that a wide range of people see.

Effective marketing is about understanding what your vision is and putting it in words that others

Table 4.2 **Sample Marketing Plan**

Week	Task	Person responsible	Due date
1	Photo shoot	Jack	
	Create written description of performance and works	Jenny	
	Gather updated biographies of cast and collaborators	Kim	
2	Create dancer and choreographer interviews for social media	Kira	
	Write press release	Nancy	
	Finalize key photos	Jenny	
	Begin graphic design	Santi	
3	Release press release to media	Nancy	
	Finalize graphic design	Santi	
	Email blast #1: announce performance	Sammi	

can understand, and this is especially true for press releases. You are searching for the clearest way to speak about your project thoroughly. As a dance collaborator, you may have lots of intellectual, artistic vocabulary to describe the work, but how can you describe it to the public? You want to describe it so most people can understand it yet still keep it accurate. A lot of this comes down to word choice and finding clear language that's not complicated or confusing. Press releases have particular formatting rules, categories, and expectations, so writing them is a skill in itself.

In the end, even after all the marketing materials, press releases, and email campaigns, your best marketing tool is *you*. Marketing is about connecting with a community, and there's no stronger connection than human interaction. You can put as much promotional material out into the world as you want, but if you're not part of the artistic community yourself, you won't be able to gain a community that supports you as an artist. To create work in the artistic community, you have to be a member of the artistic community. And to be a member of the artistic community, you have to show up and engage with that community by attending shows, talking to people at those shows, and responding to others' work. At the most basic level, when you simply show up to other productions, others are reminded of the work you're doing and ask what is coming up for you. The ability to speak clearly and passionately about what's interesting about your work is necessary as you start to build your base of support.

Summary

Putting your vision into action requires getting the ball rolling in the right direction. Choosing a venue, fundraising, and marketing for your production are crucial to taking your vision from idea into reality. Booking a venue will bring significant clarity to what production elements will be available to you, where your audience will be located, and what canvas your production will be painted onto. To make your production happen, you will need funding. Knowing the different methods of fundraising will help you decide how to best provide the necessary capital for your vision. Marketing this vision will ensure your funding plans pan out and that people come to the performance. Careful attention to all these elements can get your production on the track for success.

Part II
Process: Clarity Through Creation, Collaboration, and Conversations

The process of realizing a vision is complex and requires understanding multiple aspects of a performance at once. If the performance itself is the tip of the iceberg, the creative process is the enormous mass of ice under the water. This process brings together collaborators from many fields, each speaking the language of their own specialties and prioritizing a different part of the project. Yet they all work toward creating a meaningful performance. Knowing these collaborators and understanding how to communicate effectively is key to building a successful performance.

The chapters in this part introduce all the production collaborators that could be involved in your production and take us through a deep understanding of the necessary parts of the process. Chapter 5 presents a detailed list of the collaborators involved in dance productions as well as their responsibilities and priorities to better show their role in context with the whole production. In chapter 6, we dive into the details of creation in the studio: coordinating auditions, compensating and working with dancers, and building your creative environment. We then explore some of the production process in chapter 7: elements of stage spaces, lighting, and sound. Then, in chapter 8, we learn what the process is like for additional production elements like media, costume, and set design. After this, any collaborator will have a full understanding of what every component means in the context of each artist's process and will know how to communicate effectively about it with others on the creative team. Clear communication and a focus on effective collaboration throughout the entire creative process are the key ingredients for a successful and rewarding performance.

5

Collaborators

Courtesy of Sharon Mor Yosef/Backhausdance.

Key Terms

artistic director
assistant choreographer
audio and video editors
box office manager
choreographer
costume designer
costume supervisor
dance captain
dancer
hair designer
house manager
lighting designer
makeup designer
managing director
multimedia designer
postproduction
  coordinator
producer
production manager
prop designer
prop master
publicity creators
rehearsal director
rider
scenic designer
sound designer
sound engineer
stage manager
streaming engineer
technical director
tour manager
visual designer

LEARNING OBJECTIVES

After reading this chapter, you will be able to do the following:

> Identify the technical vocabulary associated with dance production
> Recognize the specific duties and responsibilities of dance collaborators
> Identify the roles of the production leadership team
> Understand the specialties within the production designers
> Identify the essential components of production meetings

This chapter will introduce and define the roles of the dance, production, and design collaborators. Before jumping into rehearsal or creating a lighting design, everyone involved in a production needs to understand the value and scope of the collaborators. With mutual understanding of each production team member's unique talents, the project will be on the way toward a successful event. Production meetings are where this understanding and communication take place. They are the first opportunity to address these factors and possibilities and ultimately help a production be prepared for all aspects of reality.

Organization of Roles

Figure 5.1 shows how the collaborators in a dance production might be organized. A board of directors or trustee or producer might be over the entire production. An artistic director to oversee the vision and tone of the production and a managing director to oversee the business aspects of the production would answer to them.

Artistic Director

The **artistic director** sets the vision and tone for the entire production. The artistic director can be the choreographer, but usually they are not and are there to support and oversee the artistic identity of a specific dance company or concert. A venue such as Jacob's Pillow has an artistic director for the season who oversees the vision of that season or production. In a dance company such as the Alvin Ailey American Dance Theatre, the artistic director will ensure that aesthetic continuity stays true to the company's original vision and intent. Honoring the work of the past with such Ailey classics as *Revelations* and helping to hire guest choreographers such as Wayne McGregor helps the company honor and celebrate the past while staying updated and relevant.

The artistic director determines how the work should be created and develops the system that gives the project its best shot at success. In this role, they will cross into all production elements, allocating and prioritizing resources, developing relationships with all the collaborators, managing the logistics, and making decisions about what the final product will look like. It is important for the artistic director to facilitate a healthy working environment for everyone and to make sure the work adheres to the artistic tone. The artistic director makes the decisions about the show order, flow, and quick changes. In an academic setting, the artistic director is also called the *concert director*. If the dance company were to be outlined in its various constituent parts (i.e., the branches of an organizational chart), the artistic director would preside over this department and establish, communicate, and hold the company accountable to its artistic vision and credibility.

Managing Director

Overseeing the business operations of a dance company (the second branch of the organizational chart in figure 5.1), the **managing director** is responsible for the logistical day-to-day operations to get things done. They deal with practical production aspects. Every environment is different, depending on the scale and focus (academia, concert, commercial, etc.), and this will determine the level of work. The smaller the organization, the more aspects the managing director will be responsible for. Some jobs include working with aligning calendars between the artistic and production teams, keeping the project within budget, and engaging with the venues for booking spaces and technical scheduling. During the run of the production, they are responsible for making sure everyone is in the right place and doing their jobs.

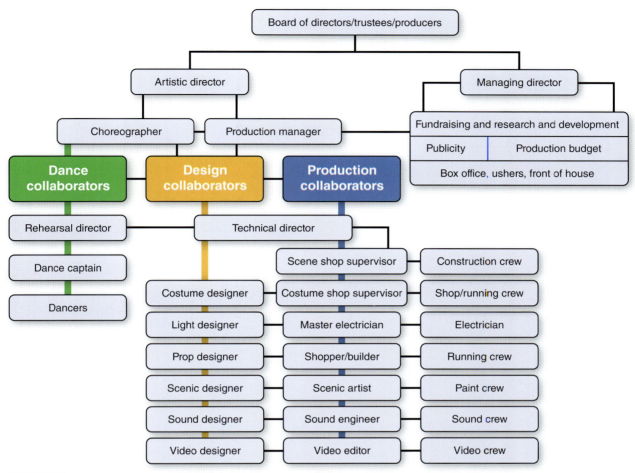

Figure 5.1 Dance production organizational chart.

Dance Collaborators

Dancers and choreographers are only a small piece of the dance production. They focus on their singular role, and to put multiple pieces together, more collaborators are needed to ensure the success of the entire production. These additional roles include the artistic director, managing director, dance captain or assistant choreographer, and **rehearsal director**. In smaller productions, you may fill some or all these roles, while in larger productions with bigger budgets, the workload can be divided into the various roles shown in figure 5.2.

Dancers

The **dancer** is the heart and soul of the dance, and dancing is the role by which you likely have entered the performing world. A studio dancer may be directed in a variety of ways, and dancing for a choreographer trains dancers for work on the artistic and production sides of performance. Each experience working on a project develops the dancer's skills in professionalism and collaboration to support future work. Choreographers have their own styles and approaches to developing work, and dancers must be as adaptable as possible to be supportive of the process.

Professional dancers who understand their roles are vital to a successful process. They embody the choreographer's vision by executing the movement both technically and artistically. During the choreographic process, it is important for the dancer to support the artistic vision. Some projects will elicit collaboration and input from the dancers, and in such cases, the dancer should offer supportive ideas to facilitate the project. If the dancer is not asked to be part of the creative process, they should be ready to produce the images the choreographer is seeking.

Often, a dancer known for a good work ethic and professionalism may book more gigs than a more technically proficient dancer who does not have the same reputation. Productions need dozens if not

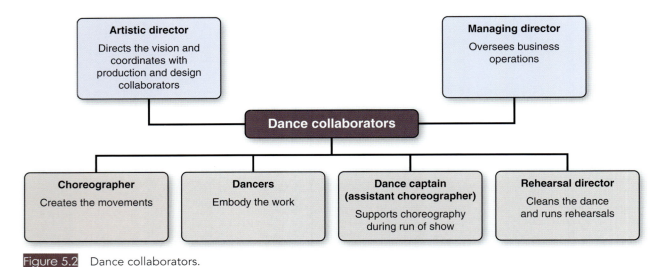

Figure 5.2 Dance collaborators.

hundreds of hours of intense group work, requiring agreeable interpersonal skills and trust among colleagues. Being a professional dancer means the following:

- Knowing the work
- Arriving early for call
- Doing your homework (coming prepared for rehearsal)
- Being physically warmed up and ready for rehearsal
- Being mentally and physically present in rehearsals
- Being reliable and practicing good time management

Poor communication can lead to frustration or misunderstanding. Dancers must communicate their concerns with scheduling or possibly the work environment. While the dancer needs to understand their role in the big picture of the full production, clear and early communication is essential. The choreographer and dancers should set up clear lines of communication at the beginning so that dancers know they are free to ask for clarity. Sometimes choreographers prefer to work without these questions and want to get the work out before inquiries are made.

A dancer should communicate with a choreographer when a sequence or movement makes them uncomfortable or is causing pain or injury. Some choreographers want input and guidance from their dancers and truly thrive in a collaborative environment. If the choreographer and the dancers have agreed to times for collaborative talks, it can sometimes help with the overall composition. If a dancer is confused or has questions about where a section is going or their role in it and they feel comfortable asking questions and asking for clarity, it can help the choreographer solidify their own ideas. It is important for the dancers to trust that their choreographer has a plan and a goal for the piece. The choreographer also has to trust that their dancers are fully committed to the creative process and the overall piece. This mutual trust is vital to success.

Choreographer

A **choreographer** composes the sequence of steps and moves for a dance performance (Oxford Dictionary). A choreographer's main responsibility is to take an artistic vision from an abstract idea to a performance actualized through dancers. The artistic vision may be theirs, or the choreographer might have been hired to develop someone else's vision. While choreographers in different settings (such as a college dance program, company, or the commercial industry) may have slightly different processes, some standards apply.

In the creation process, the choreographer is responsible for what is happening with the dancers. This starts at the audition where dancers are chosen and continues through developing the rehearsal schedule and creating in the studio. A choreographer needs to be prepared and ready to work, be respectful of the dancers, not waste time, and be aware of safety in the physical surroundings they are working in. A choreographer cannot be consumed by the rehearsal process because they must be aware of the process of bringing their dance to the stage. They need to know whom they are directly responsible for or other roles they must take on, the timeline of the project, and technical needs, and they must clearly communicate with all designers and the production team. In a dance program, the

Rehearsal is just one part of the choreographer's work on a dance production.

student choreographer typically has the support of the faculty, which allows the student to focus more on the creation of the piece in the studio; however, it does not just magically show up onstage with sets, lights, and costumes in a sold-out theatre.

Rehearsal Director

A **rehearsal director** works directly with the artistic director and choreographer and ultimately is responsible for having the dancers and the piece ready. Their job is to stay true to the intention of the work, clean the dance, warm up the dancers for rehearsal and performance, and deal with any issues or recasting. Rehearsal directors are vital when a guest choreographer comes in and sets a dance but is not there for the cleaning rehearsals or dress rehearsals onstage. In smaller academic or self-produced productions, the choreographer may take on the role of the rehearsal director.

Dance Captain or Assistant Choreographer

The rehearsal process might also include a dance captain or assistant choreographer. A **dance captain** is mainly responsible for maintaining the integrity of the choreography once the show opens and the rehearsal process ends. At that time, the dance captain runs rehearsals, assists in teaching the choreography to cast replacements, and gives notes to the cast to help keep the dance as close as possible to what the choreographer intended for it to look like. An **assistant choreographer** works with the choreographer to contribute in some part to the creative and aesthetic vision of the work. This role is different from a co-choreographer in that the final artistic choices are made by the choreographer and not the assistant choreographer. It may also be a part of their job to notate or archive the work.

ARCHIVING

Archiving a dance preserves the choreography for future presentation. Paul Taylor may have passed away, but his dance company and art live on through archived original dances. Archiving guarantees that the work will be respected and that the integrity of the piece will be followed exactly as the choreographer intended. In our digital era, this is usually done with video recordings. However, it is still vital that future generations of dancers and choreographers learn some of the original dance notation skills, such as labanotation. Documenting and archiving dance helps keep the art alive long after the lights go dark and the theatre is closed.

Before archiving work, be well informed about the rules and regulations governing the project you are working for. In many instances, written permission from unions or cast members must be acquired in advance before recording or filming any section of a rehearsal or performance.

Production Collaborators

While the dance collaborators are bringing their artistic vision to life in the studio, the production collaborators—*production leadership* and *design collaborators*—are hard at work creating the environment needed to support the vision. In academia, production leadership tends to be faculty and staff hired by the institution, but self-producing artists need to develop a production leadership team and find designers. Some venues may supply these roles for you. Production designers are specialized artists who work with lighting, costumes, music, makeup, and stage design. The larger the project, the more specialized the collaborators need to be.

Production Leadership Team

The production leadership team manages and organizes timelines, budgets, and operational structures. Like dance collaborators, several roles need to be filled for production leadership, and at times, one person may be covering multiple roles. These roles are mainly the production manager, stage manager, and technical director (see figure 5.3). Production leadership teams keep everyone focused on deadlines, coordinate the production elements, and generally deal with all the details of the actual production.

Production Manager

Managing and overseeing the work of all the production collaborators is the **production manager**. They manage the production budget, schedule, and staff, and they are also responsible for any general production requirements and overall communication, making sure every collaborator's needs are being met as fully as possible and that everyone is in the loop. They are truly the liaison and negotiator between the artistic and technical elements. They are in charge of everyone, and it's their job to make sure everyone is on the same page (see figure 5.4).

Production managers maintain relationships and communications between the administrative, dance, and design collaborators of the organization. They likely supervise a staff of their own, while working with the dance collaborators to establish goals and with the administrative collaborators to maintain parameters such as budgets and legal obligations. The production manager is a pivotal role in this process, receiving input from all sides and needing to maintain the balance of artistic integrity within the resources available.

A good production manager can meet these needs but keep collaborators realistic so everything stays on time and on budget. Sometimes this requires creativity. Their goal is to make the best version of the performance happen cost effectively

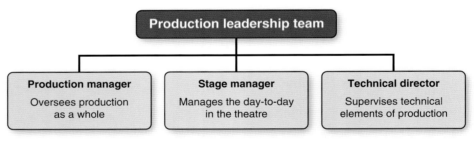

Figure 5.3 Production leadership team dealing directly with theatre aspects.

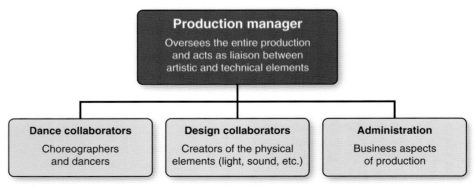

Figure 5.4 Production management structure.

and safely, so it's important for them to know why each element is key to the performance. If it's not integral, it may not be worth the money or benefit the performance artistically.

In a university setting, the production manager is usually the professor in charge of the performance. They probably simultaneously serve as the technical and artistic directors as well. In general, a production manager can be resident at a specific theatre or employed by an artistic company and come into any theatre they perform in. No matter the capacity, the production manager oversees and manages but has less direct involvement with each production element. They make the calls but hand off responsibilities to the individual technical collaborators. A production manager's specific duties may include the following:

> Create and maintain the production budget
> Facilitate communication among collaborators
> Create and update the production schedule
> Call and lead production meetings
> Procure and oversee production venues
> Oversee the lobby and external venue areas
> Send the **rider** to the venue
> Oversee the production staff
> Supervise the technical staff

THE RIDER

The rider, also known as the *production rider* or *technical rider*, is a document specifying all the requirements of the production and talent for the venue to satisfactorily prepare for the show. A rider is an invaluable asset, especially for a touring production. It arrives long before any dancer or choreographer and establishes the instructions for technical, security, hospitality preparation, and anything in between. Riders have infamously included seemingly over-the-top requirements like bowls of candy in specific colors (or without specific colors), firearms, and animals! Most of these outlandish inclusions have been said to be a test of how thoroughly a venue reads and executes the rider. Let's hope.

Stage Manager

The production manager oversees the whole production, and the **stage manager** works to oversee the stage itself. The stage manager is the boots-on-the-ground person who works alongside the choreographers and directors in rehearsals to establish and document the elements that will be on the stage and manages the progress and paperwork of the actual performance (not the entirety of the production). They report on each day's progress, asking questions, delegating tasks, and communicating the choreographer or director's needs to the rest of the organization. Each branch of the company may have an interest in these critical notes and will reply accordingly through the stage manager to advance the conversation and take necessary actions. They ensure the performance safety, call the show, and make sure it all runs smoothly. They are the go-to person who knows the show inside and out and communicates with all players. A stage manager's duties will vary greatly based on the performance they are calling. In some productions, there may be an assistant stage manager, backstage manager, or other people on their team to help with some of these duties, or they may be doing it solo. The stage manager and their team work on headsets to make sure they can clearly communicate throughout the event. Duties might include the following:

> Tape out the stage
> Manage and assign dressing rooms
> Attend some of or all rehearsals (depending on the type of performance)
> Maintain a prompt book
> Keep the tech crew on task
> Record meeting minutes, production reports, and rehearsal reports
> Document all movement and set up rehearsals
> Assist the show director during the rehearsal period
> Liaise between cast and production staff and between designers and directors or choreographers
> Create and distribute rehearsal and meeting paperwork—minutes and reports
> Create and maintain the master cue (prompt) book, from which to call cues
> Lead all backstage activity during the performance period
> Relay relevant information to performers and tech collaborators (i.e., call times for cast and crew)

LISTEN TO YOUR STAGE MANAGER

With a long list of crucial but often time-consuming and specific tasks, the stage manager is one of the hardest working people in the production. They must be heard and respected. When the stage manager comes to the dressing room to call places there is a traditional call and response between the stage manager, crew, and performers.

SM: "Five minutes to places."

Company: "Thank you! Five!"

SM: "Places, everyone! Merde."

Company: "Thank you. Places!"

At that point, the cast and crew immediately go to their opening locations.

Technical Director

The **technical director** is in charge of the technical elements of a production: everything backstage and onstage. They bring these elements together seamlessly. If the production has a big enough budget, this person would direct the design collaborators and be the liaison to the production manager. If the production is smaller, the responsibilities of the technical director may fall on the production manager instead. The venue itself may have its own technical director who coordinates with your technical director or production manager.

The theatre is theirs: the lighting, sound, scenery, and more report to them for coordination on construction, space, and safety regulations. In fact, the technical director is responsible for knowing all safety codes and regulations and enforcing them throughout the theatre. They are in charge of the dangerous parts of the performance: any rigging, special effects, or other exceptional scenic or stage pieces. Essentially, they are the director of all that is not the performance itself. Their specific duties may include the following examples:

Technical Aspects

› Generate the technical paperwork for the crew to execute (set and lighting) the design elements

› Choose the material for design elements and purchase materials for the build

› Build the design elements, from traditional scenic elements to smoke machines to flying harnesses for dancers à la Cirque du Soleil

› Coordinate scenery transport and construction (trucks, shipping, stage hands) and the space (if operating in their own space); loading into a new space and coordinating with an existing tech director

› Inform the production team of safety codes and regulations and enforce them

› Take the designers' plans and execute them within the allotted budget, labor, and time

Stage Aspects

› Work with the stage manager on tech rehearsals and time onstage for artists, designers, and technicians

› Oversee the creation, installation, and operation of scenery and props

› Run the production crew and deck crew

› Help solve problems that may develop unexpectedly so the stage is ready and all cast and crew are in the right place for curtain

› After the last performance, work with the stage manager to safely strike the production and if it is a touring show, load the truck

› After the run of show, restore all spaces the way they were

Design Collaborators

Design collaborators interpret the artistic vision through their discipline and medium. Each of these artists conceives a representation of the overarching concept with the unique tools of their trade. For example, color psychology could inform a lighting designer to use lots of red light to reinforce speed and force in the choreography. The light itself means nothing; the designer understands how light works in an audience's mind and makes the choreographer's concept of an energetic piece more tangible. In another example, the costume can instantly transport an audience through time and space, defining the setting of a dance before the first step is taken. Designers respond to the artistic vision creating elements that complement or amplify the dance. As shown in figure 5.5, designers can be divided into three categories: physical designers (sets and props, costumes, makeup, and hair), visual designers (lighting, streaming, and multimedia), and auditory designers (sound designers and sound engineers).

Scenic Designer and Prop Designer

The **scenic designer** or set designer creates the physical environment for the production. They design scenic elements based on the production team's or choreographer's artistic vision. This includes

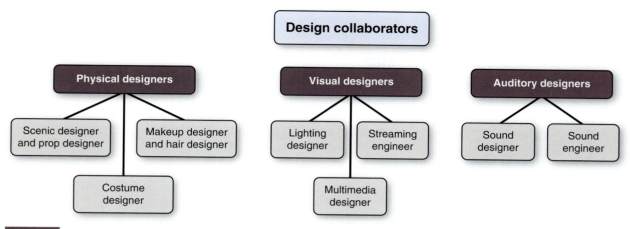

Figure 5.5 Design collaborators.

designing scenery like dancing space, levels, vertical elements like walls and drops, superstructures like canopies and truss, special elements like flying silks or slack lines, practical elements like furniture, and even hand props such as an umbrella or cane. Though dance productions are not often scenery- or prop-heavy, elements of the physical environment may contribute to the dance world or story. A scenic designer translates the abstract concept to make sure the physical aspects of the space reflect that idea. In a production, they are responsible for designing and managing the space as well as planning and documenting scene shifts and changes to the stage between scenes, pieces, or acts. The design itself manifests in the following ways:

- Scale model—a 3D computer model or physical model of the stage
- Ground plan—a bird's-eye view on paper
- Section plan—what the stage looks like from the wings; shows theatre height or vertical dimensions from the wings
- Color renderings—an artistic representation of what the audience will see
- A full set of working drawings for all scenery, furniture, and built props for carpenters and such to use
- Research—including reference photos and articles
- Paint elevations with swatches—pictures of the set with colors to be matched to other design elements

Props are handheld or portable items the dancers use onstage. If a performer does not use the prop, it is called *set dressing*. The toy rifle in *The Nutcracker* ballet is a prop a dancer uses, but the clock on the mantel is a set dressing. Scenic designers indicate what props need to be purchased or created, and other collaborators create and procure them. If they have the staff, they will work with a dedicated prop designer and prop master. A **prop designer** creates and designs the necessary props to align with the scenic designer's plan. The **prop master** rents, purchases, or builds the necessary items. The prop master is also responsible for managing the props in the space. They will provide rehearsal props for the dancers as needed. They also create and distribute a prop tracking list that identifies who gets the props and when and indicates where the props should be throughout the production.

HOW SCENIC AND PROP DESIGNERS APPLY THE SEVEN ELEMENTS OF ART

- *Line:* Is the setting more geometric or organic?
- *Shape:* Should the look be realistic or fanciful, or something in between?
- *Form:* Should there be physical objects onstage for the dancers to interact with, or are backdrops sufficient?
- *Space:* How will the dancers occupy the stage space?
- *Texture:* Does the floor need grip (for a practical safety measure)? Does the set have soft goods to create a certain effect (for an artistic approach)?
- *Value:* How will the designer apply lightness and dark values of color across the stage?
- *Color:* Are the color choices practical, psychological, or a bit of both?

Table and chairs used as props in *The Empty Room* (2018).

HOW SCENIC AND PROP DESIGNERS APPLY THE PRINCIPLES OF DESIGN

- *Pattern:* Should there be patterns on the set, or should it feel sparser and more random?
- *Contrast:* Should there be a unified appearance for the stage, or would contrasting elements add value to the piece?
- *Emphasis:* Is there a focal point to highlight?
- *Balance:* Does the piece require symmetry?
- *Scale:* Are the scenic and prop pieces natural, large, or small, compared to the dancers?
- *Rhythm and movement:* The set can supplement movement in a practical way with revolves and moving parts, or by being shaped and painted to represent motion with curves and angles, and emphasis.
- *Unity:* The entire design should have a cohesive look.
- *Variety:* Does each dance piece, scene, or act have a different set?

Costume Designer

The **costume designer**'s job is to characterize the performers. In any production, but especially a dance production, they need to understand where the artistic vision meets physical functionality (more so than other designers). For example, the 1940s zoot suit the costume shop is making needs to be flexible enough to allow for large leg movements or floor work for a dancer and might need adaptations to allow a quick change into the next piece. This requires lots of research. The costume designer needs to know the time, material, context, physical needs, and quick changes to support the statement they make with the costume. In costume design, it's all about how creative you can be to merge the visual with the functionality. This is where communicative spirit is important. The costume designer has the following responsibilities:

› Research and recommend materials
› Create a cast list with character breakdowns
› Create a design plot for each character
› Provide thumbnails or a vision board (Pinterest or similar) of each costume rendering

- › Create a color palette
- › Create purchasing and rental lists (including sources and costs)
- › Create a list for costume changes and quick changes
- › Provide rehearsal pieces as needed
- › Submit final color renderings for each character (including impressions or directions for costuming stagehands or ASMs)
- › Pull and purchase materials
- › Create working and build sketches (as needed)
- › Create patterns or drafting (as needed)
- › Provide specific requirements for hair, wigs, and makeup
- › Lead costume fittings

The dancer embodies the character, and the designer creates a visual image. A costume can quickly make or break a performance as an audience struggles to take in the visual of the costume and match it with the choreography and other design elements. Costumes have also been known to help hide the need for kneepads for a dancer or support a dancer in other ways.

Sometimes, in addition to the costume designer, there is a **costume supervisor** to oversee the creation, rental, implementation, and maintenance of costumes. This person allows the costume designer to do what they do while they manage the logistics of creating and procuring costume pieces. As we will discuss in the section about the production calendar, having costumes finished in enough time for adjustments will be essential for your dancers to feel comfortable and work out any movement issues with the costume.

HOW THE COSTUME DESIGNER APPLIES THE SEVEN ELEMENTS OF ART

- *Line:* Clothing works to emphasize or reduce the body's natural shape, and lines dominate this effect. A pant leg extended to the natural waist will have a much longer line and make the legs appear to be much longer than we observe in casual clothing.
- *Shape:* This will be the silhouette for a garment.
- *Form:* Any three-dimensional feature such as the human body is considered a form.
- *Space:* All costumes occupy a volume of space.
- *Texture:* Fabrics have infinite texture possibilities; some will be more appropriate or practical than others for the type of dance you want to achieve. This is why many dancers wear socks because the soft texture allows for easier spinning or sliding than a rubber-soled shoe or being barefoot.
- *Value:* This refers to the lightness or darkness of a hue (color).
- *Color:* This can affect everything from the psychology of the dance to the lighting choices.

HOW THE COSTUME DESIGNER APPLIES THE PRINCIPLES OF DESIGN

- *Pattern:* This may be inherent to a fabric selection or created from a variety of materials used together.
- *Contrast:* Light and dark value or intensity or using complementary or supplementary colors create contrast.
- *Emphasis:* Most of the elements of art can help achieve emphasis, such as a black spot on an otherwise white costume.
- *Balance:* Symmetry and equality in design and materials application create balance.
- *Scale:* Scale is achieved in the relative size of costume attributes or from comparing one costume to another.
- *Rhythm and movement:* Some fabrics and materials are better for movement. The fabric weight determines its ability to hang or flow or move in a certain way. The garment itself may have elements in movement as the eye is drawn across lines and attracted to the things emphasized.
- *Unity:* The entire design should have a cohesive look. The sense should be that all costumes work together harmoniously, whether that is achieved through the elements of art or simple choice. Period and genre are also critical to achieving unity.
- *Variety:* Consider each garment or collection of garments in a scene or dance piece to evaluate variety.

The costume and makeup color palettes work together with the lighting and scenery in this dance performance.

Makeup Designer and Hair Designer

Designing makeup and hair for performers is an extension of the costume design. These artists work to make the costume designer's vision come to life through the performer's hair and makeup instead of through fabric.

In a dance performance, the hair and makeup need to be functional for the dancer's movements and enhance the dance by allowing the shape of the bodies to stand out. In some instances, the hair and makeup design may be more specific to create a unique character integral to the work.

A **makeup designer** or **hair designer** may need to do the following:

› Create a cast list and character breakdowns indicating how many and which different costumes each character (dancer) has
› Create a costume plot for each character (typically a spreadsheet that identifies when each dancer wears which costume during a performance run)
› Produce renderings and visual research (a collage, Pinterest, or similar)
› Purchase and rent resources
› Create color renderings
› Provide a final product list (adjustments may occur through fitting phase, remaining within budget)

HOW MAKEUP AND HAIR DESIGNERS APPLY THE SEVEN ELEMENTS OF ART

› *Line:* Need wrinkles, a six-pack of abs, or a stronger jaw? Use lines!
› *Shape:* Many types of makeup or prosthetics can drastically change the shape of a face or body.
› *Form:* The overall makeup design will create the form.
› *Space:* Draw features together or spread them apart.
› *Texture:* Consider beard stubble or animal fur.
› *Value:* This creates shadows, depth, highlights, and lowlights.
› *Color:* Realistic or fanciful makeup all have specific color choices.

- › Create a makeup change and touch up the tracking list (updated throughout tech rehearsals and dress rehearsals)
- › Lead makeup and wig fittings or trainings for cast and crew

HOW MAKEUP AND HAIR DESIGNERS APPLY THE PRINCIPLES OF DESIGN

- › *Pattern:* A nice perm in a wig or a reptile scale sprayed onto the body can create a pattern.
- › *Contrast:* Light and dark value and intensity or using complementary or supplementary colors create contrast.
- › *Emphasis:* Prosthetics are an excellent way to create emphasis.
- › *Balance:* The classic Greek face is a study in balance and symmetry.
- › *Scale:* The classic Greek face requires perfect scale.
- › *Rhythm and movement:* Organic and curvilinear lines help create a sense of rhythm and movement.
- › *Unity:* The entire design should have a cohesive look.
- › *Variety:* Dancers should not look the same—unless you want them to.

Lighting Designer

The **lighting designer** creates the lighting, atmosphere, and overall visual environment for the production. They work with the artistic director, choreographer, set designer, costume designer, and more to illuminate the story and bring the movement, set, costumes, and themes to life. They use a lighting plot, a document that shows a bird's-eye view (ground plan) of where lights will exist physically in space, to lay out and communicate their design with other collaborators. They are also skilled drafters with experience in electronics and mathematics and use industry-specific computer software to create and print their plans.

Depending on the scope of a show, the lighting designer may design for a specific space or venue. For a touring or similar production, they may design for a single dance in a concert. The lighting

HOW THE LIGHTING DESIGNER APPLIES THE SEVEN ELEMENTS OF ART

- › *Line:* This is a beam of light exposed in midair by haze or other particles.
- › *Shape:* They use beam fields or the shape of light visible on the floor, dancer, or other object.
- › *Form:* Any three-dimensional feature such as the human body is considered a form.
- › *Space:* This is defined as the absence of light and is sometimes called negative space.
- › *Texture:* Gobos or templates break up light to create patterns or disrupt pure light.
- › *Value:* This is the intensity of light as established by being brighter or dimmer.
- › *Color:* Gels and LED color-changing lights provide hues.

HOW THE LIGHTING DESIGNER APPLIES THE PRINCIPLES OF DESIGN

- › *Pattern:* This can be achieved with beams, colors, the use of space, or physical patterns like gobos.
- › *Contrast:* This is a light and dark value, an intensity, or the use of complementary or supplementary colors.
- › *Emphasis:* A spotlight is a prime example of using emphasis because it establishes a focal point for the audience.
- › *Balance:* This is symmetry and equality in lighting features.
- › *Scale:* The size of beams or fields of light provide proportion and weight to areas or objects, including dancers, signifying relationship.
- › *Rhythm and movement:* Some lighting instruments have motors and move light around the space, often in unison with movement or music.
- › *Unity:* The entire design should have a cohesive look. A stage wash provides an even layer of light across the floor.
- › *Variety:* With each piece or movement within a piece, the show should have visual interest.

Stage gobo lighting creating textures on the stage floor.

designer's responsibility to shed light on the dance and support the vision remains constant.

Before the rehearsal starts and during the run of the production, lighting designers are responsible for creating the following:

> A light plot (done in Vectorworks or a similar program): A bird's-eye view of the theatre with symbols that represent all the light characteristics and the accessories used in the design
> A channel hook-up (done in Lightwright or a similar program): A spreadsheet indicating where the lights are powered up or plugged in
> An instrument schedule
> A list of lights and accessories (done in Lightwright or a similar program): A complete inventory of all lights and accessories that also identifies rental equipment
> A color and template list (done in Lightwright or a similar program)
> A list of gels and gobos needed
> A cue sheet: A spreadsheet that tells the stage manager and crew when the cue happens; a cue is a light change: lights up = cue 1 and lights down = cue 2
> A program for the lighting console (or they will train or pass off cues to a designated board operator)

Multimedia (Visual) Designer

As productions have evolved and more technology has become integrated into performances, other collaborative roles have arisen. A **multimedia designer** or **visual designer**, whether their job is an extension of the lighting designer's or a separate person on the team, can integrate the visuals and video (projected or LED) into a scenic or lighting design. A current example could be creating a dance shown online for a global Internet audience. The COVID-19 pandemic has forced many choreographers and designers to rethink how the art form is viewed. When collaborating and creating on a computer, designers have to come up with different ways to display the art. Digital backgrounds are now becoming an immersive part of the digital choreography and are not just a blue screen or a static background image. These new techniques in *media dance* are a new reality, and as live performance begins again, these techniques will be integrated and redefined.

Though the multimedia designer is not yet a defined role, as technology evolves and becomes more present in production and storytelling, the role is becoming popular and more necessary. This person works closely with both scenic and lighting designers, because the visual rendering would often involve the physical environment and the lighting of the piece. Depending on the scale of the performance, these roles could overlap as well.

The multimedia designer might deal with any projections, imagery, animations, and digital scenery involved in the performance and may be responsible for the following:

› Create a projection plot that shows the overall design and plan for creating the video images for the story's world
› Identify rental equipment
› Provide media for rehearsals as needed
› Create playback files and associated media
› Lead load-in work calls (as needed)
› Program projection equipment and playback device
› Hire a projection playback operator

Streaming Engineer

Livestreaming a performance has become an increasingly important mode of presenting work to a large audience, especially since the beginning of the COVID-19 pandemic. Performances streamed via YouTube, Vimeo, Facebook Live, and more have allowed theatres and performance companies to continue to offer their art to the public without gathering a large audience in the same space. To make this happen effectively, someone needs to handle the streaming logistics behind the scenes. This may be someone already on your team, or you may need to find another person to act as your **streaming engineer** to oversee the stream. As in any broadcast situation, this person is responsible for setting up all the equipment for the stream and then operating the computer or control deck on the day of the stream. They take cues from the stage manager or a director.

Postproduction Coordinator and Audio and Video Editors

Sometimes, a performance will be recorded and broadcast later, so the team may need a **postproduction coordinator** and **audio and video editors**.

These technicians are responsible for assembling the content prepared for the production and creating a product that can be broadcast to a remote audience. They may sync the sound with the video, calibrate the video color, select camera angles, make video edits, apply transitions and effects, create an introduction or credits for the piece, and much more.

Sound Designer and Sound Engineer

Depending on the production, the person responsible for the music, audio effects, and overall sound of the performance may be a sound designer, sound engineer, or one person operating as a combination of the two.

A true **sound designer** collaborates with the artistic vision to create an audio element that accentuates the performance. They may create cues along movement scripts and change tempo based on them, and create and place sound effects in the performance. They could compose music themselves or work with an external composer.

A **sound engineer**, on the other hand, often works in audio recording and editing. In a live performance, they would facilitate the effective playback of other audio media, and mix the levels and quality of the sound for the audience (via public announcement or PA system) and the monitors for the dancers onstage. They work with mixers and sound levels in the live performance to create the ideal auditory experience. Their responsibilities include curating equipment and identify the people needed to make that happen.

The job for a sound designer or an engineer job can vary. If it's a more theatrical production, the job may be more intricate and include adding sound effects, microphones, and other moving parts. In any case, the responsibilities of a sound collaborator like a sound designer or a sound engineer can include the following:

› Create the sound plot (PA, backline, microphones, monitors, hotspots, reinforcement, etc.)
› Identify rental equipment
› Create an audio patch list
› Provide rehearsal tracks as needed
› Play back files and associated media
› Lead load-in work calls (as needed)
› Create a sound cue list
› Program the audio console and playback device
› Train the soundboard operator

HOW THE SOUND DESIGNER AND ENGINEER APPLY THE PRINCIPLES OF DESIGN

- ❯ *Pattern:* Can be achieved with speaker location and sequence of sound effects or tracks.
- ❯ *Contrast:* A mixture of loud and soft sounds create depth and aural texture to a sound design.
- ❯ *Emphasis:* Specifying a particular speaker or output, or increasing volume can emphasize a location or importance of sound.
- ❯ *Balance:* Depending on the venue size, adjusting the timing (delay) can achieve balance, and under most circumstances, balance is an equal output of sound across a selection of outputs or speakers.
- ❯ *Scale:* The relative "size" of sound can be achieved through various sound effects.
- ❯ *Rhythm and movement:* Sound can pan across outputs, side to side, forward, and back. And rhythm is implicit in audio for dance, whether it is a regular beat or not—that is a choice.
- ❯ *Unity:* Selecting sounds and music that complement each other in genre or origin.
- ❯ *Variety:* Choosing sounds or music with a variety of sounds or manipulating the equalizer for variations among the high, mid, and low tones could provide variety.

Event Collaborators

Many collaborators help with the production and make sure that everything runs smoothly. These people are an important part of the production, but their primary jobs are to deal with the business end of things outside of onstage activities. The publicity staff, the box office, house managers, producers, and tour managers all ensure that the public knows that the show is happening and are there to interact with the audience and to engage with the public and future venues.

Publicity

While the artistry is happening behind the scenes, marketing content should be developed and strategically circulated to ensure there is an audience to view the final product. The **publicity creators** must understand the artistic vision and represent the work correctly so audiences understand what type of experience they are getting for their money. Publicity today has moved beyond posters and simple email blasts to let the community know about your event. Anyone working in publicity needs to be savvy about social media and know how to use these outlets to their advantage. Social media and branding in the 21st century can make or break projects even before they are performed. The materials being produced not only represent the performance itself but also the company, theatre, and anyone involved in the production. Whether you are a student, choreographer, or marketing executive, a strong understanding of current social media environments and trends will be essential to not only promote a single production but also develop a following to build on for future events.

Front of House and Box Office Managers

The venue will determine how much hands-on responsibility you will have for the front of house and box office. If you are in school or renting a theatre, this infrastructure very likely will already be in place, and it will be your role to coordinate with these managers and let them do their jobs. The **house manager** is the transition for the audience from the outside world to the performance space. They, along with their ushers, are the first point of contact for the audience and set up the mood for the event.

Responsibilities of house manager include the following:

- ❯ Direct and train ushers
- ❯ Follow all ADA requirements to ensure accessible entry and seating
- ❯ Ensure audience safety
- ❯ Work with stage managers regarding merchandise sales
- ❯ Control the flow of people into and out of the performance space
- ❯ Support concessions

The **box office manager** deals with the actual selling of tickets for the performance. This includes setting up the online ticket sale system and managing the box office, and keep the technology running smoothly. They also need to get people into seats in a delightfully pleasant manner.

Producer and Tour Manager

There may be other players responsible for the logistics of a production, like a producer for film productions or a tour manager for touring performances. A **producer** oversees a production from beginning to end. Many filmed dance productions, especially commercial productions, will have a producer at the head of the team who finds the money for the project and assembles the collaborators to work on it. This can create problems between the business and artistic sides. Potential conflicts about what's important in the show can occur when the financial backers want a specific product. The artistic collaborators may need to compromise on their vision to keep the project on budget and make all parties happy with the overall outcome.

If you have a company, a recurring program that goes into schools, or a recurring community performance or travel in any capacity, or if you're bringing in students from other schools to watch your performance, you may need a **tour manager**. Touring and bringing in other audiences are important for community engagement, getting out of your bubble, adapting to new spaces, and bringing new voices in. The tour manager makes all this happen. They coordinate everything from the master calendar and the budget to the relationship to the venue, and they are involved at every point. They often take on many of the responsibilities a production manager would for a show that does not tour. They may be responsible for the following:

› Book the venues and general events
› Facilitate clear communication with all parties involved
› Create the master calendar
› Maintain a budget for the tour and individual productions

Visit HK*Propel* to complete assignment 5.1, Building Your Team.

Defining a Collaborative Language

You may have heard the proverb "All roads lead to Rome." All the collaborators in the artistic and production areas, as different as they are, are all working toward the same "Rome," the production, but they'll each take a different road to get there. The key is making sure all collaborators are traveling to the same destination. When people aren't aligned on the destination, the production and performance quality can be compromised. Poor communication or a lack of understanding for how each describes their workflow and need can sidetrack the process, leading to a destination that's lost in translation and a performance that misses the mark.

LOST IN TRANSLATION

What language are you speaking?

› An artistic director speaks in words of encouragement.
› A director speaks in terms of certainty.
› A dancer speaks in steps and motions.
› A choreographer speaks in movement.
› A (ballet) choreographer speaks in French.
› A production manager speaks in dollars and cents.
› A technical director speaks in weights and measures.
› A scenic designer speaks in scale and dimension.
› A costume designer speaks in weaves and dyes.
› A makeup designer speaks in shades and hues.
› A lighting designer speaks in temperatures and intensities.
› A sound designer speaks in peaks and valleys.
› A multimedia designer speaks in zeros and ones.
› A stage manager speaks in stand-bys and goes.
› A tour manager speaks in meals and accommodations.
› A box office manager speaks in cash or credit.
› A social media manager speaks in 280 characters or fewer.

And yet, somehow, they all speak the language of production because that's what production is: the culmination of so many unique trades and talents.

Acknowledging the differences between production languages is the first step to avoiding miscommunication and frustration during a production. It is a mistake to assume the production team is on the same page and understand each other's language. There are different terms, sayings, and assumptions in each discipline, and taking the time to understand the others' languages and roles will clarify these assumptions for all players. Recognizing the different players in the production and knowing their language is the key to an easy process and will help determine the information everyone needs to proceed and how they need to communicate it. Each person has something valuable to bring to the table, and at the end of the day, each collaborator should be respected for their knowledge in their area of expertise, and their ideas should be heard and considered in entirety.

DID YOU KNOW?

> When a stagehand asks you, "What's your 20?," they're just asking you for your location.

> When the dancers are yelling at each other in French before the show starts, it's probably not a riot. They are most likely encouraging each other with a commonly used term to offer a successful performance.

> If you hear an electrician asking himself where he left his hammer, he's really looking for a crescent wrench.

> Stage directions: For a dancer onstage, "upstage" means what's behind you, and "downstage" is what's in front. "Right" is right, and "left" is left; but for the choreographer, "right" is left, and "left" is right, upstage is far away, and downstage is near. If a stage pipe overhead comes "in," that's down, and up is "out."

The creative brief, covered in part I, is a great way to begin effectively communicating with other collaborators and translate ideas across disciplines. A well-developed creative brief gives everyone a starting point so the group can come up with some common language about the project. The team can chime in based on their specialties during the production meetings. This sets the stage for an open line of communication throughout the production and avoids confusion or misunderstandings from the beginning.

The next important aspect is understanding the proper lines of communication. Who is the person to go through if you need to talk to another department, and who do you need creative conversations with? Creative conversations between designers, directors, and choreographers can occur informally in order to bounce ideas and inspiration off each other and confirm the artistic choices are moving in the right direction.

As mentioned previously, there are as many different organizational structures as there are organizations, but regardless of your role in the production, it is important to look for the hierarchy structure of your situation.

A choreographer working independently to submit a piece to a festival may have a lot of agency in what the specific lighting should be for their piece and may communicate this through the stage or event manager for the festival. A choreographer working to create an evening-length show with creative support from a production team will speak directly with the lighting designer and offer creative research, background, and direction to the designer, but the designer will translate that into a specific lighting design.

You need to understand the structure you are working in so you can participate accordingly. This is another place to not make assumptions. In each production, the structure can change, and knowing who has what authority to make which decision is crucial to not creating more chaos. If you are unsure, clarify these lines of communication before the production goes too far.

Be aware of your own communication skills throughout the process. As you will see in the production timeline in chapter 9, while it may seem like you have months before reaching the final production, there are multiple deadlines and smaller tasks that must be completed on time for everything to come together. Everything you communicate and act on has an impact on the final performance. Someone is liable and paying the bill, and people want to protect their interests. It's important that your intention is clear to avoid any confusion or assumptions. Making sure you are clearly communicating your needs and responding to others will ensure the best possible outcome for you, your collaborative reputation, and the production as a whole.

Production Meetings

All collaborators have a part to play in the final production. It takes an engaged team to bring the seed of an idea to an audience. Second only to opening night, the first *production meeting* is the most exciting milestone in the production process. It is the first time that the entire *company* (or all the artistic, business, and production staff) meet face-to-face (whether in person or on a video conference call) to discuss the show. Until this point, the choreographer has been developing the comprehensive artistic vision that will drive this meeting and every decision made thereafter. This *kickoff* is the first opportunity for everyone else to hear the scope and scale of the production. The purpose of the meeting is to generate action items for each participant to move the production process forward, from an abstract concept to a tangible production. Designers can begin creating drafts and plots. Publicity staff can begin advertising and gauging interest on social media. The administration and production collaborators can begin assessing the budget, staffing, and resources. And the choreographer can finally receive valuable feedback about if it is feasible to create the production as imagined or if there will be compromise.

The second and subsequent production meetings are opportunities to check the status of each department and update action items between each meeting. These meetings will typically be scheduled around significant milestones or dates within the larger production calendar. The details and deliverables will vary according to the needs of each production. This process requires that directors and choreographers collaborate with designers and production staff before the deadline dates.

No specific number of production meetings are needed, though it seems to make sense that an initial meeting would kick off the process. Meetings that offer designers an opportunity to share their designs at various phases are useful. Roundtable-type meetings offer each department an opportunity to share its status, ask questions, and generate action items to be completed before the next meeting. Those leading the meeting should be prepared with an agenda covering the important topics that the team needs to discuss. The agenda helps keep everyone on track and understand the expectations of what needs to be addressed in the meeting.

Meetings that follow rehearsals, run-throughs, or any type of cast presentation offer the production team an opportunity to reflect on what they have just observed and to make notes for updates or changes that may become apparent. A unique meeting called a *paper-tech* is useful for the director or choreographer to talk through the entire production from start to finish with the design team and make sure all the cues are accounted for. Informal meetings held between the artistic and production teams are generally called *sidebar meetings*. There can never be enough of these meetings, because communication is key to success.

To facilitate meetings, it's important to get egos out of the way, relinquish the need to control everything, learn to listen, and find your voice as an artist to clearly represent your vision. As you come into the first production meeting, remember that every production is a learning opportunity, and sometimes out of the most spectacular failures you will find perfect solutions. If you are an artist in an academic, supported environment, this is the time to explore

TRUSTING THE PROCESS

Rarely, if ever, does a dream become reality without some concessions. Even when there's disagreement, a production meeting should be a safe time and space, where the team can feel free to speak their position while respecting the people and the process, even if dreams and reality cannot mesh perfectly. Conversation brings out the perspectives of each collaborator and allows the team to make a clear decision supported by multiple viewpoints. The production team exists to execute the artistic vision, so in times of disagreement, ego must be set aside to make decisions in service of that vision.

This expansion of the artistic vision is where the magic happens. What was once an idyllic dance executed perfectly in one's mind is now a real and tangible thing impacted by the world around it. This idea must be protected, nurtured, and constantly reevaluated. Just as a person grows up and learns from experience, altering course and becoming a unique individual, so does the artistic vision. It has many caretakers on its path to maturity. Trust is the key factor in a relationship between so many people of influence over this precious thing, the dance. The choreographer must trust the production manager, who must trust the artistic director, who must trust the costumer, and so on. Collaboration means that the choreographer must hold the vision in an open palm for the production team. Meanwhile, the production team must respect the vision because it is vulnerable in this position. The production process begins here, with the artistic vision defined for the production team by a trusting choreographer, the team prepared to accept the vision with their best intentions of executing the vision with the highest production value possible and a general respect for the people and process about to take place.

outside your comfort zone, knowing that you have a safety net of teachers and professionals to help guide you in the process. From your time experimenting with producing dance, you will develop skills to support you in the world beyond academia.

Visit HK*Propel* to complete assignment 5.2, Organizing Your Team.

Summary

Your collaborators are your teammates in the process of producing a dance performance. As the creator, you may wear more than one hat in the collaboration process, but it takes a village, large or small, to bring every element together onstage. Dance collaborators like choreographers, dancers, rehearsal directors, and others work on the creative product while production collaborators coordinate and create the environment for this product onstage. Event collaborators like publicity staff, house managers, producers, and tour managers help keep everything running smoothly. Clear communication among all collaborators is key to a smooth and successful production. From the first production meeting and beyond, making an effort to understand each party's collaborative language will help your vision come to life with everyone working at their best.

Creation in the Studio

Courtesy of Sarah Delgado/Backhausdance.

6

Key Terms
audition
call back
open call
rehearsals
self-tape

LEARNING OBJECTIVES

After reading this chapter, you will be able to do the following:

> Conceptualize and plan an audition that reflects the intention of your process
> Manage time efficiently during rehearsals
> Generate a logical rehearsal schedule
> Define your leadership style in your rehearsal process
> Rent or find space for your rehearsal

For a dance production, some of your closest collaborators will be your dancers and those involved in the artistic creation of the choreography. To find and work with these people effectively, it's important to create an experience specific to your process during the in-studio rehearsals. From creating intentional auditions to help you seek out the best dancers to running a defined rehearsal process, curating a deliberate approach for your in-studio collaborations will allow your rehearsal process to effectively lead into your intended production.

Auditions

Creating a dance production? You'll probably need some dancers! You may already know whom you'd like to hire for your project, but it's likely you'll need an **audition** to complete your cast. An audition is a job interview in a creative forum. The most important goal of your audition is to choose dancers who are the right fit for your project both artistically and personally. This is your chance to make sure their work ethics, expectations, collaborative skills, and artistic abilities are what you need and what will make your work the best it can be. It's also the first time a dancer sees a choreographer's process and gets a sense of the production. This first impression allows them to see for themselves how or if they fit into the project. Overall, an audition is an important indicator of how the team will work together for the rest of the process, so approaching them intentionally is key to an effective relationship with the dancers.

First impressions are important. If you are running an audition, many of the dancers who attend are not going to be cast depending on the need of the production. It is important for those who are not cast to leave the audition feeling seen and respected and with the overall impression that your organization is one they would want to work with in the future.

An audition is where to begin to network with new talent even if you do not currently have a space for them in your project. These dancers may also make up a good portion of your future audience and followers on social media. On the other hand, if you develop a reputation of running a poorly organized audition and people leave with a bad sense of who you are, they will likely not come back to a performance and can create a negative image for you.

The production type should dictate the audition type. For example, an extensive collaborative project, where dancers will be working together for months toward a large live production, might call for an in-person, multistep audition. The dancers must collaborate with others and display their artistic styles and decision-making skills, and complete an interview process to make sure it's a good fit. That type of in-depth attention and personal dedication will be necessary for the work, and it's reflected in the audition. On the other hand, for a commercial project that is shooting in two days and relies heavily on the look and charisma of dancers on camera, a short self-tape might be a great way to get a sense of what that dancer is like in that setting and could be the perfect audition method for that project. The way you approach running an audition will not only help you find the best dancers for your project but also set you up for success with effective communication and relationships with the dancers. When an audition reflects the work environment of the entire project, the dancers will add value to your project and respect you and the process because they have clear expectations from the beginning.

There are many aspects to consider before, during, and after your audition. Making sure you address the intention of your process in all three times and curating it with that in mind will put you on the best path for discovering dancers who are the best fit for your creation process and ultimately set your production up for success. Remember, the audition sets the tone for the whole project. You are

Creation in the Studio   85

The audition should reflect your project as a whole.

auditioning the dancers and they are auditioning you to see if your project is a good fit for them. Demonstrating your professionalism, organization, technical aesthetic, and artistic expectations throughout the whole audition delivers the right dancers to the process.

Before the Audition

First you must decide the type of audition you will hold. Will it be in person? Is there a submission process? Or do you want something completely different? Again, this should reflect your project as a whole and will continue to guide the process as you create an experience for the dancers.

Next, consider what the registration process will be like. Will it be an **open call**, which is a "come one, come all" audition, regardless of technique style or skill level? Or will you invite specific dancers? What will be required of those who audition? Just as a prospective employee would not pay a fee to interview, a dancer looking for professional work should not need to pay an audition fee, so how will you cover your costs of the audition? Considering this before you host the audition will help you effectively budget and prepare for a successful audition process.

You'll also need to set up the audition logistics before it happens: Will you need to rent space for an in-person audition? Do you need to create a Google form or use a Google Drive for video submissions? What financial systems need to be in place before you hire dancers for a project? All these logistics are important to figure out before you have announced the audition, so you're not caught off-guard if anything goes wrong.

To get dancers to come, you will need to publicize the event two to four weeks before it occurs. This gives people enough notice so they'll have availability, but it's not too far out so that they forget about it by the time it comes around. You can advertise in places like local dance organizations, social media, dance newsletters, and more, but make sure the places you choose to advertise will reach the types of dancers you'd like to show up. You'll want to include the date, location, beginning and ending times, what will be expected in the audition (two combinations, partnering, collaborative creation, etc.), whether there will be a **call back** (when a choreographer has narrowed down from a large group to a smaller group but would like to see them again before making a final casting decision), and other logistics.

You'll also want to include an idea of what to expect in terms of style, experience, and commitment to the project. Letting them know when rehearsal times will be, how long the process is, what the pay scale will be like, and key skills or strengths you are looking for will help those auditioning know if they can commit to the process and if they have the potential to make the job work before they even come into the room. By narrowing the criteria for dancers to attend your audition, you are not shrinking the pool of talent to pull from; instead, you are helping yourself find the dancer that's the best fit for the project. The more specific you are with your communication, the more likely you are to find dancers in alignment with the project you are creating.

Creating a way for dancers to register in advance for your audition, rather than having them simply show up, allows you to prepare for how large your group will be and cut down on the time spent registering dancers at the time of the audition. An audition sheet should be provided for those auditioning to fill out, ideally before they arrive, with backup copies available at the audition for last-minute entries. Important items to include might be name, contact info, level of dance experience, and a space to fill in detailed potential scheduling conflicts. Depending on the type of audition (whether it's for

SAMPLE DANCE JOB POSTINGS

Read the three job postings and notice the differences. All three are dance jobs but are very different in direction and scope.

Ballet Company is looking for dancers with strong classical and modern technique.
Where: Dance Precisions, London, UK
When: August 2022
Deadline for applications: August 2022
Ballet Company seeks eight experienced dancers to join the inaugural core of dancers. We offer full-time contracts and competitive pay. Our dancers will have strong classical technique and lines, organic movement qualities, and adaptive, collaborative outlooks. We seek accomplished artists with something interesting to say who want to work on stimulating projects with a wide range of choreographers. We are committed to cultivating a working environment that celebrates the pursuit of excellence and individuality. Preliminary auditions will be held in London in August 2022, by invitation only.
Rehearsals are to begin 15th October 2022.
To apply, please email info@ with a CV and a link to a recent video.

Portland-based Dance Theatre is looking for several exceptional movement performers in physical theatre, contemporary dance, and puppetry for large outdoor arts performances in summer 2020.
Where: Portland, Oregon
When: The audition workshops and interview process will take place on Mon 14 & Tues 15 March 2020 at The Dance Space.
Deadline for applications: Monday 7th March 2020
Dance Theatre seeks professional performers to expand our pool of freelance artists for exciting projects in 2020 and beyond. We are looking for highly creative and strong individual performers in contemporary dance, physical theatre, and/or puppetry (outdoor, giant, multi-person operated).
You must be a versatile movement performer and comfortable with character work and audience interaction. We would particularly like for individuals from the global majority and underrepresented communities to join the Company for rehearsals, live performances on tour, and the delivery of creative outreach workshops in formal education settings and the community. Applicants should demonstrate at least three years of professional experience, strong dance theatre technique, partner work, and improvisational skills. These are paid opportunities. For more information, please email us directly.
To apply, please email a statement of interest (no more than 250 words) along with a CV, headshot, and a short video showcasing your practice (no longer than 3 mins).

Auditions for Cruise Line Singers and Dancers
Location: Orlando, Florida
Due to the physical requirements of our shows, cast members should be at the peak of their fitness levels. Height ranges desired for females are between 5'3 – 5'8. Height ranges desired for males are between 5'9 – 6'1. Ages should range from 20 to 39. Dancers should have outstanding performance quality and stage presence. Gymnastics, aerial training, tumbling, and partnering skills are desirable. Applicants should be versatile dancers with strong technique and experience in many dance styles. Please be prepared to learn multiple dance combinations. Ladies bring character shoes and jazz flats, gentlemen bring jazz flats.

an academic performance, festival, evening-length show), different fields may be required for you to get a sense of whether they are a good fit for the project.

Before you get started, meet with the members of your team working the audition to establish your process:

› What is the process for evaluation?
› How will you organize your data, fees, and other systems?
› What is the process of the live or submission auditions?
› Who makes the final decision of which dancers are cut and kept?

Visit HK*Propel* to complete assignment 6.1, Creating an Audition Announcement.

During the Audition

Depending on the type of audition you are running, the items that happen during the audition itself may look different. If it's a submission process, there may not even be a "during." What needs to happen to make sure you can effectively see and thoroughly consider many dancers for your production? How will you make sure you are facilitating the process so that you end up with those best suited for the project? This will differ depending on whether you are hosting an in-person audition or a virtual audition, but you'll want to make sure the instructions and structure of the audition are clear to the participants and that you conduct yourself and the event with the type of professionalism and work environment that you want to maintain throughout the production process.

Live Auditions

To get dancers into the room and on your project, you might need to host an in-person audition. To create this audition, consider what your project is and build the audition from there. If you know you'll have a live audition, consider what you will need to see from the dancers to gauge if the project will be a good fit for them. A short-term project might require a very different process than a long-term project, for example. If you are expecting to work with a dancer for a long time over an extended rehearsal process, the information they provide will differ, their work ethic might matter more than sheer talent, and their ability to collaborate with others will be a key factor. On the other hand, if you are looking for a dancer for a short gig with little rehearsal time, their ability to learn and retain the material may be of importance.

A live audition can vary greatly depending on the type of project you are creating, and it's important you include the components that will best serve your process. There may be audition components where dancers must do any of the following:

> *Take a technique class.* Beginning an audition with a technique class allows you to witness a dancer's technique, work ethic, and stamina, but it requires time from your audition. This could be helpful when there is a specific technique or style that is important for your dancers to be proficient in. Also, if you already have a company of dancers and are looking to replace one of them, having the audition begin with a company class can offer you the opportunity to see how those auditioning fit the overall aesthetic of your company and how well they work with established dancers.

> *Pick up choreography quickly and accurately.* A phrase or combo that dancers have to learn and perform within a short time frame reveals a dancer's skill in efficiently processing choreography, which could be valuable if you have a condensed rehearsal period for the dancers to learn and perform a piece.

> *Respond to improvisational tasks.* Opportunities for improvisation allow dancers to show their choices and artistic style so you can see how they fit into your project's environment. This can be especially helpful if you know you will have improvisational components in your piece.

> *Partner with other dancers (choreographed or improvised).* Contact improvisation or partnering in an audition can determine a dancer's ability to move with others skillfully and gracefully, which will be especially important if you know your piece will require lots of contact between dancers.

> *Create their own phrase or material or create material with other dancers.* A condensed creation process in an audition can help the choreographer get a sense of a dancer's creative choices and how they make them. This can be beneficial for a collaborative creation process.

> *Interview with the directors or choreographers.* As you narrow your candidates, conducting interviews is a great way to get the full sense of someone's demeanor, goals, and priorities to see if they fit with your mission as a choreographer or director.

These are options to include in your live audition, but choosing *which* exercises best reflect your expected process will be key in selecting the dancers for your project. If you've chosen the correct exercises, during the audition you get to witness how they would function within your process and get a better sense of their fit into your project.

With the structure of the audition in place, it's important to consider what's happening logistically throughout the duration of the audition. For example, who will be handling check-in, and where will that be located? Who will be in the room watching the dancers, and who will be the speaker or communicator throughout the process?

MULTIPLE PERSPECTIVES

In any audition, it's important to have multiple eyes on the dancers. It's easy for one person to miss dancers or to focus on one dancer, so whether that be in a room or on a video, make sure you have more than one person evaluating so everyone is seen from multiple perspectives. These people may be the artistic director, choreographers, company members, production managers, or others.

Self-Tape or Video Audition

Sometimes, instead of or in addition to a live audition, a choreographer may consider some form of **self-tape** or video audition. Video can be useful as a screening for an in-person audition, as supplemental audition material to get a wider sense of what a dancer is capable of, or it can be used as the only means of auditioning. To decide what mode is best, consider the attention your project needs. If you are creating a long-term production process that will require collaboration, constant interaction, and more than a visual relationship with the dancer, you'll likely want to ultimately work with dancers in person to make a decision. It still might be worth creating a video submission first to weed out dancers who would clearly not fit your process.

Consider what is important to require in your video audition. You could request many elements, such as the following:

> *A technique or class sample.* Just like adding class to a live audition, requesting a technique element in a video audition allows you to witness a dancer's technique, work ethic, and stamina and can be especially helpful to you if there is a specific technique or style that is important for your dancers to be proficient in.

> *Choreographed phrase work.* Seeing a dancer perform choreographed phrase work gives you a sense of their ability and style in performing rehearsed work as well as what their performance presence looks like on screen.

> *Improvisation.* Improvisation in an audition video helps a dancer show their artistry and decision-making skills, which can be especially helpful if you know you will have improvisational components in your piece.

> *A brief introduction or verbal explanation of their training.* Requiring a verbal introduction in the video allows you to get a sense of the dancer's demeanor and personality when you're unable to meet them in person.

Depending on the type of project, it may be unlikely that a choreographer hires strictly from a video submission. Unless it's for a short, video-based project or a commercial shoot looking for specific aesthetic, a brief video submission does not reflect the rehearsal process of lengthier projects or productions. It can, however, be used to narrow the pool of dancers for an in-person audition later. Regardless, in any video submission, you want to get as clear a picture as possible of the dancer. To do this, it's important to be very clear about what's expected in video, how long it should be, where and how to upload it, and what to expect afterward. A video submission process can be just as valuable as an in-person audition and should be treated as such.

After the Audition

After an audition, you want to make sure all parties are clear on the result and the expectations to follow as soon as possible. This means to be considerate about your turnaround time, your communication with all parties, and what the on-boarding process will be.

There is no exact timeline to follow in notifying dancers after the audition; however, it is respectful and courteous to notify them as soon as decisions are made and finalized. In the professional concert world, dancers are notified one to seven days after an audition. It is important to notify both those who get the job and those who don't, so people aren't left questioning. In both communications, it's important to thank the dancer for their time and commitment to your project for whatever length of time they've given you. In some situations, it may be useful to first notify those who have been selected for the job, wait for their acceptance, and then send out the rejection letters. This way, if someone is unable to accept the position, you can offer it to another dancer without awkwardness. In an academic setting, where the dancers are known and many decisions are made right after or during the auditions, a cast list should go out no later than 12 hours after the audition so rehearsals will start as soon as possible. The cast should either accept or deny the role within the next 12 hours. The choreographers should have their casts set 24 hours after the audition so the rehearsal process can begin.

For those who get the job, it's important to set up clear acceptance steps and an on-boarding process that they can follow. This may include updating their contact info, issuing their contract, solidifying payroll info, confirming rehearsal dates, and any other logistics that need to be put in place. The clearer you can be in communicating these steps and their deadlines, the more smoothly they will be able to transition into their role in your process.

> ### AUDITIONS AND YOUR SOCIAL MEDIA PRESENCE
>
> TikTok, Instagram, Facebook, Twitter, and other social media provide public platforms where a director or choreographer can learn about any dancer and their dance style before even meeting them. Viewers of a dancer's social media pages expect them to post content that reflects who they are as a person (or as a dancer) and may use this information to determine whether the dancer would be a good fit for a project. This doesn't mean a dancer should feel obligated to use their social media presence solely or at all for self-promotion, but it is something to keep in mind when posting public content to make sure it reflects one's identity and what one would like to express.

Rehearsals

If auditions were the first impression, the **rehearsals** uphold that impression and maintain that relationship. If you want to create a collaborative, meaningful, personal piece, those values need to be reflected in your rehearsal process as well. If you are creating an athletic, visually stimulating, precise, and clear routine, you will be emphasizing those characteristics from warm-up through choreography and until they leave the room. This comes from planning, setting goals, and being clear with your expectations from your dancers when they are in rehearsal with you.

Setting clear goals for your rehearsal process is key to creating one that will benefit your final production. To structure and lead your rehearsal efficiently, it's important to be clear on what you are hoping to gain from the process with your dancers. Do you want people to feel like a community, is it important that everyone looks and performs the same, do you want your dancers to collaborate with you in creating the choreography, or do you want them to have a shared emotional experience? Defining clear goals such as these will help you decide how to manage, structure, and plan your rehearsals.

As a choreographer, it is helpful to make a rehearsal calendar, map out how you want to structure the rehearsals, be honest with yourself and know what your leadership style is, and make sure that you have rehearsal space or venue booked.

Time Management

Remember, your dancers are your collaborators. The time they spend with you is valuable to not only your final product but also to them as artists. It's important that their expertise is valued in the time dedicated to rehearsal, just as a lighting designer's time would be valued in a design meeting.

To make sure you are setting up your rehearsal schedule efficiently for both you and your dancers, it's important to consider the whole rehearsal process before it begins. Looking at the project in full from beginning to end allows you to see the scope of the process and anticipate benchmarks along the way that indicate where you want to be. This initial layout gives you a plan for what needs to be accomplished at different points throughout the process and keeps you on track for your original goal. Of course, these benchmarks and checkpoints can be adjusted as you go because a process can evolve over time; however, beginning the process with clear goals in mind will help the process move in

Like auditions, rehearsals should reflect your production as a whole.

a direction and progress at a steady pace to ensure your rehearsal time is being used efficiently. Setting these checkpoints up and sharing them with your production team allows you to keep your team updated on where you are in rehearsals and when they need to come into the process. For example, if you have specific props, it's important to bring them into the rehearsal process earlier so that the dancers are comfortable with them. The scenic and prop designers need to be aware of your timeline. So, it's vital that the production team have a good sense of your goals throughout the rehearsal process.

Defining these goals and deadlines and rehearsal expectations early is paramount to creating a smooth and efficient process. When a dancer is clear on what is expected of them each day and knows when they can expect to move onto the next idea, they will come in more prepared to learn and ready to take on the project. The more prepared you are, the clearer your vision, the more effectively you'll be able to collaborate with the dancers and the production team.

Structure

After you've defined how you'll schedule your rehearsal process, intentionally structuring each rehearsal to reflect the values of your process is key not only to using your rehearsal time most efficiently but also to helping your dancers be best prepared for the final product.

Some rehearsals begin with a class or a guided warm-up. Depending on your process, it may be beneficial to lead this during your rehearsal time or it may be better to save the time and let dancers warm up for themselves. If you can't afford the rehearsal time, don't host a class. It's still necessary to allow warm-up time for the dancers, even if it's not organized (20-30 mins at least) to minimize risk of injury.

If you do have the time and the space, it can be extremely beneficial to provide your dancers with a class in the style of dance you'll be creating, allowing them to be prepared for the style of the rehearsal. It can also be a benefit and incentive for dancers, especially if you're not able to pay them a lot for rehearsals. It allows you to build community and a cohesive movement style for the process. Regardless of whether it's a class or a shorter warm-up, tailoring the exercises to the process can allow you to prepare the dancers for what's to come. If you're creating a collaborative piece, an explorative class can help the dancers begin to exercise their awareness and collaboration before jumping into the

process. If you are preparing for a high-energy ballet piece, a ballet class will help dancers exercise their fast-twitch muscles and technical ability. Curating this experience can heighten a dancer's ability to best practice and perform the piece later.

It's also always important to consider when you will take breaks during your rehearsals. Traditionally, breaks are not given enough during rehearsal processes because people fear losing precious time. However, breaking up the rehearsal day helps the dancers refresh, reframe, and refocus their energy so they can more efficiently take in information and perform the work. When scheduling rehearsals, a good guideline is to give at least a 5-minute break for every hour of work, 10 minutes after a 1.5-hour class, and a 30- to 45-minute lunch break after working more than 4 hours. Often, freelance rehearsals are not dictated by union rules, so it's the director's call on what is fair, but keeping the dancer's capacity and well-being in mind will allow the finished product to be better rehearsed than if there were no breaks given. Whatever break schedule you have, let the dancers know at the top of rehearsal so that they can be prepared and know that they will get time to reset in the midst of rehearsal.

UNION RULES

If the rehearsals are governed by union rules, it is important to familiarize yourself with the rules and regulations about working hours and breaks allotted. Not doing so can mean incurring costly fines and overtime fees that can have a great impact on the bottom line.

Leadership Style

As you build your rehearsals, consider not only what the structure will look like but also your role in facilitating that structure. What is your leadership style? If you're the choreographer, how are you communicating movement to your dancers? Are you an authoritarian, facilitator, collector, collaborator, or editor? Sometimes different styles may be useful at different times throughout the process. For example, you may begin a process with a high collaborative style, collecting movement from your dancers generated from the prompts you've created. As the process goes on, though, you may become an editor who decides more about what movement stays and what goes. As the performance nears, you may become more authoritative, welcoming less input from your dancers and making final decisions.

This ability to switch hats can be beneficial, but it's important to be clear about what you expect from dancers at that moment. You can do this by making sure the words, imagery, and metaphors you are using are clear and defined when you are in an explorative process. Make sure dancers are aware of the goal of a creative prompt and be clear in your goal of unison timing and aesthetic. Regardless of the hat you're wearing or what your goals are, remember to continue to communicate and treat your dancers with the respect they deserve.

> **WWW** Visit HK*Propel* to complete assignment 6.2, Planning Your Rehearsals.

Finding Space

As you get ready to begin your rehearsal process, one of the most important things that needs to happen is to confirm *where* you will be rehearsing! If you don't have a space of your own to rehearse in, you will need to rent space from a studio or school to hold rehearsals.

First, consider what type of venue would be best for both you and your dancers. It's important to consider the geographical location (what the commute will be like for you and your dancers) and to consider the parking situation at the venue. Will dancers need to pay to park when they arrive? That might mean you reimburse them for those days. Other than that, you'll want to consider the size and scope of space necessary to your process. There are a ton of venues, studios, and locations to choose from, but sometimes it's hard to know which is the best for you or how to contact them. Researching local dance studios or arts organizations is a great first step to finding space, and there are apps and resources that exist to help with this process as well. Between your own research and word of mouth, you can find space that works with your budget and provides for your rehearsal needs.

Renting space can be a hefty expense depending on the length and duration of your rehearsal process. If you want more time in a space, it may be in your interest to find ways to offset the cost of the space by opening a class for other dancers to pay to attend at the beginning of your rehearsal or trading space for an offering of your own (work,

Virtual rehearsals can be an option when limitations make it difficult to get dancers together.

cleaning, other benefit) with the host venue. Some spaces also have a nonprofit rate if you happen to have that status.

Another way to rehearse without the expense of booking a physical space is to use a video chat platform like Zoom or Google Meet. In some cases, virtual rehearsals can be beneficial for your project. It may allow you to work with a team that's in different places geographically or that has limited travel schedules. It also may give you more time to work on a project because there is no cost to rent space for a longer time. In these cases, though, it is often still important to come together at the end of a process in the same geographical space. Putting that in-person meeting at the end of the process instead of throughout saves money on space rental in your budget.

There are important disadvantages to these platforms, however. When dancers are in different spaces and dancing on different surfaces, they may have trouble fully executing movement. There may be communication difficulties in explanations and translating movement. Timing will not be consistent, and it will never equal the level of collaboration and camaraderie that will be created in person. Virtual rehearsals are sometimes appropriate for a project but not always. Consider your work and the level of collaboration, time, and financial investment you can put into rehearsals to decide if they are a good option for you.

Summary

Curating an audition and rehearsal process that reflects the intention of your production will allow your dancers to be aligned with your vision throughout the creation process. From the beginning of the audition to the last rehearsal, you want your process to embody the professionalism and dedication you initiate and expect. Even if the final product is not your masterpiece, ending with everyone feeling the hours spent were worthy of their time and open to working with you again will serve your overall career. Many companies start with a choreographer and a group of dancers who enjoy working with each other so much they just keep creating. As you move into the next three chapters and learn about the production team, designers, and timeline, realize these components are equally important. It's essential to approach every collaborative interaction with the same clear purpose you use in your rehearsal process in the studio.

Stage, Scenery, Props, and Lighting

7

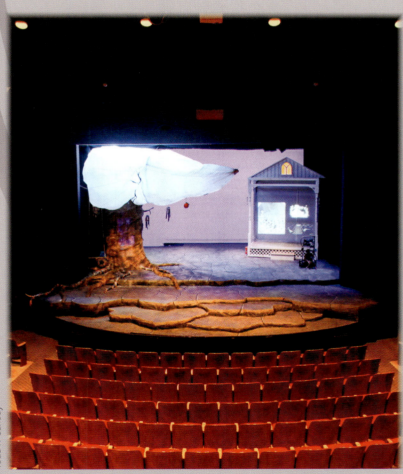

Key Terms

apron
backlight
blackout
booms (a.k.a. trees)
borders
center line
center stage
crossfade
cyc lights
cyclorama
deck
downstage
ellipsoidal reflector spotlight (ERS)
fade in
fade out
fill light
follow spot
Fresnel
gel
gobo
going dark
heads
house
houselights
iris
key light
legs
Marley
offstage
onstage
panel light
parabolic aluminized reflector (PAR) light
plaster line
rep plot (repertory plot)
running lights
scene shop
scrim
sidelight
spike tape
stage left
stage right
strip light
upstage
wings

LEARNING OBJECTIVES

After reading this chapter, you will be able to do the following:

> Describe the structure of a stage
> Understand the origin of stage terminology
> Explain how the type of show may change the level of production involved
> Understand the basic infrastructure and technology involved with the stage, scenery, and lighting
> Understand how the integration of production elements enhances the audience experience
> Understand the infrastructure and design principles for sets and props

It is cliché but true: The stage is where the magic happens. For every carefully placed dance step, there are several stagehands, stage managers, fabricators, electricians, engineers, designers, and supervisors preparing and transforming the stage into a show-specific setting. Given the various trades and departments that must collaborate throughout the process, it truly is a magical feat, whether you observe it from a seat in the audience or break it down into its constituent parts.

Understanding the possibilities and limitations of each production element is important when working toward your choreographic vision. This chapter will explore the details of stages, scenery, and lighting. We'll see examples of the differences between production types; learn the infrastructure and instruments used in each production component; explore the elements of stage, scene, and light design; and begin to consider how everything is integrated in the production. With an enhanced understanding, you'll be better equipped to communicate with the various team members.

Stages

The stage itself has many parts, each one playing a role. It is important to know these parts and understand how the stage works to improve communication and increase production value. A bird's-eye view, or ground plan, of the basic layout of a proscenium stage is shown in figure 7.1. Different areas of the stage are defined by their relationship to **center stage**. Anything closer to the audience is considered **downstage**, and further away from the audience is considered **upstage**. To remember these positions, memorize this simple diagram of the stage floor. "Up" will always be at the top of the picture and "down" at the bottom, nearest the proscenium.

Stage left is always the side of the stage that would be to the left of someone onstage facing the audience and **stage right** is the side of the stage that would be to their right. Stage left and stage right are easy for the dancer who works **onstage** and primarily faces the audience. For anyone working in the audience chamber, also called the **house**, and communicating to the dancers or crew onstage, *stage left* and *stage right* are the opposite of their typical orientations. So, the choreographer standing in the house may point with their right hand toward that direction, but they are indicating that the dancer, stagehand, light, prop, and so on move to their left as perceived from the stage facing the house! When communicating with most of the design and technical staff, understanding these directions is critical; otherwise, any element may be located, installed, pointed, or created in the wrong direction.

When a dancer steps **offstage** to the right or left of the stage, they enter the space called the **wings**. This is the open area to either side of the stage, where the scenery and props are set, the crew stand by, and the dancers typically enter and exit the dancing space. Some venues will have **legs** (see figure 7.2), which are drapes that create the alleys for travel on and off stage and help mask the wings and backstage space. A quick-change booth or corral might be built for the sake of privacy in the wings because there is too little time for the dancer to travel all the way to the dressing room and back before their next entrance in a different costume.

In a dance production, it is quite common to have lighting **booms** (also called *trees*) just offstage in the wings. Dancers must always be aware of

Stage, Scenery, Props, and Lighting 95

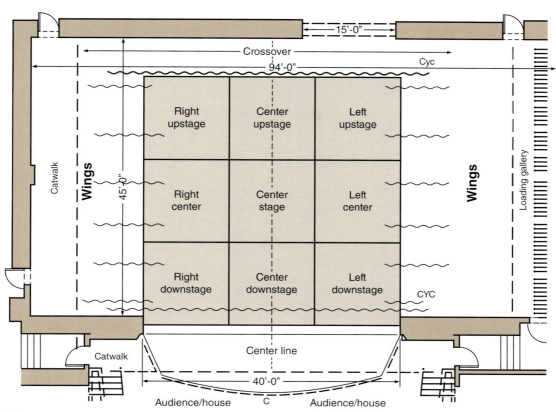

Figure 7.1 Basic stage directions in a proscenium theatre.

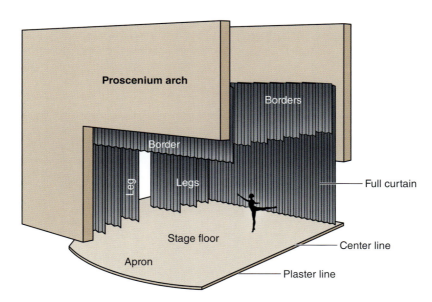

Figure 7.2 Isometric view of a stage cutaway with the parts labeled.

those lighting positions—they can cast unwanted shadows onstage if they move in front of them. Dancers can be easily burned by the hot lighting instrument if the bump it or can knock the light out of focus. Some stages will have a **scrim** along the back. This loosely woven gauze can appear transparent or solid depending on how it is lit. If there is a fly system above the stage, it is used for hanging scenery, production equipment, and drapery that further define the stage.

Many smaller venues, and some sizable ones, may not have much or any wing space. Sometimes the wings are disproportionate in size, like a large stage left wing but no significant stage right wing. This allocation of space frequently determines the logistics of how everything from the cast to the set enters and exits the stage. When space is at a premium, options can be few, and implementations can become quite creative. Touring shows, especially, need to scout every performance venue to know if the production fits into the space, asking questions like these: What are the dimensions of the stage itself? How big are the wings? How far is it to the dressing rooms?

RAKED STAGES

Raked stages are angled down from back to front and have been in use since at least the Renaissance and likely before that. This wedge profile led to the stage direction terminology of being upstage at the rear, or the higher area, and being downstage at the front or the lower area, nearest the proscenium. The rake provided a better viewing angle for an audience on a flat plane. This is a contrast to tiered audience seating most used today. Consider stadium seating as an example of tiered seating, such as that in ancient Greek and Roman amphitheaters, including the Colosseum, where the audience area is tiered and the performance space is flat.

The width and height of the portal between the stage and the audience chamber is a significant detail. This vertical plane is called the *proscenium opening*, and the physical walls that create that opening are the *proscenium arch* (left, right, and above this opening). The fourth (bottom) side of this opening is an imaginary line on the ground that connects the bottoms of the legs of this arch. This is called the **plaster line**. In a proscenium theatre, there may be more performance space beyond the proscenium—or the "pro" as the techies call it—approaching the front row of the audience. This area is called the **apron**. Dancing on the apron can indicate focus or emphasis or create intimacy with the audience.

During a production, the plaster line is typically segmented with **spike tape** (1/2-inch-wide fabric tape) markings to indicate positions on the dance floor or **deck** (see figure 7.3). At the center is a long mark denoting the **center line**. Halfway between the center line and the onstage edge of the proscenium arch is another tape line that represents the quarter mark. This means a dancer's relative position to the proscenium is one quarter of the way from the left or right edge of the stage. The final end mark is the outside mark closest to both wings.

Any number of bisecting marks may be taped down, usually in a variety of easily identifiable colors, to indicate more specific locations on the stage. In addition to the markings across the plaster line, the marks are typically repeated (reversed and repeated) all the way upstage, so dancers know where they are if they travel upstage or work facing

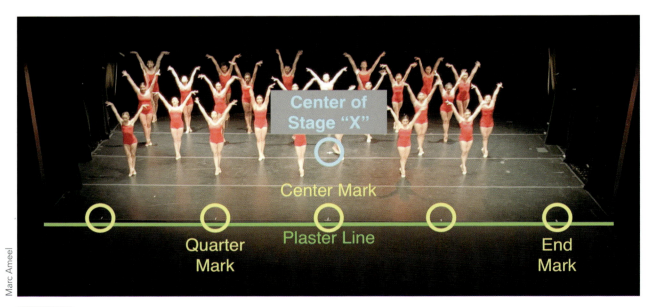

Figure 7.3 Spike tape is used to indicate the plaster line, the center line, the quarter mark, the end mark, and other positions onstage.

upstage. Usually, an *X* is taped to indicate the center of the stage—halfway up and down, and halfway left and right. Once scenery and props are added to the production, more spike tape may be applied to identify where these elements live while onstage. Stage crew and dancers may refer to these as they set for the upcoming piece or scene. Various pieces and scenes are usually represented by different colors of spike tape to prevent confusion in a busy environment.

Flooring

While dancers rehearse in dance studios, this space is rarely used as a performance venue. It is common that the flooring provided for the performance is not the same as the flooring in the rehearsal space. There are distinct advantages to rehearsing in an actual dance studio, such as the construction of the floor itself. This special type of flooring is called a *sprung floor* because it is engineered to give, like a spring, just enough to help reduce the risk of injury and give the dancer's body some relief. While there are several manufacturers and design styles for the floor, for all of them, the floor surface deflects when put under stress: It flexes when someone dances on it.

Try it. Just jump on a sprung floor, then jump on a non-sprung floor or surface, and the difference will be immediately apparent. You won't sink in, and it's not a trampoline or bounce house, but the surface bends (or deflects) just enough to help protect the joints of the dancer. There are patented designs for the floors, though most rely on layering different materials, integrating negative or open space in the layering of the floor, or a combination of these things. Foam and rubber can act like dampers or shock absorbers. A floor that is "woven" like a lattice uses the inherent flexibility of the wood along with the design and open space between solid elements to provide a flexible surface. Figure 7.4 shows one way a sprung floor might be constructed.

In addition to the sprung floor construction, dance floors are typically finished in either a wood surface for tapping (because it makes noise) or a vinyl **Marley** surface for just about everything else. This vinyl material is either rolled out on top of an existing floor or may be the top layer of a permanent floor, as in a dance studio. The amount of friction this type of surface provides is "sticky" enough to prevent dancers from unwanted slips and falls, while being just slick enough to allow dancers to slide or spin as desired. Bare feet will "stick" to Marley more than socks or low-friction shoes do. And while it can be purchased in any color, it is typically seen in matte black to minimize the reflection of very bright stage lighting.

When performing in unconventional settings, discuss with the production team whether Marley floors will be brought into the space for the dancers to perform on. This is where the creative brief comes into play. If the dance is to be filmed outside at the beach, then Marley floors will probably not be used and wouldn't work on sand anyway. If a dance is supposed to have a natural look, the choreographer may want the dancers performing on the parking garage cement, the grassy field, or an old bridge or fountain. You name it—dancers have performed there. Special accommodations may need to be

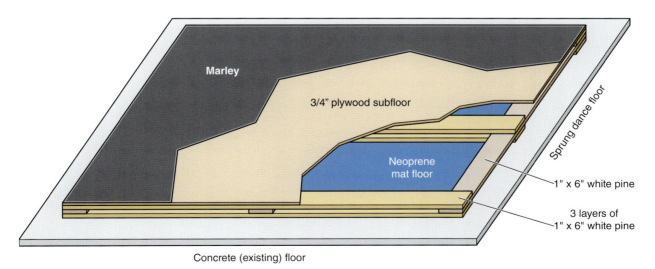

Figure 7.4 Cutaway diagram of a sprung floor.

made to protect the dancers in unconventional environments, including the shoes they wear, cleaning the location, or adjusting choreography.

Scenery and Props

Most dance companies do not have their own scenery construction shop or the staff to operate such a thing. Fortunately, dance does not depend on a well-designed set to establish the context for a performance. Certainly, *The Nutcracker* should incorporate that Christmas tree and a semblance of what the Kingdom of Sweets looks like, but this is the exception. A flash mob just shows up at the mall food court, unannounced, with no set. A dance competition is staged on an open floor with padding for safety, but there's no scenery placed on the stage. And most concerts rely on other technical elements to complement the choreography and any underlying narrative.

With all this being said, sometimes sets and props are part of a production, and you will need to know the basics for them. In this section, we'll explore the infrastructure for sets and props as well as essential design principles.

Infrastructure

When sets and props are part of the production, the scene shop, physical resources and materials, and human capital constitute the basic infrastructure to create the items required.

Construction Site

The **scene shop** is a carpentry or welding fabricating locale, such as the one shown in figure 7.5. Universities and larger companies with structural assets typically have their own shops or share one with another department or other production companies. Some dance companies hire freelance scenic and prop shops that provide their services for a fee plus the cost of materials. These types of independent scene shops may also provide design services for an additional cost; however, if you provide your own plans, they will build to the specs you provide.

Makers

Once the design is approved and the plans arrive at the shop, the dirty work begins. Set construction is literally a dirty job. Whether the set is built of wood, metal, or plastics, hands-on builders must use an array of tools and materials to execute the plans as drawn. These professional builders have skills across several more specific disciplines such as framing, finish carpentry, welding, CNC (computer numerical control) operation, laser cutting, foam work, plastic work, fiberglass work, vacuum forming, 3D printing, pneumatics, hydraulics, mechanics, electronics, automation, rigging, painting, set dressing, and general crafts.

If the designer can draw it, someone can build it—for a price. As with most labor-intensive jobs, paying the people to do the work constitutes at least half of the overall cost. Be prepared to sign more paychecks than materials purchases.

SIDEBAR CONVERSATIONS: FESTIVAL TECH

Effective communication leads to beneficial collaboration! A festival tech conversation might go something like this:

Venue Stage Manager: Hi. Do you have your tech packet, signed release forms, proof of insurance, final payment in the form of a cashier's check, and photo ID?

Choreographer (who is also Producer, Director, and Dancer): Um, yes, of course. It's right here. *(Fumbles nervously through festival-provided tote bag and drops yoga mat and water bottle.)*

Venue Stage Manager: While you look for that, please remember that you have 15 minutes to space and 30 minutes to tech. We charge $250 per hour or portion thereof if you run over. If you have any questions, refer to your festival tech packet.

Choreographer: Here is the paperwork.

Venue Stage Manager: You have 44 minutes. Merde. *(Takes paperwork. Notices something across the stage, and walks away hurriedly, screaming.)* Hey! Are you certified to be in that lift?

Moral of the story: A festival environment can bring each party's priorities to the surface very quickly. Always be prepared and professional.

Figure 7.5 Scene shop at the SUNY Potsdam, Department of Theatre and Dance.

Materials

Materials aren't free. In fact, at the time this book was written, the costs of materials such as lumber and steel have increased several times over. This issue alone has caused production companies to reconsider the scale of physical settings and use more affordable technologies and resources such as lighting, sound, video, and other media. It is common to see smaller representative scenic elements incorporated into a digital scenic design. This design is based on using digital technologies in lieu of a tangible physical set made of wood and metal. A digital backdrop or floor created with projection or LED panels might create a vivid environment for a dance. Colored, textured, and moving lighting can represent the setting for a dance. Or perhaps it is the audio that establishes the locale for a production—for example, whale sounds can conjure an ocean setting. In dance, this can be interpreted as advantageous, leaving more room onstage for the talent and resulting in more dynamic and versatile scenery.

Design

It takes time to develop a scenic design, and it is helpful when a choreographer can work from the creative brief and explicitly discuss the intention of their dance with the scenic designer. What is the statement of the piece, and why this statement? What is the story we are about to tell? Does it examine, evaluate, or inspire humanity? Is the dance based in reality or fantasy; is it more about environment or character? Is the design meant to enhance the ambiance or mood or to have a direct or more literal impact on the performance and audience? The creative brief helps to answer these questions and keep everyone focused on the same goals. As a choreographer, you want the scene design to enhance or frame your vision, to create the world in which the performance lives and breathes in harmony with all the production elements, not be a distraction to the intention of the piece. Additional information such as a color palette, indicating whether it is literal or abstract, and indicating if it's held indoors or outdoors can help the designer support the overall aesthetic.

To help expedite the conversation, a choreographer might introduce an abstract metaphor in the creative brief; this is an abstract visual representation of the thesis allowing for a center point of reference. Hearing words about the piece helps, but images, textures, and colors will give so much more context, information, and understanding. Because the scenic designer is listening and seeing at the same time, the creative brief starts the creative juices flowing. As the designer hears the vision and sees the abstract metaphor, they begin to interrupt and respond to the visual imagery. In this way, the designer becomes a part of the collaboration. Have a direct conversation at the first meeting with the designer so no one misinterprets the vision for the dance piece. The scenic designer will use the movement descriptions of the choreographer and other descriptive clues to develop their own abstract metaphor to express what they have understood in the meeting.

Ideally, in a healthy timeline, at the next meeting the scenic designer and choreographer come together to develop the concept further. Building will take time, so the sooner decisions can be made, the better for everyone involved. Timelines that honor the process of each craft are realistic and help promote timely completion of the project. The choreographer also needs to understand whatever is being built will cost money and needs to be safe. Sometimes what we think would be perfect is not monetarily or structurally feasible.

Occasionally a prop designer may be used, especially in larger productions. This may also be you if you are wearing multiple hats. The props need to be designed with the scenery and potentially the costumes. Dance productions may not have large set pieces or props, but scenery involves the whole production environment, not just the pieces created. If a choreographer specifies a weight-bearing prop for a dance, it needs to be safe for not only the performer but also the stage floor. Just taking four dining room chairs from your home may not be the best idea if they haven't been checked for safety. The use of props will also be a discussion with the stage manager regarding how these are set up and cleared. If you're working with a skeleton crew of people, more complicated props can make the transitions more complicated as well.

Integration

Dancing is challenging enough on its own. Add lighting to blind the dancer, sound to deafen them, and long nights of rehearsals to wear them out, and you can see why the last thing they need is to have a prop given to them only days or hours before opening night to make things even more difficult. Therefore, rehearsal props, like rehearsal costumes, are a part of the process and should be implemented as early as possible in the schedule, giving the dancers plenty of practice. A good rehearsal prop should be as close to the final product as possible in weight, size, and basic shape. Often, rehearsal props are just a different version of the final product, especially for hand props. It's easy to find a rehearsal umbrella or coffee mug—these items won't change much in form and function when the "real" one arrives. Larger props, like a piece of furniture, may be more difficult to procure for rehearsal, so the dancer uses a substitute prop, such as three chairs lined up next to each other to represent a sofa. Special consideration

---

SIDEBAR CONVERSATIONS: VISION

Effective communication leads to beneficial collaboration! Develop your vision statement early. Respect the people and the process by expressing your needs clearly. Even if there are unknowns at the time of the concept meeting, don't do this:

Choreographer: It's like the dancers are swimming through a marshmallow.

Scenic Designer, Artistic Director, and Production Manager: Mm-hmm.

Choreographer: And they kind of press through this invisible barrier. I don't know. Maybe not entirely invisible. Maybe there's some cool lighting or something with projections of the Milky Way, but there definitely needs to be resistance.

Scenic Designer, Artistic Director, and Production Manager: Mm-hmm.

Choreographer: And then when the strings chorus peaks in the 33rd minute, everyone drops to the floor, like the gravity just got turned on after they were floating in space!

Scenic Designer: Brilliant. Your interpretation is visionary. Just to clarify, is the marshmallow a physical construct or a metaphor?

[pause]

Choreographer: I'm not sure yet, but I don't need any scenery. Just the projections, the marshmallow, and whatever hand props we discover in rehearsal.

Scenic Designer, Artistic Director, and Production Manager: Mm-hmm.

Moral of the story: The production team's responsibility is to implement the choreographer's vision the best they can, regardless of how *unique* it may be. Choreographers, please respect the time and efforts of your team.

will need to be taken in these situations. Specialty props that are being built from scratch or that are not swappable with a one-for-one substitute (like an umbrella) will require more time onstage for the dancers to familiarize themselves. Take this into consideration when planning the tech schedule.

The set and props will arrive at the performance venue before the dancers do, or they should. This is a practical matter for larger-scale productions because it takes time to load everything into the theatre. For touring shows or smaller-scale productions that still incorporate any proper scenery, the set may arrive at the venue when the dancers do, but they should still be installed before a spacing rehearsal so the cast can get their bearings. Props should also be there, labeled and ready for use. Stage managers typically take responsibility for this, and etiquette dictates that only the person who uses the prop onstage may touch it at any time (other than the stage management and crew, of course).

Before the first rehearsal on any stage—whether there are scenic elements or not but especially if there are—the technical director should give the cast a safety walkthrough to identify all the intricacies of the space, where potential hazards exist, and how to best navigate the performance space in the safest manner possible. They will point out where the prop tables are and indicate which elements enter from which side of the stage or fly in from above. They will remind the dancers not to touch the lights because they may be dangerously hot, and they could also knock them out of focus. The technical director will denote the boundaries of the performance space for sight lines, and safety boundaries, like where the spike marks are to keep dancers from falling into the orchestra pit.

Even in the smallest venues or a site-specific location, it is critical to walk the space with a sense of heightened awareness upon arrival for the safety and well-being of everyone involved in the production. Make sure to scout that mall food court before the next flash mob!

Lighting

While the performance space is critical, it can always be enhanced with good lighting. Once upon a time, a stage light was nothing more than a candle in front of a concave reflector. Today, dance productions can incorporate thousands, possibly millions of LEDs (light-emitting diodes—tiny spots of light), moving and scrolling, flashing, twisting, and turning to create any environment imaginable, while the dancer wears a costume made of EL wire conforming to or sculpting the body's silhouette. With lighting, it seems the only limits are bound by budget. Selecting a lighting system for a dance production has many variables. Understanding lighting systems and technology with some degree of competence will enable you to discuss the possibilities with your team more intelligently and inspire feasible artistic concepts that the entire company will rally around.

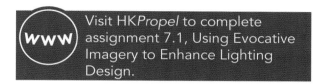

Visit HK*Propel* to complete assignment 7.1, Using Evocative Imagery to Enhance Lighting Design.

A LAMP BY ANY OTHER NAME

In the world of theatre, a light bulb is a lamp. Say it aloud: A light bulb is a *lamp*. Vocabulary competence is critical to production development. It will not only make conversations more effective but also command respect from your collaborators.

In this chapter, the lighting instruments described are based on traditional equipment, where the light source is a lamp (a light bulb). The description and application of accessories with various instruments may be different for LED source instruments, because these iterations may have color; pan, tilt, and zoom (ptz); focus; shutter; and gobo capabilities built in, reducing or eliminating the need for external accessories.

Infrastructure

The infrastructure for a lighting system can quickly become very complex and consist of so many different elements that it is challenging to understand its intricacies, let alone stay current with the new instruments and appliances that come to market in any given season. Although lights have been used onstage for a long time, their basic applications remain the same today. We use brighter lighting sources and smarter controls that allow designers and technicians to manipulate light in new ways.

Most lighting systems for everything from photography to stage performances to film production are based on the three-point lighting technique, requiring a key light, fill light, and backlight (see figure 7.6). Designers will manipulate instruments in these three positions to create the intensity, color, dimension, depth, and mood. The **key light** establishes the basic look and is generally placed somewhere in front of the subject. The **fill light** complements the key light by filling in the shadows created by the key light. The key and fill lights are often considered together, placed in front of and above the subject and offset about 45 degrees from center. The **backlight** is placed above and behind the subject to counter the flattening effect strong front lighting has on a three-dimensional subject. By casting a glow around the subject, the backlight adds depth to the visual aesthetic, essentially separating the subject from the background. If you can introduce the basic concept of how you would like lighting applied to your artistic vision, the designer can fine-tune that concept by implementing the best instruments, technology, and controls to achieve your result. Designers respond well to vivid adjectives that capture the mood, color, and setting of a dance piece.

Many lighting designs for dance incorporate a fourth significant lighting position: a **sidelight**. Lights placed directly on one or both sides of the stage and focused directly on the side (or both sides) of the subject can enhance a dancer's silhouette, emphasizing their body's lines. This concept is extremely effective for displaying a choreographer's ability to sculpt the human body into a compelling relationship to its context.

All other lighting can be grouped into a fifth category or position. This includes lighting the background, including the scenery and drapery (like a **cyclorama**). Practical and decorative lighting would also be considered in this category. These lighting positions create the environment for the dance subject and add nuance for a unique artistic expression.

The lighting instruments that are used in this three-, four-, or five-point system can also be categorized. The two most common instruments for a three- or four-point lighting system are wash and profile lights. *Wash lights* are typically used as back or downlight from directly overhead, and they cast a wide area of light in an area of the performance space, providing depth and dimension. *Profile instruments* typically supply the key, fill, and sidelight. Profile instruments output a narrower beam of light than wash lights do and are typically selected with a greater intensity (brightness) to cut through wash light when they are used together. Profile instruments may also have shutters, focus and zoom adjustments, or the capacity to hold a *gobo* or template for casting unique light shapes. Other common types of lighting instruments include **cyc lights**, which light the cyclorama drape, and **follow spots**, which are the large, easily identifiable, manually operated lights used to highlight the focus of a performance.

LED TECHNOLOGY

LED technology has made considerable progress in the world of lighting. Most lighting instruments today have an LED option. LED is preferred over traditional lamps for its ability to apply color-changing technology, its cooler operating temperatures, the lower cost and lower consumption of energy, and the subsequent ability to have more lighting instruments in a facility with the same output of power. Some designers still prefer traditional lamps because they claim the color temperature and accuracy of LED is not equivalent to their predecessors, though that gap is closing quickly and many designers are adopting the new technology.

Wash Instruments

The lighting designer uses wash lights to illuminate the space in various ways. While it will not be the choreographer's job to set these systems up, it is important to understand the purpose and use of each instrument. Types of instruments include PAR, Fresnel, strip, and panel.

When you just want a ton of uncontrolled bright light, choose a **PAR**, which stands for **parabolic aluminized reflector** (see figure 7.7). It is the original wash fixture, with the simplest construction. This

Figure 7.6 Basic three-point lighting system.

Figure 7.7 A PAR instrument.

Figure 7.8 A Fresnel instrument.

instrument provides cost-effective, bright lighting in any space. These lights are white on the visible spectrum and can be colored by inserting a colored sheet of plastic called *gel* in a frame at the end of the barrel.

The **Fresnel** light (see figure 7.8) is a bit more refined than the PAR, though it is similar. A specific glass lens is placed over the end of the instrument's barrel, focusing the light to provide a crisper, more controlled wash of light and consequently sharper shadows as well. The lens is the key here. With a tiered system of concentric circles of glass and thin grooves etched into the glass, a Fresnel lens focuses all the light in the same direction. To control the light from this fixture even further, the following accessories are often used with the Fresnel:

> A gel frame holds the gel in front of the light beam where it exits the instrument. The gel can be colored or textured to alter the appearance of the light.

> A *barn door* can be attached at the front of the instrument (just in front of the gel frame). This apparatus is essentially an optional set of four hinged shutters that offer a bit of control (shaping) to the broad wash light and can reduce "lens flare" (when you see the bright element inside the instrument, which can be distracting and disorienting).

> The *top hat* is a type of snoot, or an attachment applied specifically for controlling the beam spread of wash light and reducing lens flare. It is called a top hat because of its familiar appearance.

Another type of light is a conventional strip light. It houses a very bright lamp and reflects the light out of a rectangular housing at a relatively narrow beam angle. These instruments come in a variety of lengths (as the name *strip* suggests). They are often used for special effects, sometimes pointed at the audience, used at lower intensity to create a visually interesting backdrop, used to light paths, used to provide indirect lighting, or used to light the cyclorama drape (see figure 7.9). When the use of a cyclorama drape increased upstage, behind all the action, a specific lighting technology was created to light it: a strip light with a beam angle just wide enough to light the cyclorama and nothing else.

A **panel light** relies on LED technology arranged on a flat surface, emitting a less-controlled beam of light. It offers desirable color mixing for enhancing drapery, truss, pillars, scraping walls, indirect sources, special effects, and other less-traditional

Figure 7.9 Cyc lighting.

applications or where the intensity is not required to be too high. The output of these fixtures tends to be washed away by other more powerful lighting.

As patrons enter the space, **houselights** are used to light the audience chamber and establish a mood. This lighting helps hide the offstage area from the audience and allows the performers and crew to go about their backstage business without distracting from what is occurring onstage. **Running lights** or *working lights*, are usually a low-intensity blue light and help the cast and crew move around backstage safely. Both houselights and running lights must be considered in lighting design and would fall into a grouping of their own in terms of application, though they would be considered wash lights. House light instruments are often some version of a PAR or strip light, and running light instruments are often some version of a PAR, scoop, strip, or string light. A common example of a scoop is a generic cone-shaped work light readily available at any hardware or home supply store. String lights are the same as the ones hanging in your dorm room!

Profile Instruments

The **ellipsoidal reflector spotlight (ERS)** is the workhorse instrument of the staged entertainment

Figure 7.10 An ERS lighting instrument.

industry (see figure 7.10). Leko is an older brand name and Source 4 is the industry standard product line from the company ETC. It is versatile and complex, offering many applications, including being the instrument of choice for the defining feature of lighting for dance: sidelight! The ERS puts out a narrower beam of light than its wash light counterparts do. Depending on the construction of its lenses, an ERS can have a beam angle from 5 degrees up to 70 degrees. Any compatible ERS body can house a barrel with any of the various degrees of lenses, making this a useful instrument at any distance or height from the stage. Some barrels even have the option to zoom this angle, creating a narrower or wider beam of light. The barrel can be adjusted to provide a soft or sharp focus of light depending on the application a designer's choice.

The body of the ERS also includes unique features such as shutters to control and shape the beam of light before it exits the barrel—for example, the beam can be made square. There is also a slot for other accessories such as a gobo or template, which is inserted in the path of the beam of light, allowing the projection of a lighted pattern onto a surface. An *iris* is an adjustable gate that increases or shrinks the cone of the light beam, essentially making it narrower or wider. Irises can be manual or automated.

A follow spot is a manually operated profile instrument that rests on its own mount and stand and often requires supplemental power sources because of the extreme lamp intensities that it can offer. It is typically placed away from the stage and used to track one or two dancers in an otherwise darker scene. Multiple follow spots are typically used when more than one or two dancers are the focus of a moment, or there are multiple subjects scattered across the playing space. Follow spots have a built-in iris to adjust the size of the beam, a dowser to completely block the light when not in use (as opposed to turning the instrument on and off, which can be detrimental to the lamp inside; once turned on, they typically remain on throughout an entire performance), and a boomerang or set of gels to provide color options. These instruments get extremely hot and require a skilled technician to operate them.

Design

Lighting design begins with the venue and its resources. Many established theatres and performance venues, big and small, indoor and outdoor, have some existing lighting capability. This existing lighting system is commonly called the **rep plot (repertory plot)** and is typically designed to light the performance space to accommodate anything the company may mount from its own repertoire or to support various pieces in any given repertory (or presentation of works by multiple choreographers). If the venue is outfitted with a rep plot, and there is

> ### INTELLIGENT LIGHTING
>
> Designers have become more innovative with the development of automated or moving fixtures, sometimes called *intelligent lighting*. These lighting instruments can pan, tilt, and zoom to place the beam anywhere onstage. Some have built-in shutters and gobos like a profile instrument. Most also have color-changing technology. There are both wash and profile "movers" on the market. One distinct advantage of the moving light is that an electrician does not need to climb a ladder to focus it, adjust the shutters, or change the color—this is all done by a programmer or designer at the control console. A second distinct advantage of moving lights is the ability to repurpose one instrument in various positions and applications throughout the duration of a production. For instance, an automated instrument may be used for open, white downlight over the stage in one cue and for a multicolored, rotating gobo over the house in the next. These lights are commonly used in the commercial industry to add another layer of visual spectacle to a performance.

no mission-critical need for "specials," the design conversation may be very short and sweet:

> **Artistic Director:** *We have a repertory show with 14 student choreographers who need general wash lighting, a couple of shifts from cools to warms, or maybe an emphasis from stage left or right at moments, but nothing very specific. We want this to be about seeing the body lines, not necessarily the spectacle of lighting.*
>
> **Venue Technical Director:** *Copy that. We have a decent rep plot that can do washes, areas, high sides with texture, and sides for that contour you want.*
>
> **Production Manager:** *Does the venue provide a board operator with that?*
>
> **Venue Technical Director:** *The board op is included in your fee.*

The rep plot is a great place to begin the conversation about lighting design. Be inspired by what is available to you and use your creativity to inform your decisions. Not every transaction will be this simple, nor will every venue have fully adequate lighting for every production, so the discussion may be a bit more involved.

Director: *What is the lighting like in your venue?*

Venue Technical Director: *We have a lot of positions for lighting, but we don't keep a rep in place, so you will need to bring your own lighting package based on the design. I'll email you the venue specs and a plot of our grid.*

Lighting Designer: *Thanks. That will help a lot. What about power?*

Venue Technical Director: *Good question. We have 48 circuits, but if you need more than that, you're going to need a generator.*

Production Manager: *Do you have any references for a local rental company or an idea what that costs?*

Venue Technical Director: *I can have our master electrician get that for you.*

Choreographer: *Is it going to be possible to get the rapid color change I need for my piece?*

Production Manager: *How many stagehands would we need for that change between acts one and two?*

Lighting Designer: *We might not need any stagehands for gel swaps if I rent an LED rig. It might be a wash in the budget, but it would offer the quickest color change and help with the crowding on stage right.*

Director: *That sounds like a great solution!*

Establish a good foundation for design conversations by asking questions about the existing resources and consider the input of others. Know your options!

Most small-budget production meetings might sound more like this:

Venue Technical Director: *Our venue has a simple stage wash, and you can pretty much refocus anything you want. We just charge a reset fee in your contract. We have a few gels in the back, but if you need more color or something we don't have, then you'll need to bring that. We do have one ladder, which you can use if you provide a certificate of insurance and proof of worker's comp. The console is an old preset board, but it does the job. The sightlines from the booth are really good though.*

Lighting Designer: *Do you have any booms or anything backstage we could use to set up some side lighting?*

Venue Technical Director: *Maybe. I'll have to check. We just threw out a bunch of stuff last week.*

Choreographer: *Is it possible to light the aisle so the dancers can enter from behind the audience?*

Venue Technical Director: *You could probably turn around a Leko or two on that pipe over there. As far as the dancers' entrances, we will need to walk through that for fire safety.*

Venue Manager: *We are so happy to have you here.*

Production is a business, full of contractual and legal obligations. It's important to balance ambition and practicality.

Integration

The design and operation of the lights for the show go beyond the light plot. It is a combination of the available instruments with the other design elements, what the desired look is, and the actual choreography of the lighting that bring the final production together.

Understanding the technology available in your space allows you to work with the lighting designer to create the mood and textures of the dance. As the choreographer, you may want your piece to be bright and cheery or moody and intense. You may also be asking to define the space such as a strong diagonal or creating specific areas such as spotlights or quadrants in the space. A choreographer has integrated all these ideas into the staging of the dance, and it is the collaboration with the lighting designer that now helps accentuate these areas.

Lighting also significantly affects the appearance of the scenery and the costumes. Understanding color temperature (warmth and coolness), color mixing and theories, and value (lightness and darkness) can make or break an aesthetic and are good reasons to hire professional designers who understand how light will interact with the other elements onstage. Have you ever laid out your

TERMS USED TO DESCRIBE LIGHT DESIGN OPTIONS

accent lighting—Light put on a particular item or area onstage to highlight it or for aesthetic reasons.

backlight—Light coming from upstage, behind scenery or performers, to sculpt and separate them from the background. Useful in dance silhouette.

breakup—Adds texture and pattern to lights with the use of gobos.

color temperature—Commonly referred to as *cool* or *warm*. This is important for establishing a mood or indicating the passage of time in a piece.

crosslight—Light coming from the sides of the stage toward the center or across the stage. This is used a lot in dance lighting because it lights the body without casting shadows upstage. It also helps sculpt the body more than front lighting does.

projections—These can be slides, videos, film, lighting effects, and so on that can be rear-projected or front-projected.

sidelight—Used regularly in dance to help accentuate and sculpt the performers without lighting the stage floor.

special—A specific lighting instrument that is used for an important moment and is not part of the general lighting cover.

spot—Specific lighting that highlights a specific subject in a relatively controlled manner, often requiring a specific instrument capable of shuttering or irising of the beam.

wash—General lighting that covers a relatively wide surface area, and is less "controlled" than spot light. A wash is useful for illuminating an entire stage. Ceiling lights in a classroom could be considered a wash because they "flood" the space with even light.

clothes for the day, thinking you had a pair of black socks to match your black pants, and with closer inspection, you discover the socks are navy blue? The lighting in the room could make or break your faux pas. You might be able to get away with this mismatch, but why risk it?

There are two basic sets of primary colors, and there are two basic theories of color mixing: subtractive and additive. The primary colors of *pigment* are red, yellow, and blue; these colors cannot be made from any other colors, and all other colors are created by combining them. When they combine, they subtract wavelengths of light from being reflected for you to see, and that is called *subtractive* color mixing. Here are examples of this type of mixing:

> › Red + Yellow = Orange
> › Red + Blue = Purple
> › Yellow + Blue = Green
> › Red + Yellow + Blue = Black

All other colors are variants of these combinations.

The primary colors of *light* are red, green, and blue; when all three mix together, you get *white* light, because they combine wavelengths to be reflected. This is *additive* color mixing. Here are examples of this type of mixing:

> › Red + Green = Yellow
> › Red + Blue = Magenta
> › Green + Blue = Cyan
> › Red + Green + Blue = White

Wrap your head around this, or hire a professional lighting designer who knows how to light your set and costumes properly, so the scenic painter and costumer's work isn't all in vain.

There's even more to understand about color and light, but that could fill another textbook entirely.

Once the lighting design for texture and mood have been established, the next part of collaborating will be the cueing phase. *Cues* are a verbal or gestured signal that prompts an action in a performance. Cues are defined by the lighting designer, who shares them with the stage manager, who will transfer them into a prompt book as a script for directing the crew to execute those cues on command. A cue list may also be programmed into a computer or lighting console, and commanded to execute in part or entirely automatically. The timing of cues creates the choreography of the lights with the dancers. These effects can be used to accentuate the story or action onstage. Effects such as a **fade in** create a gradual addition of light onstage and a **fade out** diminishes the light onstage. Either of these can be fast, slow, or somewhere in between to create different moods or dramatic effects. **Crossfade** is cued during a dance to bring up new light while taking the current one down. A crossfade works with choreography to mark a transition in focus or mood of a dance. It is also a way to shift the audience's attention to another part of the dance. One of the hardest parts of choreography is finding an ending for the dance. Lighting can play a big part in this final moment the audience sees. Lights can fade out slowly as a dancer exits the stage or holds a final emotional moment, or there can be a **blackout**, which is a quick cue to take out all stage lighting at once.

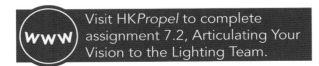

Visit HK*Propel* to complete assignment 7.2, Articulating Your Vision to the Lighting Team.

Summary

There are many types of dance production, and each lends itself to countless production variables. Selecting a performance space (or familiarizing yourself with the given space, as in a festival setting) establishes the foundation for which stage, scenery, and lighting designs are developed. Venues can range from traditional proscenium stages to outdoor spaces and anything in between. While the challenges and decisions associated with this technical puzzle are plenty, you will be at your creative best when collaborating with other like-minded artists. Having a firm foundation in understanding stages, scenery, props, and lighting will give you confidence and promote constructive communication throughout the production process. We will explore each of these elements again in part III of this book to help you see how your choices will look onstage. Beyond the scenery and lighting, there is an essential need for sound, costumes, and makeup for your dancers. Media may also be part of the production, and the next chapter will explore these components.

TECH TALK

When working in a theatre setting, it is important to understand what the tech crew may be yelling out and why. If you hear "**going dark**," this is a warning for when all the lights on the stage and in the theatre are being turned off. This is an important phrase to yell out when having a rehearsal onstage so that the performers are not injured when it suddenly gets completely dark. Also hearing "**heads**" is a warning to those onstage that work is happening above their heads. While your focus may not be on the technical aspects going on around you, there are a million things happening at once, and safety is always important.

Sound, Digital Media, Costumes, and Makeup

8

Key Terms
amplifier
audio frequency
condenser microphone
costume designer
costume shop
dynamic microphone
handheld microphone
lavalier microphone
LED pixel mapping
projection mapping
soundboard (a.k.a. console or mixer)
source device
speakers
stage monitor speaker

109

LEARNING OBJECTIVES

After reading this chapter, you will be able to do the following:

❯ Comprehend the basic infrastructure and technology used with sound, media, costume, and makeup
❯ Understand how integrating production elements enhances the audience experience
❯ Describe the current technologies available in media to enhance a production
❯ Identify the elements of costume, hair, and makeup that support and integrate the aesthetic of the dancer

The elements of stage, lighting, and scenery allow choreography to come to life as a production, and the addition of sound, media, costumes, and makeup make a production magical. These elements allow a production to become *immersive*, not just presentational, and the collaborative team works hard to create this experience. A casual observer should just be awe-inspired by the dancing, imagery, and beauty of the performance and not necessarily consider all the goings-on behind the scenes. These elements enhance that feeling.

Sound

Now that the performance space is set and lit, it is time to introduce the audio. Sound is powerful. A whisper can soothe a crying baby. A siren can alert us to danger. And it is likely that a song inspired you to dance in the first place. Of course, not all dance needs sound, but in any given production, there may be spoken words, live instruments, or other sounds to enhance the performance, and that requires additional audio equipment. From a technical perspective, audio is likely the most complex system this book will address. Consumer audio devices, including the smartphone in your pocket, have made sound and music so easily accessible that it's easy to never consider how that sound is delivered. That study is a book of its own as well; however, here we will expose you to concepts that will help you communicate effectively with designers, technicians, and your production team. You will not need to know what a transducer is, but you will need to know the difference between a microphone and a speaker.

Infrastructure

Like lighting infrastructure, an audio rig can quickly become very complex. Sound designers and audio

APPROPRIATE VOLUME

First things first: Louder sound is not better sound. Every dance production needs a good audio engineer to mix the sound because increasing the volume is dangerous. A proper mix can provide the fidelity and distinctions of frequency and instrumentation the director desires.

engineers use many more pieces of equipment than the choreographer or director need to understand. The product of the audio design, rather than the means, is more important. Having said that, everyone can benefit from general knowledge regarding professional sound systems.

The following sections will address live audio primarily, because there are more facets to this design than that of a show based on playback. The recording process for a prerecorded show could be quite extensive, and that exceeds the scope of this text. The basic components of a modern sound system, in order from source to audience, include the following:

› Source devices such as microphones, pickups, or interfaces to capture sound
› A console or soundboard to direct and modulate signal flow
› Amplifiers to provide power
› Speakers to recreate the sound as it is heard by the audience

Source Devices

A **source device** creates or originates an audio signal. The most basic analog source device would be your larynx (voice box). If you want to amplify that vocal signal, you would need a microphone, which would be the source device in an electronic audio system for a live singing performance. Some of the most common source devices for prerecorded music have been the turntable (record player), the cart or magnetic tape, the compact disc (CD), and the digital hard drive.

If you play music stored on a smartphone, its hard drive is the source device. If you stream music through your smartphone or listen to the radio, you are also likely listening to audio sourced from a hard drive, which is transmitted through a series of technological hardware before reaching your ears. A simple example of this is playing the same track stored on your smartphone and streaming it to a pair of wireless headphones, likely via Bluetooth technology. The smartphone is a source device, which transmits a signal to the receiver, the headphones. Wi-Fi, AM/FM, and satellite radio all do basically the same thing—broadcast a wireless audio signal—using unique technologies. And even though we are constantly cutting cords and working toward a wireless world, audio production is most reliable and can provide the highest production value with wired equipment. Most sophisticated live music systems today, however, incorporate both wired and wireless technology. This hybrid approach is part of why audio is such a complex art. The key takeaway here is that every sound you hear has an origin, and that is a *source device*.

There is a joke among audio technicians that goes something like this: "If I ask the dance cast for the show tracks, I'll just get a pile of smartphones on my desk." Fortunately, sound design and audio engineering are more sophisticated than having a pile of smartphones. Although a smartphone is a source device, it is not suitable for any serious production use. Keep your smartphone nearby for warm-ups, and let the professionals share the preferred sources.

Live instruments such as a piano, an orchestra, or a barbershop quartet all need a way of being amplified so they can be heard over the footwork of the talented dancers. This is why microphones might be needed as a source device in your production. Leave selecting the correct microphone to the designer or crew. People who work in the sound department are some of the most notoriously particular personalities. You could ask for a certain model of microphone, but you will get the one they choose in the end anyway.

Still, understanding the different microphone types can help when you discuss your production needs. The Shure SM58 (see figure 8.1) is an industry-standard **handheld microphone**, a term that refers to any microphone you see people hold to speak or sing into. The Shure microphone is built like a tank, but you *should never drop a microphone*, despite the popular meme. A wireless handheld microphone is exactly that: a microphone people hold that uses wireless technology.

Figure 8.1 The Shure SM58 is a common handheld mic.

Zvonimir Luketina/EyeEm/Getty Images

AUDIO FILE TYPES

Most control rooms have a computer with playback software at the center of their hub for source selection and will include both audio and video playback. In the current era, uncompressed digital audio is preferred, and playing these files from a computer through an application directly into a console is most common.

The computer can play several types of audio files to produce the necessary sound for a production. It is important to check which form is needed because the available technology or systems may require different types of input. WAV (waveform audio file format) and AIFF (audio interchange file format) are uncompressed digital tracks. This means they are big files with the best sound quality. Compressed digital tracks that create smaller files with less desirable quality are called MP3 and AAC (advanced audio coding). MP3 files can be read by almost any device, but AAC files are better than the MP3. If available, a Blu-ray uncompressed format may create a good-quality track. If the entire show was on this disc and all the operator had to do was press Play at the right moment, it could be viable. However, as an integrated option in a more sophisticated and modern system, Blu-ray is probably a headache for technicians. Uncompressed compact discs present the same issue as a Blu-ray but have a lower-quality audio. Anything analog will have a lower-quality sound and can create issues with other production technology.

A microphone selected for live performance such as the SM58 is called a **dynamic microphone**. These microphones have a *dynamic construction technology*, which does not require external power to operate and is a simple design. These features contribute to the dynamic microphone's timeless reliability and durability.

In contrast, a **condenser microphone** requires external power because of their delicate and relatively sophisticated internal structure (compared to dynamic microphones). Consequently, the condenser microphone can also deliver more accurate signals than its dynamic counterparts do, thus being superior for recording and capturing instrument audio. A *PZM* or *boundary* microphone is a special type of condenser microphone that picks up on vibrations in its "pressure zone" (PZ) rather than picking up air pressure or sound waves. They are perfect for capturing the footsteps of a tap number or the percussion inside a piano.

A **lavalier microphone** (see figure 8.2) is often clipped onto a shirt or jacket and is connected to a wireless microphone body pack and transmits to a receiver. These are also called *lapel* or *body mics*. Put one on the director during their curtain speech if they don't want to use a handheld microphone or if they threaten to "drop the mic!"

In addition to microphones, audio sources may be captured by pickups, such as one used for musical instruments like an electric guitar, or by an interface that converts computer signals into recognizable digital audio for transmission throughout the system.

Soundboard (Console or Mixer)

Cables, connectors, wireless transmitters, and receivers feed the source signals into the **soundboard**, also called the *console* or *mixer*. A sample soundboard is shown in figure 8.3. Unless you are running sound yourself or independently financing this endeavor, you will probably never have the opportunity to select a console for a production, nor even need to know your options. As of the writing of this book, with a capable console, an engineer can mostly do everything they would want to do to the source signal regarding processing. This includes actions such as gain (input sensitivity), equalizing (adjusting the bass, midtones, and high frequencies), compressing, gating and ducking (techniques for preventing the speakers from blowing up), and effects like reverb, delay, phaser, and de-esser (helpful for eliminating sibilance in speech). The console is also likely equipped with phantom power, a low-voltage power circuit delivered to equipment such as a condenser microphone through the audio signal cable itself, eliminating the need for another external power source. With a capable console, the engineer can also create unique mixes (outputs) for the contents, quality, and volume of the sound delivered via individual speakers or groups of speakers. Examples include an onstage mix for the dancers, a backstage mix for the cast and crew as they follow along with the show, a lobby mix for front of house staff to follow along with the show and to provide audio for the audience, and the all-important public announcement (PA) system, which is the speaker system set up for the audience. All speaker systems and mixes referenced here that are not part of the PA system are generally referred to as a *monitor mix*, meaning they allow people other than the audience to observe and reference the production audio as a means of tracking along with the progress of the performance. The speaker hardware used for these mixes, in these various locations, are therefore also generally referred to as *monitors* or *monitor speakers*. This can also include headsets, earbuds, and any other physical type of speaker design.

Amplifiers and Speakers

The audio signal leaving the console must pass through an **amplifier**, which boosts or amplifies the relatively low-power audio signals from the console and converts them into electrical impulses that cause the inner workings of the **speakers** to

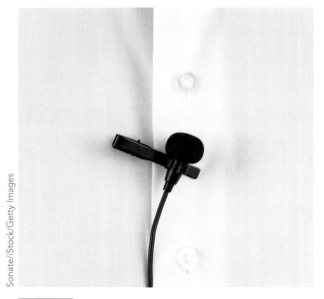

Figure 8.2 A lavalier microphone is usually worn on a shirt.

Figure 8.3 A soundboard with a show in the background.

vibrate and create sound. One type of amplifier can be a stand-alone piece of equipment with input from the console and output to a speaker or set of speakers, if the amplifier has multiple channels or paths for signal flow. In this case, external power must be supplied to the amplifier and is passed on to the connected speakers.

When speakers do not have their own amplifiers, they are called *passive speakers*. Consider the amplifier a power supply for the speakers. The amplifier receives electricity from an outlet, and the speaker receives power from the amplifier. Common examples in your life already may be a power "brick" used to charge your laptop or gaming console. You may also have a power cable that plugs directly into an outlet without a brick, which is similar to a second type of amplifier that is built into the speaker. When a speaker has its own amplifier built in, it's called an *active speaker*.

The amplifier generates a great amount of energy to "drive" the speakers, whether it is externally connected to a passive speaker or lives inside an active speaker. Amplifiers come in all types, with the number of channels (or number of speakers) it supports being the most prevalent. Modern amplifiers are also digital like the console and can process all kinds of information that only the installer understands.

Because active speakers have their own power supplies, they may have onboard features such as gain, EQ, or a "pad" button (features intended to minimize the risk of damaging the speakers). Passive speakers are typically lighter in weight because they do not contain a heavy amplifier and other controls. Passive speakers often have a feature called *signal pass-through*, which enables a technician to daisy-chain multiple speakers in sequence.

Form follows function in speaker design. The housing for the speaker might be wedge-shaped, allowing the speaker to be laid on its side and angled up toward the head or ears of the dancer onstage. In this orientation, the speaker would be used as a **stage monitor speaker**. A rectangular or cube design enables the speaker to be placed just about anywhere and multiple speakers can be easily stacked in a single location. These could be used as stage monitors or *public address (PA) speakers* facing the audience. Lastly, *speaker arrays* are typically custom made to face the audience and consist of several speakers at various angles that are usually hanging from above (though they could be stacked).

Audio frequency is a frequency that corresponds to audible sound waves. The human ear perceives frequencies between 20 Hz (lowest pitch) to 20 kHz (highest pitch). The speaker components determine the audio frequencies the audience hears. A tweeter is the smallest speaker, providing the highest-pitched sounds at the highest frequencies. Mids are relatively sized between tweeters and woofers, filling in the middle frequencies, including vocals and the widest frequency range. Woofers are larger speakers, providing the bass range of low-frequency sounds. The largest speakers are subwoofers, providing the deepest bass at the lowest frequencies

Sound Design

The first consideration of sound design should be the venue. If your production is going to take place in a venue that already has an audio infrastructure and the dance does not require anything more than playback and a microphone or two, your design conversation will be very simple, perhaps something like this:

> **Choreographer:** *I'd like to have these 14 tracks played during the 14 dance numbers in our show. [Hands sound designer a flash drive with 14 uncompressed digital files.]*

> **Sound Designer:** *Excellent. I'll throw into QLab, EQ it, set some levels, and we should be good to go. When does the show start?*

> **Choreographer:** *Five p.m., tonight.*

> **Sound Designer:** *I take cash or Venmo.*

If the production is going to be on an outdoor stage at a state fair, where everything has to be delivered by truck and set up from scratch, the conversation would be much different and perhaps like the following:

> **Choreographer:** *I'd like to have speakers that surround the audience to block out all the barnyard animal sounds during the show.*

> **Sound Designer:** *Makes sense.*

> **Choreographer:** *Is this possible?*

> **Sound Designer:** *Yes, for a price. And I will need some time to research the proper equipment, get rental estimates, and draw out a plan for the venue. It will need to be included in the rider. We will also need to*

> *hire a competent live sound engineer who is experienced with barnyard animals.*

Audio is best presented in a controlled environment. Be prepared to spend more money, time, and effort in less-than-ideal circumstances.

Integration

The range of possibilities for sound design is quite broad, and the approach will be unique for each production. The sound designer is responsible not only for what the audience hears but also for making sure the performers have what they need to perform to their best ability. The process starts with a *sound plot*. This is a technical drawing from the sound designer to designate the physical location of equipment relative to the performance space and indicate the signal flow through the system to make it work. Items included on the plot include all inputs being used, such as microphones and direct inputs from musical instruments, computers, and other devices.

An *input* may refer to the physical "input" port on an audio device (a "hole" of some shape and size), the connector *put into* that port (the device of a shape and size congruent with the "hole" into which it fits), and the source device from which that connector derives (a microphone, for instance). Outputs are also included in the sound design paperwork and include PA speakers and subs, monitor speakers, and practical or hotspot speakers. As with inputs, *outputs* may refer to the port, the connector, or the hardware at the end of the audio signal—typically a speaker of some sort, including headphones and earbuds. This information is important for the sound designer to create the acoustic environment and troubleshoot any issues.

Ancillary items to support the sound plot include the *patch* for the console. *Patch* refers to the informative spreadsheet indicating how the inputs and outputs (ins and outs) are assigned on the console, creating the signal flow through the system; and *patch* also refers to the physical connections of the various cables and connectors called out on the spreadsheet patch. Tracking where the musicians reside—in a pit, near the stage, or on the stage—supports knowing where equipment needs to be placed. A list of any rentals or purchases required for the production needs to be kept. As with lighting, a cue list needs to be developed for the production. The cue list has all the tasks required of the soundboard operator during the run of the show. This is typically given to the stage manager, who "calls" these cues during the show, and the board operator responds by executing each cue.

A choreographer needs to consider how the audio works with the performers. This could mean the dancer starts in silence, the movement and sound start at the same time, or the sound starts first and then the movement begins. The audio can be set to fade in or out and coordinate with spoken word or other performance needs. Cues for the soundboard operator are clearer when they use time markers with a dancer placement onstage. A soundboard operator or stage manager calling the show may not easily recognize a dance step as the cue for the sound to change.

Digital Media

Discussions about digital media refer to using electronic technologies—such as audio, video, lighting, computer-generated design, or software-based or streamed content—to create spectacle and add production value. Because of the exponential growth in computer processing technology, the production value for the performing arts also increases as new media and digital media devices are created at increasingly fast rates. Just as computing and web design increasingly use animation and video, so too does the world of production media. And while video and animation are not necessarily new, their accessibility and ease of use and the power of their delivery devices are constantly advancing.

Infrastructure

Digital media can be incorporated into almost any other aspect of design for the overall production value. A recent trend called *silent disco* is a dance club environment where each participant wears a set of headphones linked to a near field communications (NFC) frequency that can deliver the music for dancing and even send signals to operate LED lights on the headband or ear cups on the headphones to create a lighting show on the dancers' heads! When viewed by an external observer, patterns can emerge, and images could even be conveyed with the right perspective.

This is just one of the many recent developments in LED pixel mapping technology. The prevailing use of this technology is the LED wall, which is

Media design should reflect and serve the creative vision.

made up of many smaller panels and even smaller pixels (or single point sources of light). A video designer can display images and video *from* a wall of light rather than projecting the image *onto* a blank wall. There are many advantages to this approach: Dancers do not cast shadows onto an LED wall, whereas their bodies disrupt the light beam from a projector, casting a shadow onto the video surface. The workaround to this until recently has been rear projection—placing the projector upstage, or behind, the projection surface. The drawback to this method is that it requires a lot of space and distance between the projector and the screen, typically taking up valuable stage space away from the dancers. The LED wall is also superior in that it takes up a fraction of the floor space compared to the rear projection method. The LED wall can be flush against the upstage wall of the stage and leave the dancers with the entirety of the stage, save a few feet. Some of the newest LED panels can even bend, or flex, offering curvilinear options in a previously "flat-panel" industry.

In contrast to **LED pixel mapping**, projection mapping is layering a front-projected image onto a surface of any shape. A common trick is for designers to project onto a building during an outdoor event and have it appear to have frost, or fire, or other state of distress on it. And just as choreographers and designers have preferences in the quality of audio and lighting, media can also be layered and different technologies mixed to achieve specific effects with varying aesthetic traits. Digital media can be incorporated into or tangent to all the other production elements.

Design

Media can be integral to any other production design aspects, so the applications are endless. Designing media for a production is similar to all other design processes. It starts with a conversation with the choreographer to clarify the artistic vision and how media serves this vision. Sometimes choreographers or designers just like all the bells and whistles. But too much visual stimulation may override the dance content. Like the lighting designer, the media designer choreographs the timing and location of media to support the dance. Competing visual inputs can dilute the impact of both the choreography and media. Collaborating through the design process is essential. And while you are not building a physical set in media, considerable time goes into the media design. Collecting video and still images and designing slides and so on takes

time. In a typical production schedule, it needs to be done right the first time. A choreographer waffling between ideas will only frustrate the design team, and everyone will run out of time to make it work.

> ## SIDEBAR CONVERSATIONS: INCORPORATING DIGITAL MEDIA
>
> Effective communication leads to beneficial collaboration! A conversation about using an LED wall might go something like this:
>
> **Choreographer:** I think it would be really cool to use an LED wall instead of a physical set so we can have more space for the dancers, and we can change between locations instantly.
>
> **Media Designer:** Do you want the cues timed with the music?
>
> **Choreographer:** Is that possible?
>
> **Media Designer:** The way everything is linked through networking and time-code these days, we can go to the moon.
>
> **Production Manager:** And this costs the same or less than hiring a fabrication company to design, build, load-in, and strike tangible scenery?
>
> **Media Designer:** Yes.
>
> **Choreographer, Media Designer, and Production Manager:** *As they do their three-way fist-bump.* To the moon!
>
> Moral of the story: Media designers, including sound and lighting designers, should be knowledgeable in current technologies and production trends. It's easy to be persuaded to try something new, especially when there is little to zero net cost increase.

As this book was written, the prices for traditional construction materials continued to skyrocket; the cost of nearly all goods (and services) have increased. A concurrent shortage of computer chips compounded with supply chain delays have affected digital production. The upside is that if you already have equipment, or if you can rent it, it is possible to save money in the end by implementing some of these technologies in your production. Digital media equipment, including lighting and sound equipment, are durable goods, meaning they are reusable and have value beyond the current production. The design and implementation of digital media with this equipment may also require fewer staff and lower payroll costs compared to traditional scenic methods. If you are planning to pursue dance as a career, you already have a long-term mindset. Take this same approach as you consider financial matters as well.

Integration

The media designer must identify the technology to be used, plan how that technology will be situated or arranged in the performance space, and then create, license, or purchase the media to be displayed. For a multimedia production design, there can be a lot of overlap and significant collaboration among the designers. If the design calls for NFC integration into a costume, the media designer must work very closely with the costume designer. Likewise, the sound designer must partner with the lighting designer if sound cues trigger lighting effects. And the projection designer needs to work with the lighting designer so the stage lights don't wash out any images on the cyclorama. These are just a few examples of how closely the design teams of the modern era must work together to achieve the highest production value possible for the dance.

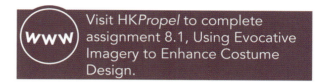

Visit HK*Propel* to complete assignment 8.1, Using Evocative Imagery to Enhance Costume Design.

Costume and Makeup

A costume could potentially be the only production element in a dance work. Consider that a dancer doesn't *need* a set, props, lighting, or even sound to create a compelling work of art. They just need their instrument—the body. Ask a dancer what they kept from their last concert, and they will likely say it was their costume. Ask a dancer if they have a leotard to wear to the flash mob at the mall—yes. Ask a dancer what they need for their next show—a costume!

Costumes and makeup help the dance tell a story.

Costumes and makeup contribute to our identity in our personal lives. You might think of how clothes and makeup contribute to one's personal "style." Do you have, or know someone that you consider to have, a great fashion sense? Do you recognize fashion trends in media or notice who's wearing what in class or at gatherings? Costumes and makeup can present a clear and immediate visual indication of one's age, sex, and culture, for instance, in our personal lives and in performance. It is easy to slip into presenting stereotypes, but good costume and makeup designers take clues from the artistic vision and use nuance to transform something conventional into something exceptional. Rather than pander to a base concept, a unique costume and makeup design is most befitting.

Costume and makeup designs also indicate an intentional response to the context to which they are applied. People regularly change their "outfits" appropriately. And so should dancers, who are essentially representing a character within a production. Salsa and hip-hop, for instance, have unique cultural aesthetic identities. Costume and makeup may be designed anywhere on the spectrum of literal representation to abstract concept and express a reflexive costume and character relationship.

Infrastructure

Costuming can be as simple as "just wear your warm-ups" or as complex as "that will take three dressers and a makeup artist two and a half hours to apply." Every production should find a place on that scale. And every production must decide how to get there. Likewise, every dancer, choreographer, and company must have a way to procure, develop, and create costumes when needed. Some productions merely require that dancers wear something from their personal closets, while the most elaborate productions require months or years of research and development to achieve their goals. Most professional productions fall somewhere between these extremes, taking weeks or months to prepare after a deliberate design process. As with all production elements, the costume and makeup design—and by definition, the designer—are beholden to the artistic vision and should be aligned to its purpose. Execution and implementation can be as varied as the design process itself, but there are fundamental tools and resources that offer support.

Costume Inventory

The backbone of any **costume shop** or **costume designer** studio is the inventory already on hand.

Even though dancers come in all shapes and sizes, having a resource of existing costumes available can expedite the costuming process. Typically, even the most modest costume shops will have some inventory. The shop will likely have inventory from previous productions. This type of inventory may seem very specific, but unless your audience is the same as the audience for the other show, you can repurpose those costumes without anyone noticing. One way to do this effectively is to alter existing costumes. A little glitter goes a long way.

Existing inventory may also include generic items such as T-shirts and character shoes. Recycling those pieces, especially the shoes, can drastically reduce production costs. Many costume shops frequently receive donations, even from other costume shops! Before you donate to your local thrift store, consider donating to a costume shop at a high school or university. If you already have your design established, you may find what you are looking for is already in stock. And even if the design is not complete, or perhaps you just need inspiration, consider taking a tour of a costume inventory. If possible, go with your designer so you can discuss your findings and make decisions on the spot.

If the company or designer does not have their own inventory, there are plenty of costume rental companies to visit. Some rental houses are located in vast industrial buildings with thousands of costumes on hand. It is an understatement to say that visiting a well-stocked costume rental warehouse is like entering the world's largest walk-in closet. Even people uninvolved in costuming are impressed by the sheer volume of items that can be racked and inventoried. Those who are interested in organization and tidiness find that professional costume warehouses label their inventories meticulously. They must—otherwise finding a particular garment would be a near impossible task. A large commercial costume rental company may easily have tens or hundreds of *thousands* of costumes in stock. At least one theatrical costume rental company lists over *one million* costumes available on their website! If pulling or renting costumes is the choice for the production, most rental houses (and the company costume manager) will allow for alterations to make the costumes fit.

Space, Staff, and Materials

If the costume design requires creating costumes, you will require a fabrication space and staff. Even an original costume may integrate some purchased or pulled pieces as the base for something more spe-

Creating costumes might require the use of a costume shop.

cific. Every costume is unique and so is its creation. A costume shop is a workshop where the fabrication and alteration of costumes occurs. This is usually a bustling workspace where skilled craftspeople cut, stitch, and adorn costumes. A full-service costume shop will be outfitted with several tools and technology and can create just about anything imaginable, and they follow the process from concept to completion. Equipment found in a costume shop may include cutting tables; measuring, cutting, sewing, and ironing tools; sewing machines, sergers, and overlocks; steamers; dye vats; and dress forms for mocking up garments. Costumes include anything and everything that a dancer can wear and hold, so the shop should also have tools and materials to build headwear, footwear, masks, and accessories like jewelry. Sometimes the line between costume and prop is unclear, and the costume shop may build or modify things considered hand props, such as fans or canes, that complete a character's aesthetic.

A designer may work alone in their creative space or *costume studio*. This distinction between *studio* and *shop* indicates that there is a design and development process in addition to the more tangible labor of construction. In the strictest sense, a shop is a work space for labor or a business that simply rents or sells costumes, while a studio is a creative space with a process from conception to completion. A studio may also be bustling with dozens of hardworking makers. There could be management, draftspeople, cutters, drapers, stitchers, milliners, cobblers, and craftspeople who can make all kinds of specialty items. These various costume studio members work with whatever fabrics and materials the design calls for. People may use these terms synonymously despite the difference explained here.

While fabrics like cotton, polyester, and rayon never go out of style, today's costumes can be much more demanding in terms of materials and features, and the processes to work with them are not yet standardized. Some more sophisticated costumes include secret compartments, quick-change features like tear-aways and reversible garments, electronics, and luminescence! Sometimes it takes the whole team to brainstorm a process for something they have not yet encountered. The designer should lead this process and ultimately provide the materials

Modern costumes can include integrated lighting.

lists and processes for developing the most imaginative dancewear.

Materials should be considered from many perspectives beyond the general look of a costume. Some fabrics do not complement each other well—that is, they do not adhere or combine easily. Choreography may determine materials selection to aid a dancer's movement. For instance, form-fitting, stretchy materials can offer flexibility, while loose garments can be a hindrance. Cotton socks can slide across Marley more easily than rubber soles, and either case could be advantageous depending on the choreography and safety concerns. The designer should research the choreography in as much detail as the aesthetic concept for an optimal design. Costume choices must often be changed during dress rehearsal because the choreography was not considered early enough in the process.

The sewing machine is truly the workhorse, but there are sergers and hand tools aplenty. The costume studio is full of cutting and mending tools like shears and needles. There are also tools like kettles for dying fabric and steamers and irons for getting the wrinkles out. Sometimes the manager needs to buy specific tools to work on specific material. Besides thread, there are adhesives, elastic, boning, and wire, to name a few things, that contribute to the form and integrity of a garment.

Costume Designer Responsibilities

Depending on the scale of production and the resources available, the costume designer role may be delegated to several team members. The simplest teams may assign costume, hair, and makeup design to the choreographer, director, or the dancers themselves. A slightly more sophisticated team structure may involve a dedicated team member who is responsible for coordinating a consistent, or at least appropriate, look for the piece. And the best production situation would provide for a formal costume designer who has the knowledge, experience, and resources to develop a fully conceived design specific to the given production. This person typically has at least a bachelor's degree or a master's degree in costume design from a performing arts or fashion school. A costume designer should be familiar with the principles of design, fabrics, construction, history, choreography, and the production process.

A designer should have an available portfolio or website with work samples to consider before a contract is signed. Likewise, the choreographer or director and the designer candidate should have a common direction for addressing the artistic vision.

Once the designer is brought on board, they should begin researching previous iterations of the production and become familiar with the genre, choreography, and key concepts. Renderings or garment pulls should begin as early in the process as possible to allow adequate time for construction, fittings, alterations, and final looks. The costume designer must attend rehearsals to understand the physical demands of the piece, because this may have a significant impact on design choices. All designers including the costume designer should attend any scheduled production meetings to report on progress and stay up to date on the overall production process. The choreographer and director will also expect to meet with the costume designer individually, and perhaps on a regular basis, to continually refine the costume design until the show opens. Throughout the design process, the designer should be prepared for traditional milestones. These include the following:

> Design meeting 1: Concepts
>> Provide research, references, and images or a collage
>> Account for each dancer and their needs
> Design meeting 2: Preliminary designs
>> Provide rough sketches and lists of items to pull, rent, buy, or build
>> Provide a cost estimate
>> Arrange to meet with shop manager or the person in charge of construction if it is not the designer
> Design meeting 3: Final designs
>> Provide final renderings or design boards
>> Confirm the design can be completed within budget
>> Confirm the fitting dates and tech schedule

Beyond these delivery dates, the designer should expect to frequently visit the shop to oversee progress, course-correct as needed, and provide timely input on questions. They should also be present for fittings (scheduled opportunities to have the dancers try on their costumes to ensure a proper fit and mobility) and create performance paperwork for the crew, including costume tracking (who wears what and when), quick-change guides (who changes into

what and how fast). The designer is also responsible for reconciling the budget at the end of the process.

Hair and Makeup

Hair and makeup design typically evolves from the costume design or is a part of the costume design. These departments work together to complete the overall aesthetic of the dancer. This means that the hair and makeup can also be as simple as daily corrective foundation to even out the skin tone, or the design could call for full-body paint applied by a professional with an airbrush.

Hair and makeup design may be covered by one person, two people, a team of people, or the costume designer. As with the costume designer position, the hair and makeup designer could be a member of the team or the cast. The most desirable option would be to have a single hair and makeup designer or a duo (to delegate responsibility while working in tandem) who is proficient in the many facets of this discipline.

Hair and makeup designers may have a background in theatrical makeup or cosmetology, or they may be an experienced esthetician. Recruiting one or more of these professionals is a distinct advantage in the production process, especially because they can proactively address tactical issues. They will also be best suited to train dancers to apply their own makeup and style their hair or fashion a wig. While dancers often do their own hair and makeup, a designer or crew member may be needed to help with relatively involved applications. Deciding how many people are required for hair and makeup prep backstage depends on how complex the design is and how much time and expertise is needed to complete the task.

Facilities for applying makeup or fixing hair will vary from venue to venue. It is a luxury when a venue has a proper dressing room with a vanity for applying makeup. Dancers often need to resort to putting on makeup in a restroom or with a compact mirror in a hallway backstage.

Beyond the inherent challenges of doing hair and makeup in less-than-ideal circumstances, there are always questions to address concerning hair and makeup. Some topics revolve around health and safety, most notably allergies and hygiene. If you, your designer, or your company is supplying grooming products to the dancers, be sure to discuss the ingredients in each product with every person to avoid unwanted adverse reactions. If there is uncertainty about a product, seek expert medical advice (the authors of this book are not qualified physicians). Doing makeup tests—sampling a prod-

Facilities for applying makeup or fixing hair will vary from venue to venue.

uct on a clean patch of skin—may be an appropriate first step but only do so under the supervision and direction of an expert.

Trust and modesty are critical concerns. Encourage open discussions about comfort and personal space. Because the application of hair and makeup products is so closely tied to hygiene, it is a very personal task, even when there is a team to assist the dancer. It can be intimidating to have someone else apply your eyeliner. And items like eyeliner, mascara, and lipstick should never be shared. Most dancers have their own makeup and hair kits and can come prepared for most traditional designs.

Prosthetics, wigs, and specialty makeup and hair products will generally be supplied for grander designs. In this case, everything that is assigned to an individual dancer would either be thrown away after the performance and replaced or disinfected and preset for the next show, with the dancer's name clearly labeled on the items so there will be no cross-contamination. Costumers and makeup artists typically wear personal protective equipment such as rubber gloves and face shields to protect themselves and the dancer from pathogens.

After a safe and healthy hair and makeup design is established, you can shift your attention to more tactical issues. Are your products reliable—will the dancer sweat off their makeup before the end of the piece? (Pro tip: Do not blame it on the lighting!) Should the hair be worn up to prevent it from hindering movement or masking the dancer's face? Are hairpieces and accessories attached securely to avoid damage, loss, or injury? In production, the simplest solution is generally the best, so be creative but don't expend so much time on any single issue that you inadvertently sacrifice the quality or integrity of the production overall.

Design

Because the scale of costume designs is so vast, it is difficult to imagine the various design conversations, though most begin with a "look" (an aesthetic) or a mood that the choreographer or director outlines in the creative brief as the foundation for their artistic goal. Consequently, the costume design is often the first design discussed, because it is intrinsically connected to the dancers, who are the objects of this art form. Considering flow, texture, and mobility in relation to the choreography is vital. As mentioned previously, this could be the only design required or feasible for the production, and is typically the key (or most important) design, affecting all others. And as with all design conversations in this text, effective collaboration is the strength of the production process.

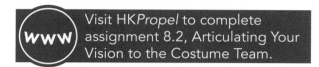

Visit HK*Propel* to complete assignment 8.2, Articulating Your Vision to the Costume Team.

Integration: Evaluating Functionality

Working with a costume designer experienced with the unique needs of dancers is essential. A beautiful costume won't be worn if a dancer can't breathe or move in it. The most intimate relationship a dancer has with a technical element is with the costume designer. In costume design, it's all about how creative you can be to merge the visual with the functionality. This is where communicative spirit is important in merging the two. Costumes and sets collaborate with scenery; if they are the same, colors will disappear. When costumes and lighting come together, some costumes allow the light to affect them more. Consider the costume design when collaborating with the light designer.

Summary

Sound is fundamental to every performance even if the dance is performed in silence. The movement and breathing of the dancers can become the score for the performance. Regardless of the sound source the patron's aural experience must be decided. A costume is the one production element after a venue that every dancer must have. Hair and makeup complete a costume design and should be considered as a supplemental part of the costume design, if not an intrinsic component. Scenery expands the context of the dance in time and location. This production element continues to evolve with the exponential increase in computing power and technological sophistication of digital media. These design departments and their staff will be addressed again in part III of this book, which will discuss how to present these choices onstage.

Now that you know what the elements of technical production are, who the creative collaborators are, and what the tools of the trade are, we need to organize this team, give them deadlines, and examine the production timeline.

Part III

Integration: Blending Vision and Process

After learning about the details of the collaborators and creative process necessary for a successful production, it's time to put these elements into a comprehensive production calendar and make each element work cohesively with all other production elements. Creating a single, integrated production calendar can be an intricate balance, but it is vital to an efficient and effective performance. In chapter 9, we dive into making the production timeline and show how to pull the timelines of each element together into a Gannt chart. In chapter 10, we explore how the production scope affects the scale and particulars of a performance and how you can curate and integrate your audience's experience into the vision you have for your production. Chapter 11 takes you through specific production elements like the stage, lighting, sound, costumes, scenery, and media and reveals key tips on relating them to other production and artistic elements. With a clear understanding of the relationship between your timeline, your scope, audience, and production elements, you are ready to sail into production week and create a successful dance production.

Production Timeline

9

Key Terms
cadence meeting
campaign
cost-out
cue-to-cue rehearsal
deliverables
designer run
Gantt chart
notes
prompt book
strike

LEARNING OBJECTIVES

After reading this chapter, you will be able to do the following:

❯ List the elements that need to be considered while creating a production timeline

❯ Structure a production timeline that integrates the needs of all production collaborators

❯ Define different types of production meetings and plot them on the production calendar

You know by now that bringing your vision to life on a stage can be a complex process requiring the coordination of many moving parts (and people). Planning can't be left to chance! With a thoughtfully considered production calendar and well-timed, high-quality production meetings, you can establish the pace of the process and create a setting for accountability among all team members for their deliverables. This increases your professionalism and will earn you the respect of the team, facilitate the collaborative process, and keep your project on track.

For the purposes of the discussion in this chapter, consider the following:

A *production timeline* is a conceptualization of the major milestones of the production process in chronological order. It represents the big idea, e.g., "The timeline for this show is early November through the holidays. We hold auditions after July 4th."

A *production calendar* is a physical or digital representation of the production timeline that identifies days, weeks, and so on of a production process. It is a type of "save-the-date," e.g., "Refer to the production calendar for the dates and times of auditions, rehearsals, tech, and performances."

A *production schedule* is a more specific document that outlines an agenda or order of show. This could be translated across departments and applications and include the who, what, where, and when, e.g., "Monday, January 1, 8:00 AM to 5:00 PM, University Theater, scenic load-in, staff names, etc."

Production Calendar

The production calendar is the most important reference tool in the production process. This calendar should be kept accurate daily and be accessible and understandable for everyone involved. You *cannot* treat it as your personal calendar. Jotting a quick note on the annual calendar inside your notebook will not create a production calendar.

The production calendar is based on the production timeline, which is created by taking a trip backward in time. It begins at the opening performance and works in reverse chronological order toward the starting point. In the broader discipline of project management, this method of calendar building is based on what is called a *workback schedule*, when we begin with opening night, and *work backward* in time, identifying the milestones and deadlines for a project. There are many ways to create a production calendar, though the most common approaches take note of the following:

› Milestones: What needs to happen?
  › Identify all deliverables required to achieve the artistic vision.
  › Create a chronological list of all the steps and deadlines required to produce the dance event.
› Production process: How will we make it happen?
  › Create a relative scale of time for how long it takes to accomplish various tasks within the chronological list.
› Communication: How will we communicate the tasks that need to be done?
  › Referring again to broader project management tactics, creating a work breakdown structure (WBS) provides collaborators with a hierarchical chart of project tasks and subtasks, assigning team members and departments to each.
  › Generate a calendar on which all of the tasks are plotted. (A Gantt chart is the gold standard in production calendaring, as explained later in this chapter.)
› Accountability: How will we make sure it happens?

> Schedule production meetings throughout the process, when team members will report on progress, ask relevant questions, develop action items, and deliver to the entire team (this includes everything from an advertising poster, to the final renderings of the costumes, to a financial report on ticket sales).

> A representative from each department or discipline should be given time to speak.

> The topics for the meeting should be outlined in a meeting agenda that's preferably issued to the team before the meeting, perhaps via email or in a shareable presentation app slide deck.

The production timeline has many parts. Each department or team that contributes to the production process has their own production calendar and task list to complete. And each of those calendars must conclude on the same date: opening night! Imagine a set of train tracks that converge upon a common destination, all originating from different cities, from different distances from the destination, moving at different speeds, making many different stops along the way. In fact, at some points, the tracks cross or run tangent for a while. It is a complex system of timing and coordination, often called *logistics*.

The speed of each train, the stops along the way, and collaboration methods are discussed at meetings. The speed of each train depends on the timeline allocated to that team. Train "stops" are *milestones*, or significant dates and deadlines. Even though each department or discipline has its own track, all must be aware of the others to avoid crashes or delays. Their interactions, described throughout the remainder of this chapter, are key to an efficient production. When the production process functions effectively, all the trains arrive at the production opening at exactly the right moment. The hardest part about creating a production calendar, however, is making sure these interactions are integrated in a detailed and thorough fashion.

Figure 9.1 shows common key leadership personnel for the largest professional performing arts organizations. They are divided into five logical groups, or teams, based on their primary functions and having common timelines and goals. All organizations structure their staff to accommodate their unique needs, and there are typically many more support positions involved that are not specified here. Some personnel may belong to multiple teams or tracks.

Milestones

All tracks lead to one goal (opening night), and a lot needs to happen within each department to reach that goal. The first step to developing an effective production calendar is identifying exactly *what* needs to happen. Each team has a long list of tasks, goals, and objectives: These are **milestones**. Communicating clear goals and deadlines ahead of time is how you make sure nothing is overlooked in the chaos of the production process.

Establishing milestones is a matter of placing your production to-do list on the production calendar. Begin with the final task. This is often the opening night of a stage performance. It could also be the first day of a video shoot or any significant moment when the preparation process essentially ends and performances begin. To plan your first milestone in reverse, you need to consider what precedes it—in this example, opening night. A final dress rehearsal usually occurs on the day before opening. (In some processes, this final dress rehearsal may be a special presentation or series of presentations called *previews*, and an audience is present.) Determine how many dress rehearsals you need or can support, and place them on the calendar accordingly. Before dress rehearsals, you typically need technical rehearsals (also called *tech rehearsals*), so you would repeat the calendaring process for that phase.

Then the calendaring gets a bit more interesting. Essentially the entire company is present for tech rehearsals, dress rehearsals, and performance, so the calendar appears as a single "track." Until that point in the process, except for full production meetings, most departments work independently of one another. Depending on the detail you require for your production calendar, you could maintain this single track and just post production meetings and design deadlines, or you could collaborate with other teams to coordinate their milestones, identifying department, venue, and personnel required. This type of calendaring is complex, and it is usually handled by a production manager or producer who is very competent in this skill and understands the process in detail. This multiple-track calendaring prevents double booking of staff and space. It also directs the tracks to merge at certain points (typically production meetings) when stakeholders can give progress reports and define the next steps.

Continue establishing milestones all the way back on the calendar to the moment that the production process begins. This initial moment can be announcing a season selection, the first concept meeting, or whatever point you deem most bene-

Administration

- Focus: Organization
- Primary objective: Lead the production process from beginning to end. This is the longest track.
- Major tasks: Select a season lineup and make the final decisions about how the organization operates.
- Key personnel: Board of directors, executive director, artistic director, managing director, director of operations, director of finance, director of human resources, director of information technology, company manager

Choreography

- Focus: Artistic inspiration and direction
- Primary objective: Lead the artistic endeavor. Choreograph movement.
- Major tasks: Complete the creative process on time and ensure the dancers are informed about production elements
- Key personnel: Artistic director, program director, choreographers, accompanists, health and wellness coordinator

Design and production

- Focus: Production value
- Primary objective: Deliver the production elements to the specifications of the creative brief. This track begins later in the process, once the creative brief is approved.
- Major tasks: Manage the calendar, budget, staff, and production resources. Collaborate internally to maintain production integrity. Consult regularly with administration and choreography teams for course correction.
- Key personnel: Director of production, designers, technical director, costume director, music director, stage manager

Fundraising

- Focus: Money
- Primary objective: Raise money to support organizational and production operations. This track may be ongoing depending on the type of company you work with, though fundraising typically occurs in waves and targeted campaigns.
- Major tasks: Cultivate and maintain a significant donor base. Organize fundraising events around specific financial needs and productions.
- Key personnel: Development director, patron services director, special events director, gifts and giving director

Marketing

- Focus: Advertising
- Primary objective: Broadcast the goings-on of the organization and create a return on the investment in advertising.
- Major tasks: Generate ticket sales. Collaborate with fundraising. Maintain relevance in the media.
- Key personnel: Marketing director, communications director, media relations director, creative director, ticketing manager

Figure 9.1 Focus, objectives, major tasks, and key personnel for five groups in a large organization.

ficial to your process. Even with all the variables involved in production, your production calendar should identify all the milestones you and your company need to remain on "track" for success.

The production calendar does not necessarily end at opening night. Performances, recordings, or broadcasts need to be included. Postproduction may need to be considered. Technical teams and venues have teardown, returns, deliveries, travel, and changeovers to consider after the performance closes, regardless of format. And a postmortem should be added, if possible, to review the process with key personnel and create action items for improving the production process. (Chapter 14 takes a detailed look at the postmortem process.)

If you scan ahead on your calendar and look at the tasks and responsibilities and deadlines assigned to the various teams and team members, you may feel overwhelmed. That is understandable. Throughout this text, it has been emphasized that producing dance is a collaborative art. For this monumental endeavor to succeed, it needs teamwork supported by a clear timeline that's synthesized through effective communication, with a solid calendar at its foundation.

Once the production calendar has been distributed by leadership, each department should develop the necessary production schedules. For example, the scenic department should schedule deliveries, builds, and installs at very specific dates and times. This minutiae is important and therefore handled at a level closer to the actual tasks being performed. The production manager or artistic director, who is concerned with the overarching timeline and the associated calendar as a matter of driving season selection, marketing, and ticket sales, for instance, is not particularly concerned with when the lumber delivery arrives at the scene shop. And that is a matter of production scheduling.

There is an old adage: "How does one eat an elephant? One bite at a time." And that is how we must approach dance production: one bite, or step, at a time.

> ### BREATHE
>
> *Breathe.*
>
> There is still a lot to take in!
> *Breathe.*
>
> How many dance productions have you seen?
> *Breathe.*
>
> How many have you been involved with?
> *Breathe.*
>
> Why then should your next production be any less feasible? You have the instruction manual in your hand!

You are likely a dancer first, so consider how you approach learning a new dance. You do it one *step* at a time. It must be approached this way whether you are remounting a famous piece or developing something brand new. And this is how to approach the entire production process. Each stakeholder is given their choreography (each movement is like a task of theirs). Everyone contributes, completing their "steps," and the entire production becomes clearer. The objective is made more attainable, and the weight of the enormity of the process lifts away, because no one has to do it on their own. This is not a solo performance.

Production Process

How will we do it? How will we make sure every collaborator's tasks and expectations are clear, in order, and—most important—clearly related to the rest of the production team? It's difficult to synthesize multiple department calendars. They influence each other, and sometimes one collaborator or team can't move forward until another team reaches a milestone. A **Gantt chart** is a type of calendar that displays these *dependencies*, or the relationships

Early in the process, it's time to get into the studio and start working on the dance.

between the various production "tracks," and clearly identifies when each influences the other. These charts will be discussed in more detail later in the chapter. Each team member needs to have their own calendars and schedules and be accountable for completing tasks and answering questions to support one another.

The following are samples of how the production process works, broken down by team.

Choreography

The choreography team might follow a basic structure like the following.

1. *Development:* Once the choreographer has an inspiration, they need to start creating their creative brief. The choreographer should ask themselves these questions: What is the piece about, or what is the theme? What is the rehearsal-to-show timeframe: How much time do we have from inspiration

to opening night? How many performers are in the piece? What venue is best suited for the production? Is there a budget for sets, lights, costumes, crew, publicity, and rehearsal space as needed? Think about assembling a team of collaborators. Create a realistic rehearsal calendar to get the work done on time.

2. *Creation:* Get into the studio and start working on the dance. Publicize and hold the audition. Once the performers are cast, get to work on creating the dance. Keep a close eye on your calendar and check it often to make sure you are staying on task.

3. *Production meetings:* Work with the collaboration team—assistant choreographers, designers, production staff, and crew—to create a production calendar that includes weekly or biweekly production meetings.

4. *Integration of design elements:* Once designers and collaborators can begin integrating their elements, schedule a **designer run,** also known as a *designer run-through.* This is not about creating new choreographic work; it is about having the designers and collaborators watch the dance in its most complete structure and discuss what they are seeing. If it is possible to have costumes, makeup and hair, props, or set pieces at these rehearsals, it will be easier for everyone to make the necessary adjustments at this stage rather than when time has run out.

5. *Marketing:* This may not be a choreographer's job, but the choreographer should be an active part of the process. Create a publicity calendar. Check in with the publicity team about deadlines and budgets. Make sure that publicity goes out at the appropriate times and in the appropriate places and spaces, using both virtual and traditional avenues.

6. *Tech:* The tech calendar should have been worked out during the production meetings. The tech calendar includes a **cue-to-cue rehearsal** and dress rehearsals. The tech calendar is created by the technical director and program or rehearsal director. A **notes** meeting will be held at the end of each technical rehearsal. The stage manager will distribute the notes to all constituents, and action items will be completed before the following technical or dress rehearsal.

7. *Performances:* After all the work that everyone has put in, it is time to let the audience into the venue and for the entire team to share their art.

8. *Strike (postproduction):* Everyone involved with the show, including choreographers and performers, need to participate in the **strike.** Once the performance has concluded, everything must be taken down, stored away, or returned. A postmortem meeting may be placed on the calendar in order to discuss any opportunities to improve the process for the next production. And around and around we go!

Design and Production

If your production team does not include all the positions identified in this example, someone will need to assume those responsibilities. For the sake of clarity and to present a complete process, the sample process that follows is based on a large-scale production company. Each team member will have **deliverables** at various times (milestones) in the process. A deliverable is anything the designer is required to submit for payment and approval.

1. *Development:* The program or rehearsal director and designers have discussions about the artistic concepts and how to achieve them. Once the administrative team approves the vision statement and the budget has been assigned to the production, the director should begin direct discussions, or development meetings, with each designer to prepare for the design phase.

2. *Design:* During the design phase, the designers should be producing deliverables, due at the end of the drafting phase. The director and designers should continue to have one-on-one or small group development meetings that include production staff to monitor feasibility.

3. *Drafting:* The drafting phase offers an opportunity for the designers to create scenic plans, lighting and audio plots with rental quotes, and makeup and costume renderings. They can also finalize the deliverables.

4. *Budget:* Because the budgets should have been established and shared before the design process, the directors and designers should already be working within these parameters. A design presentation meeting

is scheduled between when the designers create the preliminary work but before they complete their final designs for implementation. This meeting is when the designers share their preliminary designs with the entire team. The budget phase gives the production manager and technical department heads an opportunity to do a cost breakdown of all design elements and to collaborate very closely with the director, choreographers, and designers in a series of edits with short turnaround times between them. This process exists to ensure that every element is accounted for, to prevent last-minute cuts, and to establish that the final designs will not be altered in any way that increases budget, delays production, or requires additional labor. A final design sign-off meeting is scheduled to solidify the scope of the design and conclude the budget phase. Signers include the artistic director, director, choreographers, production manager, technical director, and costume manager.

5. *Planning:* With the designs now delivered to their respective departments, the technical director and costume manager will begin their preparations in earnest. A **cadence meeting** will be scheduled in the middle of this phase. Each department will be asked to provide a status update, and general production notes will be given. Detailed or specific needs and concerns should be addressed in private meetings, often referred to as *sidebars*, scheduled by the interested parties. Some designers have deliverable obligations during the planning phase because these items are needed in rehearsal.

6. *Build:* The technical director and other department heads will implement the designs. Cadence meetings will be scheduled throughout this phase. There are several design deadlines during this phase.

7. *Load-in:* Load-in refers to the time allocated to install and prepare all technical production elements in the venue. The appropriate team members will load-in the show. A cadence meeting may be scheduled during this phase. Deliverables in this phase are listed as "load-in" or "during load-in or tech."

8. *Tech:* This includes technical rehearsals, cue-to-cue rehearsals, and dress rehearsals. The technical director and director create the schedule. A notes meeting will be held at the end of each technical call. The stage manager will distribute the notes collected to all constituents, and action items will be completed before the following technical or dress rehearsal.

Production leaders will take an active role in managing rehearsals toward the end of the process.

9. *Performances:* During the run of the show, the production team goes into maintenance mode, making sure everything is set and ready by the top of the next show. The costumes will need washing, the stage will be prepared before each show, the props will be reset, and sound or lighting cues may be adjusted.

10. *Strike (postproduction):* Once the performance period has concluded, everything must be taken down, stored away, or returned. A postmortem meeting may be scheduled to discuss opportunities to improve the process for the next production.

Visit HK*Propel* to complete assignment 9.1, Create a Choreographer's Production Timeline.

Fundraising

Fundraising is not only about asking people to donate money. Successful fundraising centers around providing opportunities to create, engage, and cultivate strong relationships with the individuals and organizations that want to support the type of work you do. While working on your production timeline, you will have to answer a few questions to decide how fast funding sources need to be developed. While we would all like an unlimited budget, this is very rarely the reality, so before you start anything, you need to know how much money you have at your disposal. Can you cover your costs? The next question is what those costs are going to be. If you are submitting for a festival, is there a submission fee? In an academic setting, the student choreographer does not need to typically pay for a venue or for designers, but what if you want to film your dance and have someone edit the footage for you?

Once you have begun to identify the funds you will need, you will need to find the available funding sources. Online gift campaigns, calling for donations at the performance, donor support, crowdfunding, and grants are all ways to increase your production budget, and each will have different timelines. You may be itching to get in the studio and create the next masterpiece, but it may be worth waiting until the funds have been raised to pay the dancers and the venue and have great production and design support. Fundraising timing will differ for a one-time event versus when you are starting your company and need sustainability.

Marketing

Marketing is much like fundraising because it has to happen while all the other components are occurring. However, without marketing, you won't have an audience! If you want people to attend, they need to know when to come, where it is held, and what to expect. Marketing materials can be divided into two categories: the marketing campaign materials and the performance materials.

Marketing campaign materials will include graphics, photos, and informational materials to be released to the public before the performance. Social media campaigns, email marketing, and postcards or flyers are strategically timed to bring attention to your event and build excitement, resulting in people purchasing tickets and going to your event. The timing will shift based on the type of event and mission of the performance. All these materials will need to be created early in the process and released to the target audiences.

Performance materials include primarily the programs or other materials provided for the audience experience. Collecting artist bios, director's notes, program material, and lobby information from the creative and production team occurs while the performance is being created. Printing or other production periods mean the due dates to gather all the information will be important so the printer has enough time to create the program, and you have enough time to pick it up and have it at the theatre for the performance.

Marketing and fundraising can rely on similar information and often work together.

Administration

The best creative ideas in the world won't go anywhere if there is no direction and support. Administrative tasks such as signing contracts, paying artists, booking spaces, keeping track of communications, and liaising with the venue are just a few of the responsibilities that might be required in a production. The type and scope of production, as well as the venue, will determine how administrative duties are assigned. In an academic setting, the faculty and staff typically take on these responsibilities, leaving the student choreographers free to focus on their craft. Outside of academic settings, the choreographer will begin to take on multiple roles and administrative responsibilities. If your ultimate goal is to have your own dance company, festival, or production company, you will take on more administrative elements. As far as the timeline, the administrative component is present on the first day. After the theatre is closed, the audience has gone home, and artists move on to other projects, the administrative work will continue. We will discuss more administrative components in part IV.

Pulling the Timelines Together

After all tasks are considered, a chronological task list can emerge as well. A very simple chronological list of tasks could look like figure 9.2. Notice that this list jumps from department to department: After you create the artistic vision, your attention must go to something more business oriented, like booking a performance venue. Essentially, the right-brain creative step leads into a left-brain logical step, and so goes the production process, forever and ever.

Whether you have six months or six weeks to bring your production together, the timeline can be grouped in the following stages.

› Stage 1 (farthest from opening night)
  › Create a production budget and begin securing funds
  › Create a production timeline and schedule the first meeting
  › Determine the artistic programming (the season or performance selection)
  › Secure the performance and rehearsal spaces
  › Determine the scope of marketing and advertising
  › Identify requisite patron services support (methods and number of ticket sales, box office and front of house staffing, accessibility concerns, etc.)
  › Hire designers and determine the design deadline
  › Determine whether permission will be needed to use the selected music
› Stage 2 (everyone at work)
  › Begin production meetings
  › Schedule auditions and rehearsals
  › Determine the number of technicians needed and hire them
  › Work with designers and choreographers
  › Initiate marketing campaigns and material collection
  › Determine the tech schedule and distribute it

Figure 9.2 Sample chronological list of dance production tasks.

› Stage 3 (opening night is coming up fast)
  › Schedule costume fittings
  › Schedule designer runs
  › Load-in to the venue
  › Develop cue sheets
  › Complete all components—lighting, sound, costume, media, and so on
  › Set the show order
  › Proof and edit the production program for patrons (use about one month prior for a theatre)
› Stage 4 (dress rehearsal, opening, and closing)
  › Tech rehearsals
  › Dress rehearsals
  › Take archival photos and videos
  › Opening and run of the show
  › Closing night
  › Strike
  › Postmortem and all final administrative duties

STAGES BASED ON A SIX-MONTH TIMELINE

> Stage 1 (six months out)
> Stage 2 (three to four months out)
> Stage 3 (two weeks to one month out)
> Stage 4 (performance week)

Creating a Gantt Chart

A production manager often uses a **Gantt chart** for the calendar. It depicts various segments as ribbons of time in a "waterfall" arrangement. The example in figure 9.3 shows the timing of a company's dance productions across a season. Notice the relationship between each production as represented by a unique ribbon of color on the timeline. This chart is intentionally broad in scope to identify where effort is spent across the entire company for one season or year. It represents the big-picture span of time from inception to completion. This is good for broadly relating the allocation of time and resources within a company. Within these colorful swaths of time exist all the individual dates, rehearsals, meetings, deadlines, and moments that make up the entire production process.

Production managers in the arts use a Gantt chart, and so do project managers in almost every industry. Its most obvious feature is how clearly it represents the relationship of one task (or show or production) to the next. It is arguably the most important document you can create for your process. Essentially everything can be tied back to the calendar. Building your first calendar will be challenging, but over time, you will copy and paste and adapt new timing, strategies, and tools that will help modify your structure for each season or production.

A production manager or department head may create several Gantt charts to zoom in on greater detail for any given aspect of a production. Figure 9.4 zooms in one step from the season overview into "Production 1" and depicts how the five primary production teams relate in their given tracks. General phases of the production process and action outlines are identified within the body of the chart. Notice that design and production (D&P) and choreography have condensed timelines compared to administration, fundraising, and marketing. The latter teams are concerned with the entire season of production and remain engaged in production activity year-round. D&P and choreography focus their efforts on a per-show basis, so the time not represented in this chart is likely allocated to a different production (which would be identified on a separate Gantt chart).

Figure 9.4 demonstrates how departments operate on different times: Fundraising starts early, designers don't come in until creation starts, and admin goes the whole time until after the performance. This is a sample of a relative scale. As someone involved in a production, you need to know your own line on the chart very well and know where it fits into others' lines. The impact your department has on another, or vice-versa, is called *dependency*. A more sophisticated and detailed Gantt chart would appear more as a flow chart with lines directing the eyes across those dependencies.

Having said all this, you may not need a Gantt chart, and that's OK, as long as you have your own calendar. People planning at the highest levels and looking at how each aspect of production relates to the others find the Gantt chart an invaluable tool. Figure 9.5 shows a sample chart necessary for a technical department head, production manager, stage manager, or anyone concerned with the relative progress of the individual trades within the larger D&P team. If you find yourself in this position, start honing your spreadsheet skills, because that's how you create a Gantt chart.

2022-2023 Season

	January	February	March	April	May	June	July	August	September	October	November	December
Production 1												
Production 2												
Production 3												
End of year gala												

Figure 9.3   A Gantt chart for a company season of productions. Time is represented in months on the horizontal axis, and each production is represented on the vertical axis.

Production 1

	January	February	March	April	May	June	July	August
Administration	Announce season	Book venue/hire designers	Oversee operations	Oversee operations	Oversee operations	Oversee operations	Oversee operations	Send final payments
Design and production		Design/drafting	Budget/planning	Build	Build	Load-in/tech	Performances/strike	
Choreography			Auditions	Rehearsal	Rehearsal	Move-in/tech	Performances	
Fundraising	Contact season subscribers	Venue partnerships	Vendor partnerships			Preview audience engagement	Pre-show meet and greets	
Marketing	Season advertising campaign		Social media campaign #1		Social media campaign #2	Social media campaign #3	Final advertising campaign	Emphasize production 2

Figure 9.4 A Gantt chart for Production 1 in a company season. Time is represented in months on the horizontal axis, and each team "track" is represented on the vertical axis.

Design and production

	January	February	March	April	May	June	July	August
Production phase		Design/drafting	Budget/planning	Build	Build	Load-in/tech	Performances/strike	
Lighting		Submit final designs	Confirm rentals			Hang, focus, paper tech	Performances/strike/return rentals	
Sound		Submit final designs	Confirm rentals			Install, sound check, paper tech	Performances/strike	
Costumes		Submit final designs	Confirm rentals	Construction, fittings	Alterations, fittings	Load-in, dressing room prep	Performances/strike	Return rentals/restock inventory
Hair/makeup		Submit final designs	Confirm inventory			Load-in, dressing room prep	Performances/strike	Changeover for production 2
Scenic		Submit final designs	Confirm rentals	Construction	Construction	Load-in, paper tech	Performances/strike	Ramp up build for production 2
Props		Submit final designs	Confirm rentals	Construction	Construction	Load-in, paper tech	Performances/strike	Return rentals/restock inventory

Figure 9.5 A Gantt chart for the design and production team for Production 1 in a company season. Time is represented in months on the horizontal axis, and each technical trade is represented on the vertical axis.

If you are computer savvy or want to level up on your project management skills, you might consider a project management or task management tool. These database apps hold just about any information and can be customized to handle that data in nearly any way you want to consider it. The most popular apps currently available have user interfaces that make entering and manipulating information much easier than you might expect. When dates and times are entered, they might be viewed as a calendar, a Gantt chart, or a list, depending on your choice. Figure 9.6 is concerned with the accountability of the costume department specifically and includes specific dates that can easily be connected to a traditional calendar. This chart could also be expanded further to break down the schedule into each day, though that would create a very wide chart that is more challenging to read in book format. The task management features included help in managing the minutiae and can link a checklist right into your calendar. There are options for updating the status of a task with the click of a button or tap of a finger, and both you and the person assigned to the task (if it is not you) will know their progress in real time.

It is important that any digital calendar app or platform be easily accessible (web-based, free, and available on mobile devices of all brands), easy to read (you know a good user interface when you see one), and provide enough information to be useful (more information than just date and time). A good calendar will also be compatible with or integrated into your personal calendar. This allows you and your team to view the production timeline in direct relationship to personal, work, or other obligations that may affect availability for the events on the production calendar. Many calendar apps can add or link multiple calendars to the main interface, and the user can then turn each calendar on or off to show more or less information as needed to plan.

Just because you know how to send a text does not mean you will be proficient in digital planning or calendaring, let alone be capable of effectively implementing a project management system. So be

Costumes

	February				March					April				May					June				July			
Week # >	1	2	3	4	1	2	3	4	5	1	2	3	4	1	2	3	4	5	1	2	3	4	1	2	3	4
Concept meeting with designer*	Feb 1																									
Design phase																										
Makeup collab meeting*		Feb 10																								
Kickoff/preliminary designs due*			Feb 17																							
Drafting phase																										
Budget phase																										
Cost-out meeting*						Mar 10																				
Final designs due							Mar 17																			
Planning phase																										
Confirm rentals								Mar 24																		
Confirm hair/makeup inventory*									Mar 31																	
Build phase																										
First fittings																										
Production meeting*														May 3												
Alterations																										
Second fittings																										
Final alterations																										
Designer run*																				Jun 16						
Load-in																										
Paper tech*																					Jun 21					
Cue-to-cue*																					Jun 24					
Dressing room prep																										
Tech rehearsals*																						Jun 26 and 27				
Dress rehearsals*																						Jun 28, 29, 30				
Performances																							July 1 and 2			
Strike																								July 3		
Return rentals																								July 7		
Postmortem*																									Jul 12	
Restock inventory																										
*Production meetings in bold																										

Figure 9.6 A Gantt chart for the costume department on a design and production team for Production 1 in a company season. Time is represented in months and weeks on the horizontal axis, and each production meeting (in bold with an asterisk) and milestone is represented on the vertical axis.

honest with yourself, and find an approach that will be most effective for *you* and *your team*. And in the meantime, increase your computer skills, because they are invaluable and will only become more necessary over time.

Visit HK*Propel* to complete assignment 9.2, Create a Director's Production Timeline.

Production Meetings

Generally speaking, a production meeting is an opportunity for primary stakeholders to gather for a status update and to delegate new action items across the teams. The most common regularly scheduled meetings, cadence meetings, are most effective when each department is addressed for a few minutes only. Each department lead is given a few minutes to update the rest of the team on their progress and request what they need to move forward. For example, "Lighting just completed the hang and focus. Programming can begin on time. Does the designer have a tech schedule?" The input was a statement of progress, followed by a clarifying question. This example would occur late in the overall production timeline, but your production meeting calendar will begin with your very first discussion of your project.

PLANNING

Planning before your first production meeting with the entire team allows you to fully develop your artistic vision, gather your team, create a production calendar, and secure funding, a venue, and any other resources you will require. Contracts must be signed, schedules must be made, and rights can be obtained—it is ideal to get your legal issues addressed before commencing production. If you find out one week before opening night that you cannot use a piece of music or that the venue is already in use for something else, your production is over before it begins.

Some production meetings serve as deadlines for stakeholders to submit deliverables (milestones), such as preliminary and final designs or budget and sales reports. Most of the detailed conversations that lead up to this deliverable moment are held outside the large-group meetings in what are called *sidebar conversations*. These deep-dives and problem-solving conversations need only involve the immediately significant team members and do not need to be held during a full production meeting.

There can be different types of production meetings that serve unique purposes or have a specific focus. These meetings bring people together and keep everyone on track toward the common goal. Each of the following meetings require specific team members to show up and be ready to discuss their piece of the bigger picture.

Kickoff

The **kickoff**, or first whole-team production meeting, sets the tone for the production and gets the team up to speed with the artistic vision, the scope of the project, the calendar, budgets, and whatever else is pertinent to a smooth takeoff. As with most production meetings, time is valuable, and to respect everyone involved, the person leading the meeting should generate an agenda (and distribute it before the meeting, if possible), watch the clock, and keep the conversation focused on updates and needs and not permit off-topic discussion that wastes time.

Cost-Out

Cost-out meetings should be required of any production that has a budget for design elements or the expenditure of any significant amount of capital. This meeting is an opportunity for the designer to present their needs and for the budget manager (often the production manager, technical director, or a department head) to assess the request's feasibility. The budget manager leads the conversation to arrive at the best product and process for the amount spent. They break down the design into the resources needed to achieve that design and report back on whether the design can be achieved within the given budget. They need to consider all aspects of the build and performance: materials, labor, shipping, transportation, rentals, consumable goods, repairs, maintenance, and time! Surprisingly, labor alone can eat up 50 percent or more of a department's budget.

In a smaller-scale production, a cost-out meeting could consist of you just balancing your bank account and searching the couch for spare change. But, seriously, money handling and accounting are important skills to develop as production becomes more of a business when you ascend the ladder of responsibility.

Design

Design meetings should be required of any production with design elements. A director or choreographer can spend many hours a day just meeting with designers to conceive the right look or sound. Design meetings should focus on how to bring the director's or choreographer's artistic vision to life. Each designer's artistic approach should be grounded in that artistic vision. That concept is central to everything that happens in production, and a production sinks or swims based on the strength, clarity, and communication of the artistic vision. Similarly, a design proves successful, or at least germane to the production, if it "speaks the language of the vision." Aesthetic perception is a book all on its own, but this marriage of the conceptual and the tangible is critical to the production process and its product.

The designs will need to be approved. At the design meeting, when the final designs are presented, the director, designers, and production department heads will agree that the designs are deliverable safely, on time, and within budget.

Once the final designs have been approved, the company can hold design presentations for the cast. This is often integrated into the first rehearsal period. It is an exciting opportunity for cast and artistic team members to explore the production through the various new voices of the design team. The cast may not see a costume or prop or scenic piece again for many weeks or months, so it is important that they have some concept of what elements they will interact with or be affected by.

Designer Run

A **designer run** is a type of rehearsal that is typically accompanied by a comprehensive large-group production meeting following the run. Smaller meetings interspersed between dance numbers, choreographers, or acts could also occur. This type of meeting should be required of any production with a technical rehearsal to follow. The primary goal of this meeting is to offer the designers an opportunity to see the work of the choreographers and cast firsthand to make any final decisions on how to approach the technical rehearsal period.

Paper Tech

One last meeting before the technical rehearsals begin is called the **paper tech**. The director or choreographers and designers meet in a large-group format to walk through the show moment by moment. The stage manager changes over from a rehearsal book to creating the **prompt book**, where they will lead the crew in the execution of the cues. If the show is scripted, the cues are added into the script directly. If the show is based on written music, the cues are added into this score. If the show is based on pop music or has no real script, the stage manager must create a *cue sheet* based on some common language and format into which the designers can contribute their cues for the stage manager to organize and delegate.

In all instances, the process is the same: The director leads the team through each moment of the production, and the designers interject cues for the stage manager to record in the prompt book, from which the show is called. The result of this meeting is a first draft of the prompt book.

Cues will include audio, video, lighting, costume quick-changes, prop swaps, scenic changes, special effects, rigging or fly cues, cast stand-bys and entrances, bows, streaming prompts, camera transitions, and even communication with the front of house to determine when the doors to the audience chamber open and close!

Pro tip: If the designers can share their cue lists with the stage manager in advance of the paper tech, they can enter the cues into the prompt book beforehand, expediting the process.

Notes

Notes should be required after each technical or dress rehearsal. Usually, while the cast gets out of costume, the technical team gathers near the production table to discuss the rehearsal, giving the production manager, technical director, and department heads "notes" to be executed in advance of the next rehearsal. Here are some examples of notes:

> › The instrument in lighting circuit 25 blew out. Can we get the lamp replaced?
>
> › Dancer 3 in piece 4 needs their costume pant legs re-hemmed.
>
> › The projections at the top and bottom of piece 6 should be swapped.

Postmortem

The postmortem meeting is an opportunity for the production team to examine the process after the show has closed, with the intention of making improvements in the next production. Assessing what our strengths and weaknesses were on the project helps us learn from mistakes and get better at what we do.

Summary

The process of creating and producing dance may seem overwhelming at times, but with a clear plan and a group of like-minded collaborators at your side, it is possible to bring your inspiration to life. Understanding what goes into the process and all the important aspects of that process is the key to succeeding.

In chapter 5, we introduced the team. In chapter 6, we discussed creation in the studio, and in chapters 7 and 8, we explained all the technical design elements. Here in chapter 9, we tied them together with a process and a way to organize that process, beginning with establishing a timeline, creating a calendar (possibly in the form of a Gantt chart), then scheduling all the details. Collaboration starts in production meetings and continues as milestones are accomplished. Part of what makes moving into the performance space and seeing the dancers on stage so rewarding is understanding the enormity and complexity of the work required behind the curtain. A standing ovation recognizes the inspiring collaboration of the entire production. Now you are ready to move into the performance space and launch your dance production in part III.

Production Scope and Audience Experience

10

Key Terms

evening-length productions
festival
installation
mixed bill
premiere
repertory
repertory dance company
season
site-specific

LEARNING OBJECTIVES

After reading this chapter, you will be able to do the following:

> Define different types of dance productions
> Recognize how different types of dance productions affect the production scope
> Acknowledge how an audience's experience is shaped by elements outside of the performance itself
> Effectively program a season or show based on your mission or intent
> Curate elements of a performance with the audience's experience in mind

In previous chapters, you have learned about the roles of the production team and designers. You understand production elements such as lights, sound, scenery, props, costumes, and media. Now it is time to weave these elements together for the actual performance.

Early in this book, we discussed the creative brief and how vital it is to the overall success of the production. Part of the brief should have discussed the scope of the production and the intended audience experience. How involved a production team and designers become will depend on the budget type and production scope. As a new choreographer, understanding the differences between the production levels of a dance festival, a site-specific exhibit, or the world premiere of a long-running performance supports your success.

In this chapter, you will develop a stronger appreciation for the different levels of technical support for specific productions. Also discussed is the audience experience. While creating your masterpiece may be your main focus, without an audience, your work will not be appreciated. In curating your audience's experience, you will be creating an audience not just for a singular performance but also developing a following for a future production.

Production Scope

As a choreographer, you may find yourself self-producing or being hired to create a work for a specific event. Many choreographers begin creating work at their dance studios and then continue in their college dance programs. From there, aspiring choreographers typically begin submitting for festivals to build their reputations and repertoires. From the increased visibility, choreographers may then be booked for residencies or hired for larger projects.

While some choreographers may create exclusively for ballet companies or commercial hip-hop videos, in recent years, more choreographers are crossing over between concert and commercial dance and working in various venues including cruise ships, Las Vegas shows, film, commercials, and ballet and contemporary dance companies. Due to the huge range of potential opportunities for choreographers today, it is important to know what you are stepping into and what the expectations are for each performance type.

Mixed Bill

A common production for the concert and commercial dance worlds is a **mixed bill**, or a collection of pieces in one production. A **repertory dance company** has many works in its library to select from when scheduling a season. They may not have a resident choreographer. Instead their artistic director hires several choreographers to help build a body of work to create a season. They can also create new work themselves, but pieces are meant to be repeated to create different programming. Most works are adaptable for most venues but could need a different production scope.

Lighting

Look for a venue with a rep plot (see chapter 7), which is versatile and adaptable for different performances, or prepare a design that is flexible enough to accommodate each choreographer's vision. Decisions about lighting need to be considered from the director or artistic director's position to ensure full inclusion of each work. Good lighting designers are savvy enough to know how to repurpose instruments while using lighting methods that make each work have a look of its own. The more versatile the infrastructure, the easier this is to accomplish. Cho-

Production Scope and Audience Experience   **145**

> ### ALVIN AILEY AMERICAN DANCE THEATER
>
> The Alvin Ailey American Dance Theater is a prominent **repertory** company that is a conglomerate of two companies and many schools and community programs. Alvin Ailey's most prominent work is **Revelations**. When the company performs, they present a wide range of dances created by different choreographers. A quick visit to their website shows not only the current dances being performed in a season but also the variety of past works.
>
>
> Rommel Demano/Getty Images
>
> Famous work choreographed by Alvin Ailey, *Revelations*.

reographers also may make adjustments if specific lighting looks are not available when performing in a new venue.

Each production requires the original lighting plot to be rethought with the instrumentation that's there. If the rep plot is not sufficient for an existing plot, a rental package of lighting equipment may be required.

Sound

Mixed-bill productions rely on playback for each piece or a written score that live musicians perform. There could be extensive work preparing music or tracks, especially if original composition is included. All tracks would need to be leveled or equalized (EQd), and programmed into the playback application. Musicians may need to be hired, given rehearsal time and space, and worked into the technical rehearsal process. The venue's infrastructure can affect the production approach and lead the decision-making process, especially when recreating existing work, because the goal would be to recreate, as faithfully as possible, the original work.

Digital Media

In a repertory company producing mixed-bill concerts, the digital media department and their designs could be the most dynamic of all your tech. Projections are a cost-effective and easy way to enhance your stage presence without needing a lot of heavy and expensive scenery. If you can project some nice background images or video, your visual aesthetic increases several times over immediately. More advanced projection and media integrations can be custom-made backgrounds created in time with the dance to allow an "interaction" between the dancer (or dancers) and the projections. It's simple enough to carry a hard drive or laptop from venue to venue. The expense for this will be upfront in having it created. On the other hand, if the venue isn't outfitted with projection capability, you might just skip this altogether.

Sets and Props

You or your company may have a basic stage setup that you can use repeatedly for almost any kind of dance show. Maybe you rely on a blank stage with plenty of room to dance, and you gather a few appropriate hand props as required over the years. And maybe you have something a little more visually interesting, like boxes or risers that offer levels to the dancers and can be used in just about any performance. The key to the designs is to be discreet, nondescript, and adaptable. If you build an inventory of stock scenery and common props, you can focus your energy and money on integrating the unique elements of future productions while pulling from your existing resources for most of your needs. For both physical and digital scenery, it is important to remember that the dance is about the dancer, and the environment should exist to support the choreography.

Makeup and Hair

Less is more when it comes to hair and makeup in a repertory company. Changing hairstyles mid-performance is a tricky thing, especially if wigs are involved. The reset and prep time for wigs is lengthy. Simple hairdos and easy changes from a low ponytail to a bun with real hair are not difficult and can give dynamic looks in a simple and time-efficient manner. Corrective makeup can be applied to just about any piece and keeps things simple. Be careful and intentional about anything beyond this, because you might overwhelm the cast and crew.

Evening-Length Productions

The performance you're creating may not be a collection of smaller pieces; instead, it might be a large-scale **evening-length production** that stands alone. These evening-length productions can be performed only once or can become a piece in your repertoire and tour to various locations and venues. Productions like this can vary in scale themselves, from a touring production of a Broadway show, to a Cirque du Soleil show, to a lower-budget evening-length premiere.

This can be the largest scale and most expensive type of dance production. Especially for large touring productions, the casts can be large and the costumes most extravagant (and may need to be a specific type or period). Because the venue is likely large, all the technical elements will be expanded: You will need more lights, more speakers, more media, and so forth. For this type of show, you will need to think big. Larger audiences mean the performers need technical elements such as lighting to direct the audience's attention. At this scale, you will be working with professional designers.

Lighting

Unless the production is taking place in the same venue as the previous mounting, the existing lighting plot will need to be recreated in the new venue, or a new lighting design will need to be created. There may be too many variables from location to location for the lighting plot to translate, especially when considering scale (large venue versus small venue, indoor venue versus outdoor venue). This is not to say, however, that the cuing and overall look cannot persist in each iteration. It is more a matter of relocating instruments, perhaps renting or buying new ones, or reconfiguring based on power, space, and position. As opposed to a repertory show, where each piece may need different lighting considerations, an evening-length production has

Evening-length productions are often grand in scale.

the potential for higher production value because the decisions are all dedicated to the singular work. Choreographers need to talk with lighting designers in new venues to make any necessary changes.

The lighting design for this type of production will likely be of the highest production value, including any possible lighting equipment and methods. The lights may move as much as the dancers do. Coordinating with the designer will support the artistic vision.

Sound

You may be at the mercy of the venue for the direction you take for sound design when remounting something. You will want to maintain the original score or soundtrack, but you may not be able to include live musicians. You might have to record them or resurrect a previous recording. If you are performing in a familiar venue, or have performed this piece in this space before, the process will be easier as you have already figured out how to be successful.

Sound design is a very precise, often finicky science. At this level, sound designers do not just throw a playlist together. Multiple elements need to be considered to ensure the sound is appropriate for the performance. Is the music live? How large is the band or orchestra? Is there acting or speaking involved? How about singing? How big is the venue—200 seats or 2,000? Is the performance held indoors or outdoors? There are major infrastructure considerations to be made and efforts should be made to keep the stage mix reasonable for the dancers while creating a house mix for the audience that is comfortable and clear.

Digital Media

The great thing about projections and media in a repertoire is that after you have them designed and paid for, you should own them outright and never have to pay for them again. If you hold on to them too long, the physical media becomes damaged, lost, corrupted, or even outdated! Make sure to back up any digital media you have, including your music and sound.

Until recently, scenery and props would have been most critical to the physical storytelling of a narrative dance, but today projections and media are being integrated into or replacing the scenic department entirely! There may be a large animatronic prop or some wagons that roll onstage periodically through a pop music concert with dancers, but the stage will likely be configured around an LED wall or curtain display that can change from one song to the next instantaneously. You could be dancing on a beach one moment and literally standing in front of an iceberg the next. Even traditional ballets like *The Nutcracker* can have a digital makeover in the scenery department. How efficient and simple would it be to have that Christmas tree grow on screen versus in a more traditional manner? Season after season, that gag would get cheaper, too—you don't need as many crew, there is less physical material to load in and out, and there is no maintenance on the mechanics and paint.

Sets and Props

The most challenging part of overseeing sets and props in a repertoire is finding space to store them all. As an independent artist, storing large items will likely be nearly impossible, so if you develop a repertoire, focus on other areas for production value. The university you attend or a professional company with their own studio space may have room to store a set or some stock scenery and a modest number of props for repeated use. Even a school or dance institution has to be judicious about storage. Space comes at a premium, and when the decision comes down to studio or practice space versus storage space for some platforms and hula hoops, the former will always win. It might be possible to find an industrial park where you could get a great deal on a space that could have rehearsal and performance space in the front and some storage in the back, but this is becoming increasingly difficult to find, especially for a reasonable cost.

DEFINING YOUR BRAND

Some companies have developed a brand with a signature look. If you want to be known and recognized, you may think of using unique scenery, media integration, audio, or logo, or you may even be known for site-specific work. Look up the following companies and see how they make themselves stand out: Chunky Move, MOMIX, Pilobolus, DIAVOLO | Architecture in Motion, and BANDALOOP.

Makeup and Hair

At this scale, and on the largest stages, makeup and hair play a critical role in dancer expression and aesthetic. Everything, including makeup and hair, is just bigger (bolder, brighter, more saturated, and even exaggerated) in the narrative evening-length productions. What would look silly on the street looks quite natural and is even difficult at times to discern from the cheap seats in a 2,000-seat opera house.

A makeup design is simple enough to repeat on just about anyone (not considering the adaptations for skin tones), but you never know what hairstyles will be en vogue the next time you produce your repertoire. Having said that, you may want to design so that hair is less important or buy some wigs that can be reused. But, again, you have to consider storage, and unless treated well, wigs won't last long on the shelf.

Festival Performances

For both new choreographers and experienced creatives, a **festival** setting is a great way to showcase work to a large, like-minded audience. In terms of scope, a festival is usually a mixed-bill production, but each work is submitted from a unique context and creator. When each work is created with a separate vision in mind, the evening may not have a clear flow, but the audience is able to see a wide variety of performances. Sometimes there is a theme or criteria for works that are submitted, but for the most part, programming is based more on who applied to the festival and less on the content of each submission.

There are large, nationally established festivals, like Jacob's Pillow Dance Festival, Joyce Theatre's American Dance Platform, and the Fall for Dance Festival in New York City, all of which attract established companies and choreographers and allow a more in-depth production value for performance. Others are regional and are accessible for both experienced and emerging choreographers to apply to. For example, the Palm Desert Choreography Festival in Southern California has divisions for both professional and preprofessional dancers and allows choreographers from around the world to showcase work. There are also plenty of small, independent festivals created by dance companies in every major city where choreographers can come together in their local dance community to showcase their work.

In any capacity, the festival setting is unique production-wise because of the wide variety of creators involved. The collaboration between production designers and choreographers may necessarily be less because of the nature of the production. Designers have not been to every step of each work's creation process. Instead, the choreographer brings the finished work to present at the festival and must coordinate only at the very end of the creation process with the lighting, sound, and set designers to bring their work to life onstage. Depending on the type of festival, the production elements available to a choreographer for the performance may vary. If it is many short pieces, there might not be much room for play, but a large festival with fewer, more substantial works involved may have more technical elements available for use.

Lighting

In a festival setting, the lights will "focus" on the dancing. After all, it's dancing and choreography that probably got you into the festival in the first place. Because of this, lights will be less important to your overall production design.

Sound

Most likely, there will be less discussion about design and more discussion about engineering—playback, setting levels, and timing. Festivals generally require submitting your playback tracks by a certain date, in a certain file format, and with a certain way of naming the files. You may be offered a microphone if there is any talking, Q&A, or a curtain speech.

Digital Media

Digital media is doable as long as the festival supports it. The venue will send out tech requirements and options well before you attend, so make sure you read this paperwork closely and plan accordingly.

Sets and Props

If less were ever more when discussing sets and props, it would be in a festival environment. Just consider transporting any scenic element or prop in your personal vehicle. Now multiply that by the type of set you see in your head, times the number of dancers who hold props, times the number of pieces in your set, and it's easy to see the appeal of keeping it simple. See the note from the lighting section. This is an opportunity to show off your dance skills. Literally no one ever went to a dance festival because the scenery was so amazing. It is manageable to take along a prop or two if they fit in your vehicle and are required in the dance. Be smart here. While you juggle your festival tote and water bottle as you search your email on your cellphone, the festival coordinator at check-in will not be concerned or interested in assisting you if you drop all your props at the door.

Makeup and Hair

Changing rooms and makeup mirrors might not be available, so consider whether you want to put on all that glitter and glam at the hotel and walk down the street or across the campus in full onstage makeup. Again, refer to the venue notes as you plan your trip to the festival.

PREMIERE

The first public performance of a dance work, also known as its **premiere**, can be an important part of the art of dance. Sometimes, the press is invited to the premiere, and if the work receives accolades, it can propel the company, the dancers in the work, and the choreographer's work into the public eye, giving all those involved more career opportunities. For companies, the premiere also can help with marketing their shows. The fact that a show is a premiere can be packaged for an audience as an opportunity to be the first to see a new work.

In a premiere, you can create the lighting, sound, set and props, media, and hair and makeup designs. Every choice in a new production will be unique, so make sure you are intentional with your decisions and expenditures. Premieres come in all budgets, so be creative and find a designer who can work with you from the very beginning of development. Who knows what you will discover!

Site-Specific and Installation Performances

Performances that are created for a specific space (often not a theatre space) are called **site-specific** works. An **installation** is when a work originally created for the stage or another site is "installed" in a new, often unconventional site. Some performances aren't meant to take place in a conventional theatre or stage. Site-specific and installation performances may take place outdoors, in homes, in nature, or in other nontraditional performance spaces. In both cases, as it was mentioned before, dance can and does occur everywhere. Any production elements added to a performance space should add value to an already invaluable thing: dance. The art of dance does not depend on these things but should thrive in their midst. To dance is necessary but where and how is only secondary.

However, with site-specific work, the *where* and the *how* take a different type of precedence. Site-specific dance aims to break down conventions regarding what theatrical elements are needed for dance to exist. This breakdown of "the standards" challenges the status quo beyond using lighting, sound, and scenic design. It also introduces what the relationship between performance and audience ought to be. In a traditional setting, there are specific guidelines for what the role of the audience is during a performance. For site-specific work, the audience brings an unpredictability that must be considered.

FLASH MOBS

One of the most dominant subgenres of site-specific dance to emerge in recent years is the flash mob. Dancers and choreographers are establishing companies dedicated to this (not) impromptu style. Have you heard of flashmobamerica.com? You have now! Theatre students effectively execute a flash mob in the quad, raising awareness of an upcoming musical performance. Onlookers get a surprise and enjoy the (song and) dance. Flash mobs may be marketing stunts or be presented as a unique performance unto themselves.

MARC AMEEL

Theatre students stage a flash mob on the quad to raise awareness of an upcoming performance.

Visit HK*Propel* to complete assignment 10.1, Planning the Audience Experience.

Audience Experience

As the production creator, you not only are responsible for the movement and production elements on the stage but also are in control of the audience's entire experience inside and outside the theatre. As you dream big, you must also think about how your choices influence your audience experience. From the big picture when you are programming your season, to the impact of programming your production, to the little details for the audience's experience inside and outside the theatre, the entire audience experience comes from intentional choices a creator makes.

As choreographers, dancers, and designers, we create art because it is who we are and what drives us. But we always have to be mindful that what we do is a visual art that is meant to be seen. For better or worse, being seen is the culmination of the work. Without audiences, we would not be able to do what we do. To put it bluntly, in most venues they pay our bills. There is also something beautiful and magical when a performer is up on the stage and can feel the audience's energy. That energy is sometimes the most important element and is the final piece of the performance puzzle. All the collaborators work for months and can occasionally lose sight of what is happening onstage. However, an audience will let you know if you have a hit or a miss. Most audiences are not shy about expressing their opinions, good and bad. Artists will wait for hours after opening night for the reviews to come out. Having our work seen is also the most influential way to inspire the next generation of artists and performers.

When creating your initial creative brief, the interaction between the performers and the audience needs to be considered. What is the overall audience experience? Will you have traditional ticketed assigned seating or possibly unassigned seating? Is the audience stationary as the dancers perform, or does the audience walk through the space, experiencing the performance from different angles? Is the performance space a dinner theatre, and where does the audience sit in relation to the dance (theatre in the round, proscenium, or a runway style)? Or is the performance livestreamed, meaning the camera angles and cueing need to be choreographed as well as the dance? Most have experienced the traditional theatre setting with the audience in assigned seats watching the performance on a proscenium stage, but choreographers willing to challenge the status quo have shifted the experiences to create different impacts on the audience.

Planning a Season

Unless you own a theatre, your concert will be part of a **season** or series of events in a particular venue.

When planning a season of theatrical work that will include dance performances, it is important to remember that dance should never be an afterthought but a vital and important part of the season.

Dance performances in college programs tend to be later in the term or semester since the time to plan, cast, and choreograph is packed into a relatively short time. If there are student choreographers presenting their work, they need all the time they can have. The same can be said for student designers learning their craft. They need the time to work and develop their vision. Dance performances need to be fully supported by the tech and design teams, whether it be faculty, staff, or students. Where the dance performance is in relation to the theatre or music performances is an important conversation to have.

Whenever a venue is a shared space between different performance types—music, choir, dance, musicals, theatre, and so on—the needs for each production will vary. This is something to consider when looking at how much time you may be able to book in the space for the tech run, dress rehearsals, and performances. Theatres have crews that can flip the space, but it takes time to remove the previous show's scenery and lighting and then install a dance floor, bring in any built scenery, and rehang lighting. Ensuring the crew has enough turnaround time will be a discussion for the venue production team because this will inform your process and schedule.

If you are developing your own company, your season likely will include performances in multiple venues. As you are building your company or repertoire of work, think strategically about what performance opportunities and locations will best serve your goals. You may do several low-tech lecture demonstrations to provide performance opportunity and community outreach. You may enter your work in a few festivals and then at the end of your season, produce one full-scale show with all the bells and whistles.

When planning your season, remember your budget! While everyone loves to perform frequently, you might not have the funds to support this. As a young choreographer, look for opportunities throughout the year to collaborate with other artists to maximize your finances.

Lastly, be respectful of your dancers' time and other obligations, especially if you are not paying a full salary. Many dancers pick up work during the holidays with a local show like *The Nutcracker*, and if you plan performances or rehearsals during this time, you may lose dancers due to their need to make money.

Seasons of theatrical work often feature productions of *The Nutcracker* in December.

Programming a Production

When you are dealing with a performance that has multiple pieces as opposed to just one piece, you need to think about what your show order will be. Creating the production is like planning a holiday meal. You invite people in with something that catches their eye. Then you offer an opening first course, a main course in the middle, and leave them with some dessert. The biggest goal in creating a show order is to keep in mind what you want your audience to experience and when those experiences happen. Here is a list of questions that you should think about as you are creating the order of pieces:

› What is the first and final image or thought that you want them to experience?
› Do you have several different styles of dance represented in your production? Or at least different feelings and vibes throughout the performance? Where are your light or less emotional moments and where are your heavy or more thought-provoking moments? These different pieces or moods need to be placed strategically to keep the audience engaged and let them breathe after a very heavy piece.
› Are you going to have an intermission or multiple intermissions? How long will they be? Will intermission be 10 minutes, 15 minutes, or more than that?
› What are the major scenic, costume, or lighting shifts? How much time do these take to accomplish?
› Do you have dancers who are in multiple dances? Do you want them dancing in back-to-back pieces, or does that not matter?
› A good rule is to have a maximum of two minutes between pieces. If you can cut it down to one minute, that is ideal. You should only give your audience enough time to check their programs. If you take too long, they get restless and disengaged and pull out their phones or wrapped candies. Or they leave altogether and might not come back.
› Do you have pieces that are longer than 20 minutes? If you do, think about giving the audience a break by either having an inter-

mission after a long piece or placing a shorter piece after and then going into intermission.
› What is your last piece? What do you want the audience to experience as the very last thing and usually the most memorable moment?
› Are you doing bows after each piece? Or is there one large group bow at the end of the show? Or both?

As you can see from the list of questions, there is no absolute right or wrong way to program a production. The key is being thoughtful of your choices, your artistic vision, logistical considerations, and the overall audience experience.

Curating a Performance

Everything that happens on the stage is under the control of theatre staff. Everything that happens outside of the proscenium is someone else's job (house manager or patron services) because they are in charge of the patron experience. An audience member's experience from when they hear about the performance, walk into the building, and leave the theatre is part of your production and is driven by your creative vision.

Now you have developed a program order to support both the audience experience and logistical considerations of the technical staff and dancers. The experience for the audience begins before the dancers take the stage and continues after the final bow. As soon as the audience begins to interact with the venue, the event has begun. If you are in charge of the overall feel of the production, deciding on what the preshow, inside the theatre, and post-show aesthetics will be is part of your job. Here are some questions to consider:

Preshow
› How are you going to bring the audience into the performance and prepare them for what they're going to see? Is it big and spectacular, or are the dancers warming up onstage (casual and intimate)?
› Are you letting the audience see the scenery (take in information), or will it be a surprise?
› How can you build anticipation and create the right tone and increase audience engagement?
› Are there materials in the lobby to inform the audience about you, your dancers, the company, future performances, where they can find you on social media, photos of the cast, bios of the performers, and so on other than what is in the program, or is it just a program?
› Do you want to adhere to or disrupt traditional expectations of how a show begins?

Inside the Theatre
› Will there be assigned seats? Is there a VIP section? If it's open seating, how is this being handled by the house manager?
› Is the curtain down so the stage setting is a surprise for the audience, or is it up and we see the stage, scenery, even dancers?
› Is there a fourth wall, or not? Do dancers move in and out of the audience to include them, or is the audience watching from the outside?
› Is there spoken word? Does the director, choreographer, or someone else speak before the performance?
› Is there an announcer? Is the program projected between each piece? Are there houselights that go up and down between dances, or if it is a larger show, is there an intermission? If so, how is the transition into the intermission?
› Is there a Q&A or lecture component at the end or beginning of the show? Grants many often require interaction like this.
› Who is involved with any speaking components, and how do you handle any audience questions, runners, standing microphone, and so on?

Post-Show
› Is there a meet-and-greet area for performers to meet family and friends?
› Is there a place where the audience can talk with performers? Is this structured or casual?
› Is there a formal or informal reception after opening night to thank donors?
› What is the overall impression you want your audience to walk away with, and how do you get them to be interested in supporting your work in the future?

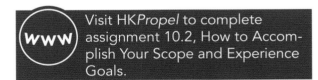

Visit HK*Propel* to complete assignment 10.2, How to Accomplish Your Scope and Experience Goals.

Summary

A major component of the creative brief is deciding the production scope. When starting out, you may be a part of a bigger production. But if you stay in the industry long enough, you could be the one calling all the shots. As a choreographer, understanding how your work is being showcased will influence your artistic decisions.

While it may be attractive to stay focused just on your own choreography, it is important to understand where your work fits into the full audience experience. Walk yourself through all aspects of being an audience member for your event. You can create the most brilliant choreography but all your work will fall flat if you ignore how you want to engage the audience before, during, and after your show.

11

Integrating Elements Onstage

Key Terms
color temperature
EQ
gain
ground row
high-side lights
hue
routing
SFX
sky cyc
volume

Vipin Kumar/Hindustan Times via Getty Images

155

LEARNING OBJECTIVES

After reading this chapter, you will be able to do the following:

- Recognize the elements of a stage and performance venue that may affect your performance
- Identify key components of lighting, sound, scenery, props, media, and costumes that can directly influence your performance
- Acknowledge what production components tend to be beneficial for dance or adversely affect the production
- Make educated decisions and collaborations to ensure the production element integration ultimately benefits your work rather than overpowering or hindering it

Once you've established the scale and intended impact of your performance, it's time to put the production elements in place to make your vision come to life. At this point in the production process, most of the administrative and business dealings are either complete or on autopilot. And even if they are not, your attention must now be fully on the final phase of preparation.

Design choices have been made, the costumes and props have been purchased or built, the lights are focused, the sound has been checked, and the projections calibrated. All this happened during the days and weeks dedicated to load-in while you were leading the cast in rehearsals and having those one-on-one meetings with the designers to make the final adjustments before this phase.

Now, theory meets practice, and everything you thought you wanted will prove its practicality in the next several days. This chapter will take us through the production elements. It will show how you can effectively integrate their components to realize your vision and avoid conflict with it. Much of what is suggested in this chapter can happen during the build phase or the load-in at the venue, and every choice affects the impact of your performance on the audience.

Stage Considerations

Walk the performance space. Then walk it again. You should do this immediately upon procuring the space, because your rehearsals should be spiked to the stage (or performance space) dimensions. It is also a good idea to take pictures of the performance space and venue so you can remember where the entrances and exits are; see where the dressing rooms are located in relationship to the stage; see how much wing space there is for people, staging, props, and quick-change booths; note how close the legs are; review what the sight lines look like from the audience and backstage; and evaluate any other aspect that may affect your choreography or staging.

It is important to know the performance space well because its parameters might require you to change your work or eliminate a segment in the show altogether. Although in preproduction we try to answer all technical questions before arrival, there is no substitute for walking the space. Spaces can change in real life more than you can imagine on paper. As reality dictates movement, the choreographer may have to add a phrase to allow the dancer more time for the crossover, or the stage space is smaller and an exaggerated movement such as a leap may need to be reduced but must hold the same emotional impact. Touring companies may have to eliminate a dance sequence altogether because the space simply can't provide the necessary technical support—such as when a dancer is flown out over the stage like Peter Pan or Cirque Du Soleil and the venue can't support such an elaborate presentation safely. This is also why a touring company will have several options in their repertory; you substitute one for another to accommodate for that particular stop on the tour and still have a complete show to present.

A venue that presents dance probably has a sprung floor installed or has one on hand to lay out before your performance. It is important to note what kind of floor surface you will be performing on. (See chapter 7 for a refresher on flooring for performance spaces.) This is probably the most important thing for a dance production to consider. A sprung floor is about the best you can expect. A hard floor with Marley will not have the same give, and it will be harder on the body, though it will be

Integrating Elements Onstage   **157**

nice for spinning and sliding. A polished wooden floor would be great for tap, but not much else. Do you have your own Marley that you can bring and lay down in someone else's space? A concrete, tile, linoleum, Steeldeck, or rough wooden floor or platform each has disadvantages and risk factors. You may find that if the venue cannot change the floor options, you need to adapt your choreography so that dancers are not executing moves that could be potentially dangerous or unnecessarily hard on their bodies. This may be especially true in a site-specific or found-space scenario.

Indoor venues have the advantage of climate control, at least theoretically, so temperature and humidity should be relatively comfortable, and you should clearly understand what you will encounter. Even if the venue is prone to high temperatures, you can have extra ice packs, electrolyte drinks, and fans to help combat heat exhaustion. Humidity is another thing altogether and may require shortening your performance. You can always pack more blankets, mats, and layered clothing to combat a cold venue. Indoor venues will typically have a stable technical infrastructure, meaning that the lighting system should be reliable, the speakers should work, and the changing rooms would provide adequate privacy.

Performing outdoors is always a gamble because the weather can be unpredictable. Just because you scheduled your performance in the summer does not mean you won't get rained out! The weather you may be used to at home will likely not be what you encounter if your production is moved anywhere else. Watch the weather forecast constantly, and plan for contingencies if you choose to perform outdoors. That could mean just having sneakers to combat light rain and prevent slipping, or it could mean wearing an entirely different costume made

Dancers exploring found space.

of lightweight, breathable fabrics in a heatwave. An outdoor venue may have portable, rented, or temporary technical infrastructure. These setups are prone to more issues because they are put up and taken down, often the day of the performance, and can have more fail points. Lighting and projection is not as effective outdoors in the daylight as it is indoors, where there is simply more control. A high-quality LED wall could be a good solution here. Sound can easily get lost outdoors or just be difficult to mix against the ambient noise—again there is less (or no) control compared to an indoor venue. And indoor dressing rooms could be available near the stage, but that is not a given. Warm-weather locations or professional amphitheaters may be the exception and have permanent weatherproof gear and a better layout for nearly year-round outdoor performances.

Altitude is another factor that can drastically affect your performance. If you are a sea level–based company on tour and find yourself at 4,000 feet or more above sea level, you will not have the same lung capacity and endurance as you do at home. You may need to schedule a few extra days in the venue city before your gig to allow for acclimation to the altitude. If this is not an option, consider breaking up your dances or plan to perform shorter pieces.

Scenery and Props

Scenery and props are usually designed and grouped together because the world of the dance should be consistent. The set is the environment in which the dance takes place: an urban street-corner, a 1950s diner, or the surface of Mars, to name a few. *Props* is usually shorthand for the term *hand props*, which refers to anything a dancer might hold in their hands: an umbrella, a waiter's tray, or a space-ray-gun. But what about things like trash cans, diner booths, and Martian rocks? These are all props as well and must seamlessly integrate into the scenery, so they are an extension of the scenic design. Therefore, an urban street corner + trash cans + umbrellas = unified sets and props. Traditionally, the scenic designer will call out or refer to the trash cans on their design plot, and then a prop master would source the trash cans. Common objects like this can usually be purchased and then distressed or modified to fit the final look. The umbrellas may be an integral part of the dance, so the choreographer would identify them from the beginning. This item may just go directly to the prop master, though the scenic designer may be consulted on the appearance. And if the umbrellas need to be stowed in the trash cans, further conversation between the choreographer, prop master, and scenic designer can reveal how they should do this, which may influence the final construction or modification of the trash cans. Perhaps the lid needs to be hinged or attached in a certain way. Perhaps the trash cans need to be padded inside with foam at the bottom so they don't make a loud noise when the umbrellas drop in. All these details will be approved by all three stakeholders and executed by the prop master or their department, depending on the size of the company. That is the effort it takes to add just two elements to the environment. This much consideration must be given for *everything* that ends up on the stage.

Your attention to detail is key. Regardless of your budget or circumstances, you may have colleagues to help. If your show is so bare bones that you only have the dance cast to assist, that is enough. The dancers can be excellent partners. You can bounce ideas off them. You can get their feedback on how the scenery and props are working together and how they are influencing the dance itself. If your cast is not outspoken, you should encourage them to participate in the refinement of the sets and props, if for no other reason than making the dance space as safe as possible.

The scenic and prop construction teams build with a safety-first mindset (or at least they should, and if they don't, find new ones). But there is always room for feedback. That's not to say that everything can be recreated from the ground up once you enter tech week, but notes can always lead to those tweaks that make the final touch. Sanding down a rough edge, applying some glow tape, or greasing a squeaky wheel can make a world of difference in the end. In the best of circumstances, you will have designers, crew, and staff to help identify those notes, and, in some cases, they will make and execute notes that improve things overnight that you will never even know about!

Your primary consideration as a member of the scenic and prop construction team must be how the dancers will be able to move around the performance space. Elaborate scenery may look great from the audience's standpoint but can severely limit the usable dancing space. Keep in mind while an actor walks around a performance space dancers leap, jump, kick, and throw their limbs through the space.

Dance concerts are often on empty stages because of the following:

› Dance can require a lot of space, and anything on the floor or in the way can be a hazard (and the larger the cast, the more space is required).

› Nothing should be added to production unless it adds value.

Notice the utility panel on the upstage wall of the theater. The choreographer has opted to fly out all the soft goods (drapes) to allow the most danceable stage space possible.

› In a digital world, projections and LED walls can provide excellent settings without occupying valuable dance floor space.
› Sets are expensive to build, move, and store.

The type of show you are doing will dictate how critical physical scenery is to the overall production. A show in a found space is interesting because of the improvised nature—adding shop-built scenery to it is probably inappropriate. A well-conceived prop or two could add something, but a full set won't. If you are creating a dance for film, however, the circumstances change, because the scope has now changed and so has the production value.

If you are shooting in the desert and you need a crashed flying saucer in the background because otherwise your dancers just look like green people in spandex, you have a reasonable request. This same sci-fi–themed dance may be better served by a digital backdrop on a proscenium stage, where the dance floor is limited. And then, perhaps a scaled-down version of the same alien ship could be suitable for a staged environment. Other considerations must include the following:

› Is the entire dance production set in the same locale?
› Does the saucer need to move on and off the stage?
› Do the dancers ever interact with the set?
› Does the set need to incorporate lighting and sound or other technical elements?

Context makes a difference, and one question always leads to another. Remember the most important question: Does the production element add to or subtract from the dancing? In theatre, directors often start adding props and costume accessories and asking for lots of technical elements late in the process if they feel the acting isn't good enough, if they've lost their vision, or if they are just too inexperienced at what they are doing. To avoid this, hold the dancers and the dancing above all else. If the scenery or the prop doesn't need to be there, don't add it. Sometimes, less is more.

Scenery or set elements can add beauty and visual interest and help accentuate the story of a dance piece when it is appropriate to add them.

Set elements can add beauty and visual interest to a dance performance.

But you always have to consider what the scenery or set elements do for the space itself. Once a choreographer adds a piece of onstage scenery, there is less available dance space and issues of where to store it before and after the dance come up. If the choreographer desires a hanging set element, the floor is clear, but other problems can arise. This is why it's important for all the collaborators to talk about scenery or set elements from the very beginning of the process. If communication breaks down, the choreographer is not educated about technical aspects of theatre, or a choreographer changes their mind in the middle of the process or at the last minute, things can go horribly wrong.

The best collaborations are ones that fully support the creative vision. The image from Solitary Moments explored the feeling of being trapped and hopeless with what was happening in the world and the world around the dancers. The set designer created an isolating space, and the lighting designer added lighting that accentuated both the choreography and the set pieces. What they created together is greater than what could have been created if they hadn't collaborated.

ADMIT WHEN YOU DON'T UNDERSTAND

As a choreographer, it is important to educate yourself about all the components of the theatrical process. You don't have to become an expert in everything, but you do need to know enough to be able to communicate with your collaborators. A young choreographer may have little technical knowledge to understand exactly what the designers are showing when they bring technical drawings and ground plans to production meetings. The classic mistake is pretending you know what they are saying by just nodding and agreeing. If you don't know how to read and understand the measurements, you may end up with a set piece much bigger than imagined. By the time you are in tech and the set is hung up in the air, you may be stuck with it. Scenery items rarely can change in their size once completed, and your dancers are not going to grow overnight to match the enormous set piece that seems to be consuming the stage.

This scene from *Solitary Moments* (2016) illustrates how set pieces and light can support the artistic vision. (Choreography and costume design: Kerri Canedy; set design: Todd P. Canedy; light design: Dan Gallagher)

Visit HK*Propel* to complete assignment 11.1, Learning From Great Examples of Integration in Dance Productions.

Lighting

In chapter 7 we discussed components of lighting technology and basic design. Now that you are in the performance space and starting to see the production elements come together, one of the first elements to take note of will be the lighting design. The principles of a successful lighting design can be considered within the following two categories:

› The function of lighting
  › *Visibility:* Can we see the action of performers? Better yet, is the visibility or invisibility supporting the story? Sometimes we don't want to see the action.
  › *Revelation of form:* How is the audience presented with the subject matter or dancers? Some designers call this *selective focus*, the visual tour guide through the story.
  › *Mood*: Lighting has a direct influence on the overall feeling of the piece, and how one manipulates this design element can create dramatic emotional responses from the audience.
  › *Composition*: This principle refers to the overall look: Is it pleasing to the eye?
  › *Reinforcing the story:* Does the lighting support the story being told in the dance?
› Quality of light
  › *Distribution*: Where is the light placed, and where is the subject matter it is lighting? For example, a lighting instrument may be placed above the audience, aimed at the dancer on the stage, providing front lighting. At the same time, another instrument may be placed downstage left for angled, or off-axis, front lighting on the dancer, providing a dynamic combination of light and shadow, color, and focus.

- *Intensity*: How bright is the light?
- *Movement*: Every light has to come up (turned on) and go down (turned off). In addition, the lights themselves may move to create additional choreography. Moving instruments run by an electrical system are called *intelligent lights*. A spotlight is a moving light powered by a human, you see these frequently in musical theatre or in ice skating.
- *Color*: This refers to the **hue** or literal color of the lighting effect (as discussed in

Even the most *(a)* visually interesting physical structures are enhanced by the lighting applied to them. Observe how the aesthetic, mood, and production value are affected by adding *(b)* lighting to the set. The vertical panels are calibrated for projection mapping, further enhancing the use and impact of the space.

chapter 6) and to the **color temperature** (warm or cool). The color qualities of the instruments used will affect the design of a dance piece.

There are three main lighting concepts. A key to successful lighting for dance is a *sidelight*. The second most important concept is using *high-sides*. And to round out the trifecta of awesome dance lighting is the effective use of a *cyc* (that big, seamless off-white muslin drape discussed in chapter 6).

Sidelight is installed as a three- or four-light system on a vertical pipe called a *boom* or *tree*, just offstage, between the legs in the wings. Figure 11.1 shows an example of this configuration. When light is directed from the wing and illuminates the dancer at a perpendicular angle to the audience's sight line, the most beautiful contours can be seen. Sidelight can make the dancer appear to glow.

Sidelight positions are typically referred to by their relative positions to the dancer's body:

› *Highs* are usually hung on the boom at about 10 feet from the deck (floor).
› *Heads* are usually hung on the boom at about 6 feet from the deck.
› *Mids* are usually somewhere around 3 to 4 feet from the deck.
› *Shins* are usually about 1 foot off the deck.

High-side lights add to the sidelight effect at an angle closer to 45 degrees from above. They are typically hung in a three-light system from a batten, truss, or pipe, as opposed to coming straight from the wings at body height. High-sides add contour to the head and shoulders. They are also very useful for adding texture to a design. By putting a template, or gobo, in a Leko lighting instrument, the light beam can be broken up and made to appear patterned. This is often considered more visually interesting than a typical circular field or light on the stage floor and can also create dynamic shadows as the dancers pass through the light beams.

POPULAR LIGHTING EFFECTS

- Moving lights can add motion.
- Templates or gobos can add texture, shadow, and mood.
- Haze allows the audience to see the light beams, which can be a very striking effect.
- Follow spots add emphasis to the subject of the dance and can draw the audience's attention to a specific location (even distracting the audience from seeing something on another part of the stage).
- Lights focused on the audience directly ("blinders") can have the same effect, temporarily "blinding" the audience as the stage changes or dancers enter and exit the stage. When the light dims, there is a new visual in front of the audience.

Cyc lights refer to any lighting used to illuminate their eponymous counterpart: the cyclorama drape ("cyc" for short)—the massive, light- or neutral-colored upstage drape that provides a blank canvas for backdrop lighting and visual effects. Though

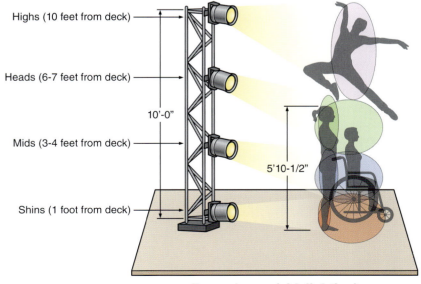

Figure 11.1 Dance boom.

any lighting instrument could be used to light a cyc, there is an instrument type created specifically for this purpose. Regardless of whether they are modern color-changing LED instruments or a traditional set of incandescent "cells" (one cell being an individual light source intended to work as part of a "gang" of three or more other cells to allow for color mixing) they are uniquely designed to provide a saturated wash of light across the drape. This wash is achieved by the narrow beam angle the instrument provides. These instruments are designed to be set on the floor or hung from above, within a foot or two of the cyc itself, spanning from each end of the drape across the entirety of the stage. The results are best when a "ground row" (floor-mounted strip) is combined with a "sky cyc" (hung from above).

Ground row is where the lights are set on the floor, from edge to edge of the cyc curtain. They are focused to "scrape" up the vertical face of the drape. A ground row of lights can be placed upstage (or behind) the cyc or downstage (in front) of the cyc. A ground row of lights downstage of a cyc typically requires a little 12-inch or 18-inch wall or flat of some sort so the audience can't see it. This little wall or masking is also called a *ground row*.

Sky cyc lights are hung from above the stage, in front of or behind the cyc. The advantage is that this clears stage or crossover space on the deck or floor. A ground row and sky cyc can be used together, and this usually results in the best saturation and coverage of the cyc, offers more options for effects, and isolates areas of the cyc for illumination. Advantages for lighting the cyc from the front or rear are negligible and may depend on designer preferences.

There is another tricky way to light a cyc, and that is to put all the instruments upstage of the cyc (ground row or sky cyc or both) and focus them on another cyc or light-colored drape upstage of the lighting instruments, allowing the light to bounce onto the rear of the cyc. This helps smooth out beam edges and make the light blend more evenly across the cyc. Ask your lighting designer if they want to use a bounce for the cyc, and you will earn instant respect. This concept is identical when using more contemporary LED instruments, but the construction of the instruments will be different.

What Works With Lighting

With the cyc lit, and little to no other light onstage, you can create some of the most amazing silhouettes. The drape is bright and vivid while the dancers are nearly pure black forms. Have the designer slowly draw up the sidelights and watch the contour of those featureless voids come into focus for a truly inspiring aurora outlining the muscle tone or costume of each performer. Then, snap out the cyc and use strong front lighting with full backlight to reverse your aesthetic. You will see the faces, expressions, and details of the dancers pop in a 3D-like effect (that is mostly the backlight doing the work).

What Doesn't Work With Lighting

What doesn't work is putting a primary color of light on its complementary pigment color. Consider the following examples:

> › Red light on a green costume makes everything look gray.
> › Green light on a purple costume kind of stays purple, but everything gets redder, not greener (this is science).
> › Blue light on an orange costume turns everything brown!

If the lighting designer follows the guidelines of the color wheels and knows the underlying theories, the lighting color can enhance the costumes' appearance. Usually, the goal is to complement the designs of the other departments, so lighting should make the costumes pop and the set (or dancing space) match the tone of the dance.

"FLASH AND TRASH"

In the modern stage entertainment era, there is a controversial design style: *flash and trash*. This style is characterized by a lighting designer throwing every effect and gimmick at a production for the sake of showing off the capabilities of the lighting rig, rather than designing to the aesthetic, tone, and message of the performance. They "flash" all the lights and "trash" the show. In most cases, this is the sign of a poor designer. Or perhaps the choreographer or director asked for too much, and the designer appeased them so as not to cause a tech kerfuffle. Either case is a lack of good communication and indicates a bad production. Ironically, this can work in cases where things are chaotic or intentionally distracting. There are solid cases for using "flash and trash," and that usually accompanies productions where neither the producers nor the audience are concerned with story or nuance.

The bottom line with lighting is that it should never distract from the action on the stage; it should support it. If you walk out of rehearsal thinking about the lighting and cannot remember the dance, fire your lighting designer!

Sound

It's important to be familiar with the music used in your production. Listen to the tracks or, if using live music, attend the musicians' rehearsal. (Record the rehearsal if you can, but be sure to ask for permission.) Then listen to it all again. You need to know what the production sounds like. You need to know what the dancers hear (the monitor mix), what the live audience hears (the PA), and what the world hears (a recording or stream). This means you may need to observe the rehearsal or listen to the playback from the stage, the house, and perhaps behind a monitor, maybe listening through headphones or from a control booth. Every live performance sounds different depending on what role you play. Keep in mind that louder does not mean better and being exposed to noise at levels over 70 decibels for extended periods of time may cause hearing loss.

Dancers are used to practicing with mostly poor-quality audio. Actually, *most* people listen to poor-quality audio. Why does audio quality matter? It probably does not matter to the casual listener, but if your goal is to choreograph a live dance performance, it can have a serious impact on the end production value. Do not confuse audio quality with the live mix. Also, audio quality in this sense applies only to recorded tracks; a live band or orchestra relies solely on a good live mix. Common sense should tell you that if you start with the highest-quality audio, you have the highest quality chance of delivering the highest quality product. So, when pulling media for a show, get the largest sound files you possibly can. Larger file sizes tend to imply better quality audio. Using a baseline of about 10.6 megabytes per minute ensures you are using a higher-quality uncompressed audio recording. Check the file sizes of your audio tracks, and you will know if you are listening to gold or garbage.

When assessing audio, if you are not sure about the file size, it is important that you trust your ears. If it sounds good, then that is good enough. The average person, and that includes you, cannot discern much of what a sound designer or engineer can do with their equipment. The console and the computer can analyze sound in ways most people cannot even conceive. Close your eyes and listen. If you like the way the audio sounds, that is what it should sound like for the production. It is your artistic choice at the end of the day. And no sound designer or engineer will ever be satisfied with the mix; most sound designers will ultimately find at least one thing that could have been improved.

If your dance requires sound, you have to find a way for your audience and your dancers to hear the audio. If you are doing a planned site-specific piece or an impromptu flash mob, it is OK to use a portable speaker and a cellphone for track playback. In more technical theatres, sound and lighting can be synced together electronically with common and easy-to-use modern technology. Production software like QLab can be programmed to sync an audio track with a lighting console cue list, and using time-code ("what-happens-when") automatically triggers lights to change with the beat!

Recorded audio tracks for playback are great. They save time and money. They are portable. They just work. But when available, live music for a live dance production can bring a higher production value to your performance. Assuming you have the time and money to integrate live music, *and* you have high-quality backline and sound equipment, you will need a proficient audio engineer to mix your sound. (Someone has to mix playback audio also, but it is not nearly as complex or nuanced as a live band or orchestra mix.) An oversimplification of audio signal flow states that the mix has five main parts: **gain** (loudness in), **EQ** (equalization), **SFX** (sound effects), **routing** (which speakers the sound comes out of), and **volume** (loudness out). Here are the explanations for these settings:

› *Gain:* Setting this correctly establishes whether the mix will sound good at all. It can also determine if you will destroy your equipment by pushing "too much sound" through it.

› *EQ:* Want more bass? Want to hear that spoken word section more clearly? Do it all with adjusting which wavelengths of sound are featured in the output. In other words, increase or decrease the low, mid, and high tones individually.

› *SFX:* Add reverb, or echo, or any effect that your mixer or your designer has in their inventory.

› *Routing (also called bussing):* Assign the outputs, which is where any given input will be heard. This is also where monitors and other types of mixes can be added to the overall design.

› *Volume:* The loudness of the end output. This is not a substitute for a proper mix using all the steps and tools listed previously. Louder is not better.

All these elements when considered carefully and correctly can be combined to create a score that perfectly reflects the environment you are trying to create.

CHOOSE YOUR WORDS CAREFULLY!

Listen closely to the lyrics! If a choreographer has chosen music with lyrics, it is important to know what words are being said. While the focus is predominantly on the dance movement, sometimes an explicit lyric or two can slip past everyone. Depending on your audience, explicit lyrics may need to be edited out, a clean song version found, or a program note added to warn the audience. Choreographers who work with music sung in a different language need to find a translation of the lyrics. It is possible the song's meaning for anyone who understands the language can completely change the impact of your dance.

Digital Media

Productions today increasingly rely on digital media for the scenery, using technology such as LED walls, pixel-mapping, and projection-mapping. This technology is becoming more available, economical, and user-friendly. Technically savvy choreographers and directors can apply these technologies to their productions even without having a proper designer on the team. It is always preferable to have expert designers and technicians; however, it is hard to argue against having some experience of your own. Depending on the scale of what you'd like to do with the technology, you might be able to curate a still projection, video clip, or other media source to accompany your performance.

Regardless of whether you have a designer or not, it's important to make sure any media elements included in your performance enhance the work and aren't just added for show. Because of its recent ease and availability, projections, video, or flashy media might seem like an easy and cost-effective choice to add some production value to a piece, but it's only adding value if the content reflects and enhances your vision and intention of the work. Adding technology or media because it's "cool" or "trendy" will not have the desired effect and can overpower the work you've put on the stage. However, when approached intentionally, media or video can bring more information to a work or highlight the intention by providing scenic or thematic context to the piece when it's implemented. A good way to tell if the media is overpowering or not is to have a friend, an outside eye, watch the piece while it's on the stage and get their feedback. If the audience is more inclined to watch the media elements instead of the dancers onstage, media might not be serving the piece the way you intended. If the audience is drawn even more to the dancers and the story they're creating, it's probably enhancing the world you're creating onstage and accomplishing its purpose.

Costumes

Costumes are essential in dance. They don't just help portray the story. They can add so much to the dancers' performance quality. Once a dancer puts that costume on and feels the fabric move with them, it can change their entire demeanor and inspire the dancing and storytelling. The function of a dance costume is multifaceted and depends on the vision of the work. The costume supports the physical choreography by providing additional visual movement, being restrictive and purposefully creating tension and limitations for the dancer, or being neutral. Characters and character relationships are also depicted in costume design. If you want to show a family grouping, the parents' costuming will contrast with the dancers portraying the children to demonstrate an age difference. Using color palettes to link dancers visually in groups and show relationships can be striking. With a cast of dancers where the ensemble is all in black and the main character is in white, you immediately support your choreography in highlighting the importance of a specific dancer onstage. Costumes can be used like a prop as a scarf, jacket, shoes, or possibly all the layers come off except for the nude leotard underneath.

TEST THE DYE

Dying costumes to create a unique color for your dance takes experience and time. A secret to dying fabric is that not all fabric will take the dye and make the color you want, and sometimes the dye can change the texture of the fabric. *Always* test some of your fabric first! Just imagine you are only a few days before the performance and you take all your freshly sewn costumes and dump them into the dye without testing it first. What could go wrong? If you are lucky, nothing. But there is a good probability the color won't take. If it turns out looking awful, now you don't have enough time or money to fix the mistake.

Costumes can define the setting. Without a physical or digital set, the costumes can convey the period. Costumes can depict the location. Costumes can suggest cultural context, age, status, and interests. The costume is a powerful tool for storytelling or establishing a tone. Think of the musical *West Side Story*, where there are two specific cultural groups being depicted during a specific era and location. If the costumer mixed the color palette between the Jets and the Sharks, they would not be readily identifiable by the audience. This is another example where era-specific costuming is important to establish the time and setting.

Chapter 1 discussed how costumes were used to support storytelling and define male and female characters. Depending on the dance industry and the vision for your work, you may use costumes to define gender roles. In the commercial industry, it is common to accentuate the physical attributes of men and women. In the concert dance world, the trend is to allow more flexibility with costume design. Men may be wearing skirts and women pants, and the entire cast may be a mix of designs, changing the stereotype of what men and women should wear as a costume for a dance work.

Typical base pieces for costumes include a leotard, a unitard, a biketard, pants, skirts, tutus, a bodice, tops, and dresses. Costumes can range from pedestrian, everyday looks (pants and a shirt) to a uniquely designed dance costume. If your dance is about a busy day in New York City, the costuming will probably look more business professional, but if your dance is about being an animal in nature, the costume choice may be a dyed unitard. Aesthetics are the easy part. What "works" for a production must also take into account practicality, safety, and synthesis. Can the costume fit through the set? Is the fabric slippery and dangerous? Is the color complementary to the lighting? Does the fit allow the dancer to move adequately? Regardless of the design of the costume, it must be functional for the dancer. Poorly placed decorative items, fasteners, and seams can create injury risk and limit the dancer's expressive ability.

Working with costume designers can be very rewarding, but if you are on your own for costuming, don't be afraid to trust your gut. Ultimately the dancers are players on the stage—literally during a performance and figuratively from day to day. They dance throughout the day, choosing what outfit to

Dynamic costumes creating character and mood.

Courtesy of St. Lawrence University.

THE GREEN DRESS

Imagine a beautifully choreographed large group piece where all the dancers were going to wear green. The costumes would flow, swirl, and be ethereal. You may think requesting green hues in the lights only makes sense to make everything match and enhance the effect. The light designer may have mentioned that the costumes and lighting should not "match" one another but should work together to help accentuate the colors of the costumes. You hold your ground, just knowing the extra green lighting will make all the difference in your vision. Once you see them onstage in their green dresses under the green lights, it is not the beautiful image you had thought. Instead they look like a zombie apocalypse onstage, all green and undead. This is a key lesson on how important lighting is to the overall effect on costumes. If you make one of these mistakes, swallow your pride and ask the light designer to please fix the mistake.

wear, whether to wear makeup, and how to comb their hair. And then they make a different choice the following day. You have an intuition and experience about how to costume a dance.

Costuming is a more personal and intimate technical element than lighting or sound; it is an extension of the dancer and a part of the character they play. Properties of dance costumes that affect both the aesthetics and functionality of the costume include the following:

Properties of Dance Costumes
> *Fabric:* Is the choice natural or synthetic? Natural fabrics take dye more easily, and breathe better, but synthetic materials last longer and hold up to the wear and tear of multiple uses.
> *Construction method:* Are the costumes easy to get into, or will the dancer need assistance? Fasteners to avoid costume malfunctions need to be sturdy and well secured while avoiding impact points for a dancer. Also, are there any special adjustments that need to be built into the costume? For example, keeping a dress shirt tucked in while dancing will require the shirt be sewn into briefs.

> *Line, shape, and form:* These elements accentuate or deemphasize the body of the dancer. Asymmetrical versus symmetrical lines in the fabric and the costume design can change the visual aesthetic.
> *Color, texture, and patterns:* These can catch your eye on the fabric bolt, but once made into a costume, if the flow and movement of the fabric doesn't facilitate a moving body, you have a problem. Collaborating with the lighting designer is especially important with these elements because lighting can make these elements stand out or blend into the background.
> *Movement:* The type of fabric combined with the cut of the garment can add flow or structure to a garment. A garment with flow can accent movement, and garments that have structure can highlight shape, line, and character.

Makeup and hair design is an extension of the costume and puts the finishing touch on your aesthetic. Whether your makeup and hair design is simple corrective makeup and a ponytail or a wig and prosthetics with full body paint, you need to incorporate makeup into your production package.

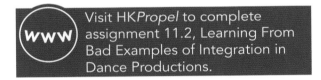

Visit HK*Propel* to complete assignment 11.2, Learning From Bad Examples of Integration in Dance Productions.

Summary

As you get closer to being in the theatre with your performance, you will have to consider not only the design and impact of production elements but also how the production staff will implement them to create the desired effect. While curating and working with designers to create the specific technical elements for your production, it's important to consider the logistics of the theatre space and what particular components of lighting, sound, costumes, scenery, and media will serve your production best. When approached with an educated and intentional eye, these elements will highlight the dancers and the intent of the piece without overpowering or obscuring the work with details that are too flashy.

Part IV

Culmination: Performance and Beyond

The performance takes everything from the process and puts it into action. As the culmination of an enormous amount of work by a team of collaborative artists, the performance and dress rehearsals leading up to it can feel short. Without the proper preparation, this week can lose some of the fullness of the artistry it was built on. Chapter 12 discusses the production week leading up to a performance and shows you how to make the most of your time in a venue by creating a detailed tech and performance timeline. It discusses tech and dress rehearsals, where there will be constant working and reworking of both artistic content and technical elements. In chapter 13, we dive into the performance itself, where your problem-solving skills kick into high gear. In these culminating moments, the product of a process filled with cooperation creates a positive environment, allowing the vision to come to life onstage. When the performance concludes, your process does not. Chapter 14 discusses a postmortem: the time after a show for reflection, evaluation, and growth. Being able to reflect on and evaluate your process is a valuable part of any creative endeavor, because it allows you to learn from each project, build on your experiences, and integrate lessons learned into your larger body of work so your artistic voice can grow with each dance production you produce.

Production Week

Key Terms
dress rehearsal
paper tech
production week
technical (tech) rehearsals

Courtesy of Tim Agler/Backhausdance.

171

Producing Dance

LEARNING OBJECTIVES

After reading this chapter, you will be able to do the following:

- Understand the timeline for the week leading up to a production
- Identify the key elements for cue-to-cue, tech, and dress rehearsals
- Effectively plan and schedule cue-to-cue, tech, and dress rehearsals
- Be prepared to address unexpected situations that may arise during production week

You have finally made it to the performance space! All the weeks of working in the studio, designing and creating in the production shop, and meeting with your collaborators are about to pay off. The week of the show is often called **production week**, and this is when all final rehearsals in the actual performance space occur. Cue-to-cue, tech, and dress rehearsals allow dancers and the production crew to get used to the work in the space and become familiar with all the technical elements and cues that need to happen during the performance. Walking into the first technical rehearsal is exciting for everyone who has been a part of the project. With the excitement may come some fatigue, stress, and worry about how it will all finally come together. Remember to breathe. At this point, everyone wants the show to be a success. Having clearly laid out tech and performance timelines will provide the structure for all the chaos. All participants in the performance need clear direction about what is

A lighting technician programs a cue into the console, generating a brilliantly lit cyc.

happening and when, and these timelines should be worked out as early as possible at production meetings.

Timeline

The length of the tech and dress rehearsals, and, eventually, the show run time circles back to the creative brief and what the artistic and logistical teams determined was feasible and appropriate. When shows are expensive to produce, the tech and dress rehearsals may happen on one day and the single performance on the next day. In larger or more supported productions, the tech and dress rehearsals may last a few days, and the run of the show may be a weekend, several weeks, or a month. In this example, we are working with what is typical in most academic settings. Regardless of the time allotted, it all needs to get done. You may have the luxury of time or be time-constrained and scrambling. Plan accordingly.

All productions need similar elements in their production preparations to ensure a successful opening night. They will need at least a cue-to-cue, tech, and dress rehearsal to ensure everything will run smoothly during the performance.

CREW VIEWING REHEARSAL

- WHEN: This is held one week before opening night.
- WHO: All choreographers, cast, designers, production staff, and crew must attend.
- WHERE: This rehearsal is typically in the rehearsal studio.
- HOW: Pieces are performed in show order in costumes as complete as possible or in clothing the color of the costumes. Recording this is a good idea. Choreographers meet with designers after the crew viewing. The stage manager starts compiling show cues.
- Note: In an ideal world, this is an organized event, and everyone is in one place at the same time. Occasionally designers may come in to view the dances during rehearsal times because of scheduling conflicts.

Cue-to-Cue Rehearsal

Cue-to-cue, technical, and dress rehearsals each have unique goals. Together they complete the production phase of preparing for the production.

CUE-TO-CUE REHEARSAL

- WHEN: This is held the weekend before show week.
- WHO: Production staff and crew as well as choreographers and cast should be in the theatre at designated times.
- WHERE: This rehearsal is held in the performance space.
- HOW: All technical elements need to be finished (i.e., costumes, video, sets). Dancers don't perform the whole show but move from cue to cue for the designers and crew. Choreographers sit at a tech table with the designers and stage managers to talk through the cues as they are being decided. The stage manager finishes compiling show cues during cue-to-cue. If time allows, the performance can be run with all the technical elements. It may not include costumes and makeup, depending on whether these elements are essential for the other design elements.

Note: This is about the technical aspects, design, and cueing, and not about the dancers practicing anything other than knowing where the light will be onstage and how to work through the cues.

A cue-to-cue rehearsal is a run-through of the important moments or cues in a piece to establish the timing and execution of each cue so the technical elements flow smoothly. It's extremely valuable because this rehearsal is usually the first time the entire company is together in the performance space (other than a design run or crew watch, when there is no tech). The stage manager should have a prompt book, which is a script or outline of the performance with all the known cues identified and linked to specific moments. These moments are typically identified with a timestamp, a line of dialogue, a physical movement, or another recognizable trigger action. This rehearsal is an opportunity for the stage manager to observe each cue event and practice calling the associated cues. Once a cue or sequence of cues has been set and the stage manager is satisfied with the execution, they will call a brief "hold" and ask the company to advance to the next trigger event and rehearse the next cue. The dance or performance does not play out in its entirety but jumps from cue to cue.

This day can be long, depending on the size of production, and can be scheduled on a long *10-of-*

12 hour schedule, when the company will work for ten hours out of a twelve-hour call, allowing for two hours of breaks—typically a one-hour lunch and a one-hour dinner. Other breaks will be called to satisfy labor and union laws or if the designers and technicians need to troubleshoot something. Because this day, and tech week in general, is for the stage management and technical crew to perfect their parts, it is common etiquette during those scheduled breaks to allow the crew to eat first and have preference on amenities.

The cast is expected to be on standby and ready to jump to any given point in the performance at the stage manager's discretion. Because the work is not being run in its entirety and is only being viewed for specific cues, dancers do not need to perform the entire dance and can warm up as they see fit instead of participating in a formal warm-up. Dancers are expected to be quiet backstage and focused on the process so they do not hold up the process when they are called. They do not need to be in costume, unless it is a special garment or will affect other technical elements. These unique pieces will definitely need to be available at the cue-to-cue rehearsal. With coordination between the stage manager and costume department, things like quick changes may also be rehearsed during a cue-to-cue rehearsal. Makeup and hair and safety protocols are common uses of time this long day. Some companies find it advantageous to use a minimum cast in the cueing process to allow for simultaneous backstage preparation.

By the end of this exhausting day, the stage manager's prompt book should be almost complete, with only minor tweaks expected in the days ahead, usually for timing, as the performance runs in real time. Likewise, the crew should have their tracks or list of tasks recorded and prepared for the first tech rehearsal, when they will have relatively very few chances to perfect their own choreography of scene

The stage manager refers to the prompt book and asks that the crew execute cues on command. The stage manager jumps from the current cue to the next cue in sequence, asking the dance cast to set in a new position as the crew updates the tech to the new look.

shifts, sets and resets, button presses, rope pulls, and technical magic. And the cast should be expected to know all their entrances and exits as well as those special moments when they themselves cause a cueing event.

Cue-to-cue can be stressful and physically draining, so it is important to maintain hydration, energy, and awareness. This is a team effort, and every task is critical to the production value and proper execution, so everyone be supportive. Respect and patience will make all the difference in the general mood and takeaway from the day.

The best-case schedule would be a week in which you have at least an entire day dedicated to cue-to-cue or at least enough time to cue through the entire performance, plus multiple days and evenings of tech rehearsals and dress rehearsals. Practice makes perfect, right? But what if you are in a festival or other situation when there just isn't much, if any, time for rehearsals? You should still make sure you do a cue-to-cue rehearsal if possible. If you have cues within your performance, you have to make sure the stage manager has had a chance to call them at least once, in sequence, with the elements. And in the strictest situations, when there is literally no technical period, have the stage manager work with whatever designers are available to have a **paper tech**. Paper tech is a cue-by-cue, page-by-page walkthrough of the entire show in the prompt book, when the stage manager can confirm the cues on paper—it's better than nothing! In the academic setting and beyond, the paper tech is typically held after the design run so the designers can solidify their cue lists and before the first cue-to-cue or tech rehearsal so the stage manager can establish a first draft of a complete prompt book.

The cue-to-cue is when the choreographer works with the designers to finalize their vision. As the choreographer, you finally see all the pieces slowly come together in the space. It is important to be ready to adjust the choreography and to give your dancers clear instructions for onstage placement, entrances, and exits. There will typically be times where there is a pause while a light is being refocused or the music track is being worked on. In these moments, you can talk to the dancers about spacing, find out if they need spike marks on the stage, and work out issues with sets or props. It is important to remember this day is not about you or the dancers but about how the technical elements come into play for the performance. So, when the stage manager says they are ready to move on, tell the dancers you will provide more notes later. Avoid stress by scaling your production value and techni-

cal needs to the venue and performance type so you do not force too much tech into a time or space that is inadequate. Sometimes less is more.

SETTING DANCER EXPECTATIONS FOR CUE-TO-CUE REHEARSALS

It is important for the choreographer to prep the dancers for what to expect during the cue-to-cue tech. From the dancers' perspective, everything will seem like it takes forever and they never get to where they get to dance full out. They need to understand they are moving from one technical cue to another and may be asked to show a movement, formation, or facing for the stage manager to note. While this day can feel tedious for the dancers, it is essential that they are focused and listening for directions, not talking to each other onstage. If the dancers are not clear on entrances and exits, crossovers, how to work around or on a set piece that has suddenly appeared in the center of stage, or need spike marks for staging, this is the time to ask the choreographer for assistance. As time allows, the choreographer can clarify questions and work with the stage manager in blocking the dance.

A typical cue-to-cue rehearsal or *10-of-12* schedule looks like the following:

› 9:00 a.m. to 12:00 p.m.: All called. A safety orientation is likely. Typically, the stage manager will ask to set for the top of the show, and they will begin cueing from the top until lunch.

› 12:00 p.m. to 1:00 p.m.: Lunch (remember, if it's catered, the crew eats first!).

› 1:00 p.m. to 5:00 p.m.: All return to the venue, and the stage manager will typically pick up where they paused, unless there is a moment that they decide with the director and artistic staff needs to be repeated.

› 5:00 p.m. to 6:00 p.m.: Dinner.

› 6:00 p.m. to 9:00 p.m.: All return for the final session to continue cueing.

› 9:00 p.m.: Hard out, which means that security locks the door at this time, and if you overstay your welcome, you will be charged large overages in your venue contract. If you are in an academic setting, it could mean repercussions against the students' sleep and study as well as discipline for faculty or staff.

Technical (Tech) Rehearsal

Once the cue-to-cue rehearsal is complete, a **technical (tech) rehearsal** begins. A tech rehearsal is different from a cue-to-cue in that the tech rehearsal typically runs from top to bottom without skipping and only pauses for mistakes or a need to redo something better or safer. In a perfect world, the technical rehearsal is run in real time so the company can begin getting used to the pace of everything. However, do not rush. The goal is to run through the performance, not to force your way through it. There are often tricky sequences in any production, so it is better to mark through (walk or step through slowly for accuracy) these sequences and build speed, rather than to go full speed and make learning the sequence impossible.

If there is a complex cue sequence that requires action by several people or departments, it is likely going to take multiple attempts to perfect it. There is a balance of time spent on learning the sequence with finishing the rehearsal, and that is something a good stage manager should bring to the team. They will hold the run just before the complex sequence,

announce what is about to happen (everyone should remember this sequence from cue-to-cue), and then mark through the sequence, methodically, so everyone starts to get it in their muscle memory. Sometimes, a sequence can (and should, maybe for safety reasons) be broken down and run through for each department once, layering elements on top of each other with each subsequent run. Once you have all the elements incorporated, you can repeat the process to increase speed. This sequence is often the following:

1. Mark through
2. Quarter speed
3. Half speed
4. Real time

Other than stumbling through these most challenging cues, try your best to continue working through the show from top to bottom with as few holds as possible. The only people calling holds should be the stage manager (because at this point, they own the performance), the choreographer, director, or technical director. Sometimes a dancer

---

SCHEDULE FOR WEEK OF TECH AND DRESS REHEARSALS AND PERFORMANCE

- ❯ WHO: All dancers, choreographers, and crew must be present at the following dates and times. Every participant must sign in at the call board upon arrival.
- ❯ WHERE: This is held in the performance space.
- ❯ Monday: Dancer call is at 5:15 p.m. onstage or in a studio for warm-up and a possible run-through of dances. Crew call is at 6:00 p.m. to sweep, mop, and prep the stage and backstage as well as conduct a sound and light check. Technical rehearsal (start and stop as needed) starts, in costume, at 7:00 p.m.
- ❯ Tuesday: Dancer call is at 5:15 p.m. onstage or in a studio for a warm up and possible dance run-through. Crew call is at 6:00 p.m. to sweep, mop, and prep the stage and backstage as well as conduct a sound and light check. Technical rehearsal (start and stop as needed) starts, in costume, at 7:00 p.m.
- ❯ Wednesday: Dancer call is at 6:00 p.m. onstage or in a studio for a warm up and possible run-through of dances. Crew call is at 6:45 p.m. to sweep, mop, and prep the stage and backstage as well as conduct a sound and light check. Dress rehearsal in full costume and makeup begins at 8:00 p.m.
- ❯ Thursday: Dancer call is at 6:00 p.m. onstage or in a studio for a warm-up and possible run-through of dances. Crew call is at 6:45 p.m. to sweep, mop, and prep the stage and backstage as well as conduct a sound and light check. Final dress rehearsal or preview night is at 8:00 p.m.
- ❯ Friday: Dancer call is at 6:00 p.m. onstage or in a studio for a warm-up and possible run-through of dances. Crew call is at 6:45 p.m. to sweep, mop, and prep the stage and backstage as well as conduct a sound and light check. The show is at 8:00 p.m.
- ❯ Saturday: Dancer call is at 6:00 p.m. onstage or in a studio for a warm-up and possible run-through of dances. Crew call is at 6:45 p.m. to sweep, mop, and prep stage and backstage as well as conduct a sound and light check. The show is at 8:00 p.m.
- ❯ STRIKE: Meet immediately following the last show; all must participate and meet in the scene shop for assigned duties.

The choreographer stands on the plaster line for an intimate look at the dancers' movements as the accompanist (left) and the production team (bottom) run through the technical rehearsal. The choreographer may request multiple attempts at a technical sequence at variable speeds to make sure everything is safe and accurate.

may call a hold if they are feeling unsafe—that's OK but should be rare. Likewise, a stagehand or crew could call a hold but only in an emergency, like a fire hazard or other safety-related issue. Protocol and etiquette dictate that anyone else who would want to call a hold complete the sequence and make the request to the supervisor on headset. The stage manager would then make the call to hold. Remember, the idea is to *not* hold and get through the performance. If you have a second day or evening or more of technical rehearsals, rinse and repeat, getting better and faster with each run.

A typical tech rehearsal schedule looks like the following:

> 6:00 p.m. to 6:15 p.m.: All called. Company addresses show notes from the previous evening and new items to bring awareness to, including safety notes.
> 6:15 p.m. to 6:30 p.m.: Cast warms up and crew sets.
> 6:30 p.m. to 8:00 p.m.: Run through the performance.
> 8:00 p.m. to 8:15 p.m.: Break.
> 8:15 p.m. to 8:30 p.m.: Notes.
> 8:30 p.m. to 10:00 p.m.: Run though the performance or work trouble spots.
> 10:00 p.m. to 11:00 p.m.: Notes, tech work, and shutdown occur.

Any combination of these elements can make a productive tech rehearsal schedule. The key is to get one decent run in with few if any holds and to gather and disseminate good notes that will improve the run the following day. These notes should be shared among the departments before the end of the night and included in the stage manager's rehearsal report so the day staff (if there is one) can make any fixes, adjustments, reprogramming, or tweaking to improve the tech for the next rehearsal.

In the cue-to-cue and any other preliminary run-throughs onstage, the dancers would have warmed themselves up for what they needed in that run, but beginning in the tech rehearsal, a formal warm-up should be hosted to allow dancers the time to fully prepare their bodies for performance. Tech rehearsal is the first time the work will be performed to its fullest physicality, so a warm-up becomes a necessary part of the tech rehearsal schedule. There is another benefit to having the full cast warm up onstage before the show: Asking either senior dancers or a rehearsal director to run a warm-up helps bring everyone together and focuses the energy of the entire cast to build a sense of community.

GENERAL WARM-UP GUIDELINES

Dancers need a space to warm up before performing. Warming up not only prepares the body for action but also brings the entire cast together in a shared space and energy. Having a rehearsal director, choreographer, or company member lead a structured warm-up ensures everyone is ready to go. This may also be when some dancers mark through some of the trickier choreography.

Depending on the philosophy and the resources of the production company, costumes may not be worn during tech rehearsals. If your cast is not wearing their costumes, they should wear something similar in color, weight, and form as their costume. This helps immensely with lighting and offers a similar movement experience for the dancer. Specialty

Visit HK*Propel* to complete assignment 12.1, Create a Production Week Calendar.

Crew work in the booth as the cast warms up onstage.

costume pieces, especially shoes and head or face coverings, should be worn throughout tech (and as much of the rehearsal process as possible), regardless of whether the remainder of the costume is worn at that time. All props should be in use throughout tech and be tested for safety and durability.

If your dance has props or a set that the dancers interact with, it is possible you have not had the final product to work on during rehearsal. For example, you have created a dance where dancers look through a window, move on a couch, or throw hundreds of balls across the floor. In the rehearsal process, you may have been using blocks or chairs to represent the furniture. In the studio rehearsal process, as a choreographer, you provide as much of the choreography as possible, but it may mean that additional time during the tech rehearsal needs to be set aside to work with the final set or prop and the dancers. Once you add a prop or set the dancers need to interact with, it immediately creates a greater challenge and risk for the dancer. They need time to become comfortable with the items, and choreography may need to be adjusted to fit the reality of the finished product.

MOVING PROPS

When you have props or moving sets, it creates unpredictability in every performance. Whether you are dropping feathers from the rafters, rolling balls across the stage, climbing ladders, or leaping from one set piece to another, rehearsals are essential for anticipating issues. Ideally the dancers have been working with the actual props and sets before going into the theatre, but many times this is not the case. Dancers will need time to become familiar with what they are interacting with. Rushing the process puts everyone and the overall performance in jeopardy.

For dancers, the tech rehearsal is the first time they can find their rhythm for the dances and the overall show. Some coordination of the dressing rooms and quick-change areas will need to be worked out at this point. The quick changes may include costume, hair and makeup, and shoes. Dancers with quick changes need to begin to practice these quick changes during the tech rehearsal. Choreographers may need to make some changes if the time it takes to change a hairstyle from a bun to a French braid, to switch lipstick colors, or to change from pointe shoes to heels is too long

between dances. It is important to remember that once you are in the theatre, the success of the overall performance depends not just on your dance but on how all the dance pieces come together as an entire concert. Tech rehearsals are a great time to recognize what changes may be needed to keep the flow of the entire evening going.

At this point, the choreography shifts should be at a minimum because any shift in formation, movement, entrances, or exits can directly affect the work already done to develop all the cues for the show. If the stage manager depends on your last dancer taking three steps toward the audience as they cue lights and the music fades out and you change the final choreography, this creates a very stressful moment for everyone. If changes must be made, discuss them with the stage manager and possibly run a quick cue-to-cue before the tech run to make sure everyone is on the same page.

To an artist, choreography may never seem finished, and it may be tempting to continue to make changes up until the final moment. However, there is a point where the choreographer has to let go and give the dance to the dancers and ultimately the audience. To alleviate stress and foster trust, this letting go should happen during tech and dress week, not only for the sake of the performers but also for the designers and the crew who have designed their art around what they perceive to be a finished choreographed product. If a choreographer changes things at the last moment, it has a real and

THE BOW

Dancers are amazing performers and horrible at bows. The bow is the last moment the audience sees the dancers onstage. A poorly rehearsed bow can create an awkward and embarrassing moment for everyone. Rehearse the bows when you are still in the dance studio. Already know how the bows will be cued with the stage manager and teach this final moment. This can be as simple as once the lights go completely out, move quickly to stand in a line centered across the stage, with your feet together and arms by your sides. Once the lights come up, take a gracious bow to the audience, stand up, and wait for either the curtain to close or the lights to go to black. A show can become amateur quickly when dancers move before the lights completely go out or before the curtain closes. Rehearse the bow!

significant effect on what the designers have created and what the performers and crew are expecting to happen onstage. If a change is absolutely necessary, make sure that you, the choreographer, are keeping your entire collaborative and performance team in the loop. In general, choreographers are perfectionists, and they are never truly satisfied with their work. However, suppress the urge to change everything up until the curtain rises on opening night.

Dress Rehearsal

By the time a dress rehearsal is held, the cues are set so the whole company knows their choreography and their tracks, and the technicians have clarified their jobs throughout the performance.

A **dress rehearsal** is intended to show what an actual performance will look, sound, and feel like in every aspect. Everything from the call schedule to the final bows should be performed as if there was a paying audience in the house. Only in the event of a major technical catastrophe or a legitimate safety issue should the dress rehearsal be paused. This is the best opportunity to troubleshoot something in performance conditions, so it is most edifying and proper to work any kinks out behind the scenes.

If the costumes were not worn during the tech rehearsals, the costume department is eagerly waiting to make sure there are no costume malfunctions while dancing. If there are concerns, the earlier a costume is worn in the rehearsal process, the better. During the first rehearsal, the costume designer will be watching to ensure all appropriate body parts are covered and supported, checking to make sure the shirt stays tucked in, checking that the appropriate undergarments are being worn, and watching anything else that catches their eye. This is also the time for dancers to express very nicely what is and is not working for them. If a dancer has to move and the costume is restricting the movement, the designer may need to add slits to a dress, add pleats, and make general adjustments so that the dancer can move. There are also times that a seam rips open, a strap breaks, the shoes are not the right color, or something falls off. During the dress rehearsal, clear communication between the choreographer, dancers, and costume department is essential to make sure everyone is happy with the final product. At this point, the costumes have been made, and they will not be able to whip up something new on the spot.

COSTUME THOUGHTS

During the design phase, it is important to think about the movement of the dancers and what functionality you need from the costume. If a designer created a beautiful costume made of a slippery material and your piece has partnering, this costume may be an issue. What if you need the dancers to wear kneepads due to floor work, but the costume is a dress? Do you want the kneepads hidden or shown? Is the dance extremely athletic, so dancing in wool may give everyone heat stroke? Once you are in dress rehearsal, the money and time has been spent. There will be limitations as to how much can change in the last few days before opening night.

A typical dress rehearsal or performance schedule looks like the following:

› 5:30 p.m.: Crew is called.
› 6:00 p.m.: Cast is called.
› 6:15 p.m.: Warm-ups are held.
› 6:30 p.m.: Cast goes to wardrobe and makeup.
› 7:00 p.m.: House is open (stage and first cues set).
› 7:30 p.m.: Curtain opens.
› TBD: End. The official run time of the show won't be known until after a few consistent run-throughs.
› After run-through: Notes for cast and production are done.

Expecting the Unexpected

Production week is one of the most exciting times in the process because the entire company is now working together in the venue. This is when all the meetings, planning, and effort will begin to pay off. Yet, despite all the good intentions and spreadsheets, there will always be some things you cannot predict and some things that your experience should lead you to prepare for even though you do not expect them to happen.

Category A: Things You Cannot Predict

› Who will get ill and call out
› Who will get injured and step out
› Force majeure (natural phenomena)

- Power outages, loss of HVAC, and leaky venue roofs
- Faulty technical equipment or faulty venue technicians
- A lousy audience

Category B: Things Your Experience Will Prepare You to Handle

- Someone will be ill—you need cast understudies.
- Someone will be injured—you need cast understudies.
- A pandemic will break out or a tornado will tear through town, so practice your mantra: "It's *only* a dance. It's *only* a dance." Contingency plans based on the conditions you can predict are a good idea.
- The power will go out and some part of the venue will fall apart—know the emergency protocol of the venue for performers, crew, and audience.
- The dimmer rack will overheat and a speaker will get blown out, and the venue staff will not be able to fix it before opening. Practice your other mantra: "It's about the *dance* (not the tech). It's about the *dance* (not the tech)." Decide whether the show can still go on with what is available and consider whether doing so would put the performers/audience at risk and the show needs to be delayed, postponed, or rescheduled.
- The fire marshal will visit at the top of dress rehearsal and threaten to shut your production down because you never submitted critical paperwork—always keep critical paperwork on hand so you can show it to them, and then they will leave.
- The audience won't "get it." They came to support *you*, but they don't understand your modern *interpretation* of a leaf on the wind. Practice your other mantra: "Modern dance is ripe for interpretation. I am a good choreographer. I don't need to be understood. I just need to be appreciated." In the future ensure your marketing targets the right audience and ask yourself if a preshow talk or program note could help support your vision.

ALWAYS BE PREPARED

The most important person in a dance company may never perform onstage: the understudy! Illness, injuries, and life events happen, and they are unpredictable. In sports, there are always players on the sidelines ready to step in for an injured, ill, or missing player at any time. Having one or a few understudies for your dance is a way to ensure you don't have to rechoreograph the entire dance or teach a dancer overnight. The understudy attends all rehearsals and learns specific roles. While they may never make it into the performance, they can then become great note takers during the performance process and support the choreographer. If you are cast as an understudy, never throw away the opportunity. Who knows if someone goes out and you step in? That is your moment to show your talent onstage!

Visit HK*Propel* to complete assignment 12.2, Defining Responsibilities.

Summary

When you are in the theatre with your work during production week, the dancers and production crew can finally see the work in the space it will be performed in. Rehearsals during production week allow everyone to become familiar with all the technical elements and cues that need to happen during the performance. Cue-to-cue rehearsals allow the crew to assign and lay out those cues, a tech rehearsal solidifies all the technical elements, and dress rehearsals are a chance to see everything working together and ensure that everything runs smoothly before the performance. The timeline of a production week helps prepare the dancers, production crew, choreographer, and everyone in between for a successful and smooth performance.

Performance

13

Key Terms
box office
front of house

LEARNING OBJECTIVES

After reading this chapter, you will be able to do the following:

- Understand the overall flow of a performance
- Identify the responsibilities of the front of house and backstage crews before, during, and after a performance
- Acknowledge what's expected of performers to be effectively prepared for a performance
- Effectively strike the production elements of a performance after it's finished

Opening night is here! Because it has the same schedule as the dress rehearsal, the performance should be a smooth process. It can include anywhere from a handful of friends and family to thousands of your biggest fans. As a choreographer or director, you should have handed the keys to the kingdom to the stage manager at the first tech or cue-to-cue rehearsal, but by now, you absolutely need to step back, pick out a fabulous outfit to wear on opening night, and let the production team do their thing. It will be all right, and if it isn't, that's the joy of live performing arts. There's nothing more you can offer than some words of encouragement and a "Merde!" or two.

The company should be confident, prepared, and ready to execute at a high level. You can visit with friends in the lobby and buy flowers for the cast. Keep in mind that these performers *want* to do a good job, and they are motivated to do so in front of a critical audience. As you watch the performance, keep your notes to a minimum; you can't rechoreograph the dance.

Those last few moments before the stage manager calls "places" are special. An audience is about to witness weeks, months, and even years of work for the first time or for the hundredth time. On performance nights, three groups are working diligently to make sure the show starts on time and runs smoothly. While the backstage crew and dancers are prepping for the performance, the house manager and ushers are managing the audience.

Front of House

While the dancers and stage crew have been in the venue for days doing cue-to-cue, tech, and final dress rehearsals, the house manager and ushers typically arrive on site on opening night. This is when the marketing and publicity team become part of the actual performance. The **front of house** team is completely in charge of the organization and movement of the audience. Depending on the venue, you may not directly participate in the events occurring in the front of house. In most academic settings, the choreographers either stay backstage or blend in with the audience members to enjoy the show from the house. If and when you run your own show, it is important to understand how the audience moves through a venue.

Tickets

The first step is knowing where your box office is and how tickets are being sold and distributed. If tickets can be bought by cash only, do you have a cash box with enough change available? Do you have someone responsible to be in charge of the cash box? If you are allowing tickets to be purchased through an electronic source such as Square or Stripe, do you have the necessary equipment set up, and is there good Wi-Fi or cellular service where you are to run the apps? Do you have prepurchased tickets being held at will call? Do you have a VIP section? Each of these transactions can take time, and it is essential the audience can quickly obtain their tickets, make a quick bathroom stop, and be in their seats on time for the start of the show.

After the logistics for tickets have been worked out, you may find the best option to move people through the ticket line quickly is to have multiple lines designated for specific types of ticket sales or pickups. This will take planning and adequate staffing to cover all the options. Typically, the box office opens at least one hour before the start of the show, but regardless of how early it opens, there will always be those last-minute people thinking a dance performance is like a movie where you can walk in during the credits.

Audience Management

Once the audience members have their tickets in hand, the questions are, Where do they hang out, and what do they see before the seating opens? The publicity or marketing team is in charge of what the lobby or waiting area looks like. Is there a table with promotional materials for the dance event? In larger venues, vendors sell merchandise, and some venues may offer refreshments. If refreshments are available, it is important for the audience to know if everything must be consumed before entering the seating area. You will have a very upset audience member if they waited in line for a drink only to be told moments before the show is to start that they have to throw the barely touched drink away.

The time available for the audience to find their seats will vary based on the venue and type of performance. A traditional theatre may open its seating 30 minutes before the curtain. Regardless of when the seating is open, the ushers need to be ready, especially if the seating is assigned. Ushers need to be aware of all emergency exits and assist anyone who needs extra help getting to their seats. At this point, the house manager has their watch in sync with the stage manager to count down to the start of the show. The house manager has an eye on the flow of the audience and five minutes before curtain may ring a bell or make an announcement asking the audience to please take their seats. Once the house manager sees that it seems the whole audience is in the venue and seated, they will then hand over the control to the stage manager to start the show.

If there is an intermission once the houselights come back up and the audience begins to mingle around during the break, the house manager synchronizes their watch with the stage manager again. A bell sounds or an announcement is made five minutes before the start of the next act. Audience members having great conversations in the lobby are politely asked to take their seats, and once everyone is seated once again, the stage manager takes over and the magic of the performance begins again.

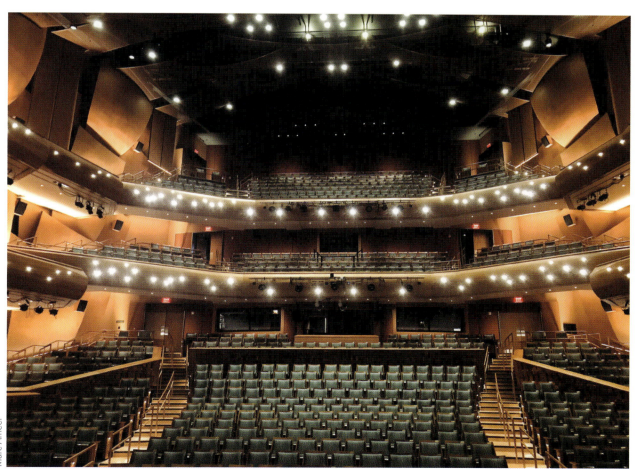

The audience chamber or *house* at the Musco Center for the Arts at Chapman University in Orange, CA.

Clearing the House

Sometimes the hardest thing after the show is getting the audience out of the venue. Once the final bow has been taken and the houselights have come on, it's time to clear everyone out. Ushers can stand at the doors, thanking the audience for coming and directing the audience to a designated meet-and-greet area typically in the lobby or outside the venue. The audience buzz is great, and you want everyone leaving on an inspired note. But if they linger in the venue, this can cost overtime. It can be helpful to have a few ushers go to the front of the seating area and kindly encourage lingering talkers to take their conversation outside because the space needs to be prepared for the next performance. Once all the people are out, depending on the venue, the ushers can quickly pick up random programs and trash to leave the space as clean as possible. If there are chairs, the ushers may need to straighten rows and reorganize the seating. The key is to leave the space ready for the next performance. The house manager will release the ushers and will talk through any notes with the stage manager before locking up the venue for the evening.

Backstage Crew

At this time, most of the designers have moved on to other jobs, and the show is left in the very capable hands of the stage manager and crew. Even if all the tech and dress rehearsals went well, it is typical the cast and crew may have a few butterflies before the curtain, but all should feel confident that they know their jobs and are ready to go. The stage manager has posted a sign-in sheet for the crew and the dancers to make sure everyone is present and on time. Each member of the crew has specific jobs before, during, and after the show.

> ## PERFECT PRACTICE?
>
> They say that a perfect dress rehearsal is a sign of a rough opening performance. Try to keep all the mistakes in tech, so opening night goes off without a hitch!

Before the Curtain

While the stage manager is counting heads and coordinating with the house manager, they trust their crew knows what to do to prepare the space. The deck crew ensures that the backstage area is clean and ready for the performers. If the theatre space is used for classes or other activities during the day, sometimes things need to be moved or picked up. The quick-change booth may need to be set up again, the crossover space needs to be checked for hazards, and the stage needs to be cleaned. Any gels or set pieces need to be ready for the first dance in the concert, and all the other props and sets need to be triple checked to confirm they are in the preset areas and ready to be moved on cue.

In the booth, the light and soundboard operators may review cues and go over any notes from the previous performance. The light board operator will run a dimmer check, test tricky or atypical cue sequences, ensure that all systems are working properly, and set the preshow lighting look for the venue. Likewise, the soundboard operator will do a sound check, make sure all the music is cued in the system for playback, run a mic check if appropriate, and stand by for the stage manager's cue to play preshow music. If media is a part of the show, a test run with the computer system, projector, and any other elements is important.

Never assume everything will work just fine. Maybe the cleaning service tripped a breaker or accidentally hit a button on the board while dusting. Even a cue from the end of the show could still be active in the system, and if it is not checked, it can create a moment of sheer panic at the beginning of the show for the crew and performers. Once everything has been checked and prepped, it's time to set the preshow lighting, start the preshow audio, and sit back and take a few deep breaths.

Showtime

The stage manager will call places three times before the start of the show. This is a standard practice to keep everyone aware of the time and make sure people are where they are supposed to be on time. The first call is 15 minutes before the show, then 5 minutes before the show, and then the final call for places means everyone is ready to go. The stage manager is in constant contact with the assistant stage manager, who sits backstage and is the liaison for communication between what is happening backstage and the booth. Once all the dancers are in place, the assistant stage manager will let the stage manager know everyone backstage is ready to go. The stage manager will get the OK from the house manager and then the show will begin.

In a perfect world, from the start to the end of the show, everything will flow smoothly. However, this is not always the case. The stage manager needs nerves of steel to be able to make quick decisions if

At last—it's showtime!

there are technical issues in the booth, such as the wrong music playing or the media freezing. They may also have to pause the show or announce a change in performance order if a dancer becomes injured or is unable to go onstage. While we all hope none of these things happen, their possibilities are a part of being in live performance. If your event is being filmed and edited later, you can stop and start more easily, but time is still money, so efficiency is key.

Clearing Backstage

At the end of the night, the crews quickly clean up and reset for the next performance. The set and props need to be found and reset for the top of the show. This may mean tracking something down that a dancer carried off with them into a dressing room. One of the biggest activities at the end of the show is wardrobe reset. At the end of the night, costumes that can be cleaned are collected, washed, and prepared for the next performance. This may also include mending items that were torn or damaged during the performance. After everything is clean, the costumes are hung back up on the costume racks, waiting for the dancers to return the next day. Specialty makeup or hair supplies need to be reset, organized, and possibly cleaned before the next performance. Dancers need to realize their costumes don't magically become mended or cleaned overnight but that a crew of wonderful people are doing this work. Thanking the crew goes a long way.

At the end of the night, the stage manager will go over any additional notes and clear the backstage area of any lingering dancers or crew members. It's time to go home, rest, and prepare to do it all again the next day.

Visit HK*Propel* to complete assignment 13.1, Creating a Show Day Checklist.

Performers

Weeks of rehearsal and hours of tech and dress rehearsals all to get the production to opening night. This is an exciting time—all your hard work finally has an audience. The performance now becomes about the dancers onstage, so it is important to remember you are all a team and to continue to thank the crew and stage managers throughout the show's run. Both the dancers and choreographers need to be aware of standard protocols and etiquette during the run of the show.

Regardless of whether your crew is students or professionals, patience and understanding are vital to having a positive experience. A choreographer's job is to be straightforward with the collaborative team so that the crew knows what they need to do. It is not the choreographer's job to reprimand anyone or take charge backstage when something goes wrong. The choreographer needs to make a note and give that note to the appropriate person at the appropriate time. That person will most likely be the stage manager, but it depends on how the structure is set up in your specific theatre dynamic. Say thank you to your crew and let them know that you truly appreciate all the hard work they are doing to make the show a success. A little chocolate and a thank-you note never hurts. The crew should always know that they are just as important as the performers.

Once the performances have begun, the designers may be off to other projects and are no longer a part of the nightly shows. If the choreographer has been clear with their design team, those last few moments before the show opens are a time for gratitude and congratulations. Choreographers should always write a thank-you note to each of their designers. This is a personal touch that fosters respect and builds bridges to future successful collaborations.

Arrival and Preparation

Once a dancer arrives in the venue, they need to organize their space, pick up their costumes, preset any items in the quick-change booth or backstage, and get their mind and body prepared to perform.

Dancers are typically responsible for their stage makeup and hair unless otherwise specified. Shoes and undergarments are also the responsibility of the

Dancers gather for the final circle and receive encouragement from a choreographer before they retreat backstage and get into costume for the evening's performance. *Merde!*

dancer to clean and bring to the theatre each night. If there are any issues that a dancer needs help with, they can talk to their choreographer or go to the assistant stage manager, who will work to solve the problem. Always be respectful and note the chain of command. If a dancer can't hear the sound onstage while dancing, they don't go tell someone to turn up the volume. They convey the issue to the assistant stage manager, who then provides the information to the stage manager, who then makes the call on how to support the dancers but not affect the rest of the show.

Other etiquette reminders for dancers include remaining silent backstage; if someone tells you to be quiet, you just do. Dancers backstage need to keep an eye on the time and know how long it will take them to be ready to perform. While the stage manager is providing time-to-curtain reminders and then calls for places, it is ultimately a dancer's responsibility to be ready before they are called.

Preparing for the performance each night is a unique feeling and is very difficult to describe. The preparation should include a warm-up, final notes, a final circle exercise, and time to prepare. Depending on your role in the show as the choreographer or artistic director, you can have a role in organizing the preshow process.

Final Notes

After everyone is warmed up, making a circle on the stage is the easiest way to bring everyone together to share any necessary information. The stage manager may offer any general technical production notes to the cast, including reminders about sight lines, holding for the lights to go out, and final bow reminders. There may also be specific notes for a performer or cast that can be delivered at this point. Once the stage manager offers notes, the director of the show—that may be you if you are wearing many hats—will usually offer performance notes. All notes should be kept short and simple, and changes are only made if absolutely necessary.

As a final activity, this huddle or group circle helps ease nerves. Just take a moment to reflect and breathe together. Examples include the following:

1. After warm-ups, a quick activity like Pass the Dance can help connect everyone. Have the performers get into small circles of four or five or however many works for your specific needs. Turn on some fun music and have one person in the circle start by doing a dance move such as jumping up and down. The next person joins in doing that same move, and so on until it gets back to the first person. Then the next person chooses and does a new dance move while everyone is still doing the original move until the new move gets to them. This continues around the circle until everyone has contributed a new dance move.

2. Form a circle with all performers and crew. Hold hands and pass the energy by starting a single hand squeeze. The next person does the same and so on. You can feel and see the energy being passed from one person to another until it makes it back to the start.

3. Before every single performance, try saying, "Today is [insert the actual date], the only [insert the actual date] there ever will be. Take a moment to breathe and look around at this amazing group of people and enjoy this moment."

4. Lastly bring them all in very close, all start pounding the stage or studio floor and say, "On the count of three, everyone yell 'Merde!'"

These final moments are important to make sure the cast is ready to perform and that they know you trust them to do the work. The most important thing you can do for your performers is to give them the confidence they need to let their muscle memory take over. As a choreographer, you need to let go and let them bond as a cast so that they know that they can count on each other and have each other's backs out there under the lights.

Visit HK*Propel* to complete assignment 13.2, Developing Health Protocols.

Strike

All performances will eventually come to an end. This may be after a single show, weeks, months, or years, but eventually the final curtain will come down. While the performers and choreographers may be ready to pack up and move on to the next project, there is still work to be done to completely close out the show. Strike is the teardown and return of production elements. Costumes go back to the shop or rental house. The set is disposed of or stored away. Props go back to the prop house (and no one should ever walk away with their favorite prop from a set—props are not souvenirs!). Strike involves all production departments, and each has their own department head, or crew leads, and will operate a little differently. Strike should be planned by the technical director or an equivalent competent person before the final performance day, and that plan should be shared with everyone ahead of time.

All cast and crew, including choreographers, need to be a part of strike, even when it means rolling up your sleeves and getting dirty. Of course, if you are physically unable to dive in with a hammer and screw gun, there are plenty of other jobs that need to be done for an efficient and productive strike to occur. Get in there and offer your assistance. It is also your job as the choreographer to ensure that your performers know whether they are required to participate in strike, and if they see you working, they know that it is a team effort and not just a job for the crew.

Strike usually occurs immediately after the house clears at the end of the final performance. In some cases, the strike begins *during* the final performance. Some departments, like costumes and props, can begin packing up as dancers drop off a costume or prop for the last time, if it is not needed again in the show. For example, anything from act I that isn't brought back in act II can be packed, labeled, and staged by the cargo elevator. That is a grand model of efficiency.

Since everyone is expected to strike, and it has likely been a long day or days leading up to this final phase of production, providing food is a good idea. Pizza may not be on the top of the dancers' diet, but it makes for a great motivator when a person is expected to jump into a fast-paced demolition and packing extravaganza! Keep the company hydrated as well. It makes sense to provide caffeinated beverages when working a late-night shift, but make sure to have plenty of water and electrolyte drinks on hand as well. One exception to the "everybody works" philosophy is that you should never require anyone to participate in a strike who is injured or who cannot physically engage in such activities. Perhaps those people can help delegate and track tasks, run logistics, manage attendance, or throw away the pizza boxes.

Sets and Props

If the production is in a school setting, there is most likely a regular strike plan, lots of tools, storage space, and staff support. These strikes can go very quickly and be extremely efficient. The set may be stock scenery, and that would just be absorbed into inventory. Odd set pieces or things that will not be used again often just go straight to the dumpster. Props are almost always saved and added to an ever-expanding inventory. This collection may be shared with a theatre department and be quite extensive.

Breaking down the set may involve relatively safe tasks like unscrewing things and could include smashing things with a sledgehammer or cutting things down with an open-bladed reciprocating saw. Consider assigning tools and tasks based on three factors for safety: the person's experience, their comfort level, and the availability of personal protective equipment (PPE, like safety glasses or leather gloves). Never give a tool to someone if they have never used it before (without proper training) and never force a person to do anything they are uncomfortable with—this refers to fear as well. (Doing a new task can be uncomfortable because one is not used to it yet. That's awkwardness.) Someone who is afraid of operating a saw or climbing a ladder is very likely to get hurt because their fear is greater than their competence. Let these people mop the stage or work in a less-risky environment.

If the strike is in a rental venue, you likely have a set and props that will be moved back to a rental house or to your home base. Demolition is less of a factor, though you might need many hands to pick things up, load them on a truck, and manage what is too large for people to handle. Teamwork is the name of the game. Be sure to look through every room and in every corner before you leave for the night. You don't want to leave anything behind. If it is valuable, you probably won't see it again.

Lighting, Sound, and Media

These departments are grouped because they rely less on deconstruction methods and more on rearranging, resetting, and replacing equipment. There are often rental packages of equipment in these departments as well, so pulling that equipment, inventorying it, and packing it for return is a priority. Rental packages may be a part of a production in any venue or production type. If you are in your own school or studio, the heads of these departments or a technical supervisor or the equivalent will want to have the equipment reset, the booth cleaned, and the repertory reestablished. In tech, *repertory* refers to the setup of equipment that is always readily available in the space. If you are at a festival or in a rental, you might just need to grab your laptop and go. Just make sure to thank the house staff before you disappear—those people work hard for you.

Costumes, Hair, and Makeup

Depending on the size and type of show, there could be no costumes to wash or there could be hundreds! If laundry is needed, then the strike could be a marathon for the wardrobe crew. If everyone else leaves before them, make sure to give them the remainder of the caffeinated beverages and some praise—they made the dancers look awesome. It is also important that if you leave anyone in the venue, be extra diligent about locking up and practice the buddy system. No one (in any department) should ever work alone after hours.

If you are in your own venue, the laundry and restocking of costumes may take days or weeks depending on the staff-to-costume ratio. In a rented or temporary venue, you need to check under every chair and behind every door for every last sock because this will be your last opportunity to take it. Costume designs, like technical designs, often incorporate rented elements. Prioritize inventorying and packing rental items so you do not get charged late or loss fees. Everything else can be dealt with at a slower pace.

Hair and makeup stations and supplies need to be cleaned and sanitized. Dancers might take some or all of their "glam" supplies with them. In larger, more involved designs, however, wigs, prosthetics, and specialty makeup will need to be tended to. Again, make sure you get everything that belongs to you out of an "away" venue if you want to use it again. If the show is in your own venue, and you have lots of wigs to restore and such, the process of returning items to their original condition can turn into a long-term project. Be patient, pace yourself, and be delicate with the resources.

Summary

After the show has been struck, it is time to breathe and enjoy the moment. If you are a student choreographer and your choreography was for a course, you will probably have a feedback session with your professor, mentor, and classmates. If you are a faculty choreographer, you will most likely have a postmortem with your entire team to go over the triumphs and pitfalls of the show. These postmortems are an important part of the process and should not be overlooked or put off. It is vital that the show is talked about while the memories are still fresh. Dance and theatre are an ongoing, never-ending cycle of preparation, implementation, and evaluation. Even as we are opening one show, we are in the process of thinking about the next.

Postmortem

14

audience

LEARNING OBJECTIVES

After reading this chapter, you will be able to do the following:

> Recognize the purpose and value of a postmortem meeting
> Acknowledge the important elements that the technical, design, and choreographic perspectives address in a postmortem meeting
> Recognize the value of a mediator or third party in a postmortem
> Effectively give and receive constructive feedback in a postmortem meeting

After you walk away from the final performance and strike, it's not uncommon to start looking for the next project to focus on. Maybe you have projects overlapping, and finishing one just cleared the way for a deeper dive into the next. However, before you jump to the next thing, it is important to pause and complete a postmortem. Postmortem is Latin for "after death." If you are a fan of true crime dramas, the postmortem examinations are performed to determine the cause of death. In the performing arts, the term refers to an examination or discussion that occurs after the event. This meeting involves the production team, artistic team, and any other invested parties. The goal of the meeting is to review the process and identify what was successful and where are areas for improvement and even more importantly develop a plan to make the next event more successful.

Technical Production Perspective

For the production team, the postmortem is a way to formally "close out" the event. The quicker the postmortem can be held after the final performance, the better. This is because the events are still fresh in everyone's mind. The production and administrative teams might still be chasing down final details. The production team is making sure anything rented or borrowed has been returned. All scenery, props, and costumes being kept have been inventoried and placed in storage. If the dance floor is not permanent in the theatre, that has to be accounted for and stored properly. The administrators for the production are counting ticket sales and matching the amount of money spent with the amount of money raised. Understanding where you come out on the money side of each production will drive what is possible for the next production. If one department went over budget, the next production may have to cut back on expenses based on

projected income. All contracts and payments need to be completed and signed off to ensure there are no loose ends that could haunt the team later on.

There is no right or wrong way to structure a postmortem, except to say that it should lead to action items intended to improve your processes and ultimately your production value. The production process is based on the following four areas of concern.

Budget

Just because a production came in on or under budget does not necessarily equal success. How the budget was handled and on what the budget was spent may be just as, if not more, important. For example, if the show came in on budget, but there were unreturnable purchases of goods that did not get used in the production, money was wasted. If the show came in on budget but it took longer than allocated to reconcile the budget, which then caused the company's administration to get behind on allocating the next budget, that is a negative collateral effect. If you make purchases and do not get receipts, it is a big problem and can come back to haunt you if you are ever audited. If you make purchases with cash, be sure to log this immediately (and get a reimbursement or follow your company policy), because mixing personal and professional monies is a big no-no. It is essential that all money matters be handled with attention, precision, and efficiency. How you spend money and what you spend it on are critical to the short- and long-term success of your company. If you are not good with money, hire someone who is.

Calendar

Your production will open on time, but how was the time spent leading up to the curtain and what was the quality of that time? Was your time spent joyfully crafting your art, accomplishing tasks on time, hitting your milestones with ease, and confidently sitting in the house on opening night knowing everything was on track? Or was every day of production a struggle to keep up with the never-ending punch list of to-do's, sleepless nights trying to make up for lost time, and apologizing on every phone call for being late? One of these scenarios is obviously better than the other. How will you manage your time?

People

It's easy to see how tempers might flare and insults might fly in a postmortem, where everyone in the meeting is looking at their collaborative project with a critical eye. Working with other people, especially other opinionated people and especially other opinionated and sensitive artists, is tough business. But that is not an excuse to tear anyone down. If and when there are issues with people in a production, remember the professional approach is to focus on the issue, not the human—this should never be personal. It is perfectly acceptable to criticize someone's performance (cast or crew or administration or staff) as long as it is objective, contextualized, and respectful.

People are indeed the most important part of your production, and if you treat them right, respect them, and communicate well, you will find yourself surrounded by loyal partners in your next venture. On the other hand, if you subjectively call people out, leave people out of the communication loop, and forget to pay them on time (just to name a few amateur mistakes), you will be a solo artist throughout your career. The Feedback section in this chapter has more information about how to constructively share and receive feedback in the context of the postmortem.

Physical Resources

Physical resources are all the tangible components such as the scenery, props, costumes, and technical production equipment. Did you have all the things you needed? Were they procured on time? Were they

People are the most important part of a production. With respect and trust from all, *(a)* the process will result in *(b)* collaborative work that everyone can be proud of.

economical? Can you reuse them? Can you get any value back for them in sale or trade? Where will you store them? Can you donate them to a school, community center, or church? Were your resources as significant to the production value as you had imagined? Would you use them again if you were to do this a second time? Did the cast and crew adapt well to using the things? Was there any **audience** feedback regarding the things? Did the things make or break the production? Sometimes less is more, and in production, sometimes more is more, but there are always "things" to consider.

Reflection

Postmortem is an opportunity to reflect on a production to apply what can be learned from the current experience to the next one. It is important to work through both the successes and the areas of improvement, so that the positive outcomes do not get lost in an attempt to only fix problem areas. Incorporating a SWOT analysis, as discussed in chapter 3, can be a useful tool in this process.

As a designer or collaborator, it is helpful to spend some time evaluating your role in the production process. What in your control went well, and what maybe could you do better next time? Try to identify solutions to problems, not just a list of complaints. As a professional, the time you spend in purposeful self-evaluation will support and sustain your career. Here are some important questions to observe while reflecting:

› Did my concept support the thesis of the story and choreographer?

› Did I fully commit to the goal?

› Did I explore all avenues of the design?

› Was I true to my vision?

› Did I effectively communicate my ideas to the team?

› Did I meet my deadlines?

› And, most importantly, did I listen to the other team members?

While self-evaluation is important and you can improve on your own successes, no one works in a silo. We create, work, and produce as a team. There may be things you did not know about or see that affected other team members in positive and negative ways. As a team, it is important to come together and build a consensus evaluation of the entire production from multiple points of view. This may be the most important step in the educational and professional development process.

Here are some important questions to present in the group reflection:

› Did we support the thesis of the story and choreographer?

› Did we commit to the goal as a team?

› Did we explore all of the avenues to find a successful resolution and production?

› Were we true to the group vision?

› Did we effectively communicate our ideas to the team?

› Did we meet our deadlines and our goals?

› And most importantly did we listen to each other?

While postmortem meetings are rich with valuable information and growth potential, unfortunately this is not always the outcome. The negative side of postmortem meetings is that most of them are not completely honest or are not as effective as the players want them to be. There are sensitive artists involved, people are human beings with different motivations and degrees of honesty, and

EGOS

The postmortem had all the intentions of a fruitful exchange for growth. It was an open forum for people in all the departments to listen in on the choices that were made to create the production. Scenario: A choreographer goes to a postmortem to ask a simple question to the light designer about their color choice for the final tableau: Why green?

› **Ideal outcome:** The choreographer asks the question and the light designer is able to explain their creative and artistic choice. Maybe the green provided a natural environment feel that supported the artistic goal. This creates a dialogue between the designer and choreographer to see if there was a misunderstanding. If they work together in the future, they will have a great place to start from.

› **Unfortunate outcome:** The whole conversation became a platform about complaining about this and that, and egos collide. In this situation, the choreographer is not able to ask their question, and communication and trust has broken down. The team may be less excited or trusting to work with each other in the future.

they see events from varying points of view. In its pure form, it is a wonderful tool to reflect and grow as a unit; however, when people are *not* fully honest with themselves about their work, can't communicate openly and honestly with the team, or have a different agenda, the entire postmortem process can be quickly hijacked. It is unfortunate that you will find some people have an axe to grind or want to have a platform to air their personal complaints instead of staying focused on the bigger picture.

If you are fortunate enough to be in a healthy situation, the egos are left at the door, and there isn't a hierarchy in place. This allows junior members of the company the ability to speak honestly and for everyone to grow to better and greater success.

Visit HK*Propel* to complete assignment 14.1, What to Bring to a Postmortem.

Choreographer and Artistic Perspectives

For the choreographer, the postmortem is a time to reflect on the entire process from the initial inspiration through the completed performance. Looking back at your artistic process can sometimes be difficult. As artists, we are hard on ourselves and always strive to improve our work. But it's important to look back at the whole picture and try to separate yourself from it.

Depending on your level of involvement in the overall production, you may not be a part of postmortem with the design and production team. In academia, this may be reserved for the faculty and directors where students are not necessarily included in the meeting. The greater your involvement in the overall process, the more likely a postmortem will be an essential part of your growth as an artist. This is a time to work with the design and production team one last time to close out the show, celebrate what went well and improve on communication for future events.

Topics may include the following:

> A discussion about deadlines could include something about how the production team wasn't clear on deadlines or there was a breakdown in the communication with the dancers, so it created some unnecessary stress for everyone involved.

> It could be simple things such as "I hope that next time we add five minutes to the intermission to let the performers rest and change."

> Budget is also an important item to discuss once the show is over. Did the team stay on budget? How can the budget be used more wisely in the future, or how can we find ways to stretch the budget if needed?

There can be more difficult conversations about artistic differences, breakdowns in communication, inappropriate handling of situations, and being honest about relationships that just don't work. These are uncomfortable things to talk about, but they need to be brought up so that the pattern of bad energy or hurt feelings doesn't just keep going. Not everyone will agree with everything that is said, and that is OK, but if it is not said or discussed, it will fester and become a bigger problem next time. Remember that no one can read your mind and you can't read anyone else's mind. So, the issues that are brought up now may not have even been on the radar, but once they are talked about, they can be resolved or at the very least acknowledged. When people come to the table with solutions and not complaints, strategies are put into place for the next production.

As your dance company grows or the scope of the productions increases over time, there will always be areas to reassess and improve on procedures and processes. This is the joy of the creative arts. With each show, we are inspired to grow and challenge ourselves for the next event.

Self-Reflection

Some personal reflection is important before having a group discussion. If you were an audience member and you were seeing this piece for the first time, what would your reaction and thoughts be about this piece? Some questions you can ask yourself are the following:

> Did the work bring specific emotions out?

> Did this work make you laugh or feel uncomfortable?

> Will you remember this work after you have left the theatre?

> Would you recommend this show or work to a friend?

Keeping a journal throughout the process is something that you may find helpful. This can be a written or digital journal. Recording your progress at the end of each rehearsal keeps both you and the dancers on track while you are in the process and allows you to go back and evaluate the process. These written and digital remembrances are important as a way to reflect and evaluate.

Group Reflection

You may also decide to have a postmortem meeting with your cast, especially if these are dancers in your company or you plan on working with them in the future. It can be helpful to hear feedback from their perspective on the logistics of the run of rehearsals and production week. It is possible the dancers were dealing with costume or backstage issues and didn't bother you during the run of the show but would like these to be addressed in the future. Now the run is over and they are assessing the physical impact on their body, so they may have questions about how to best support their health moving forward. It's possible there was a lift or moment that they felt was too risky or harmed them. Some may express concerns for the costumes being clean or repaired properly before each show.

Again, the postmortem is not a complaint session. As the choreographer, it is your job to set the tone, ground rules, and keep the conversation on topic and focused toward finding solutions for sustainability. Dancers will appreciate having their concerns heard and solutions decided. They will also appreciate you even more if you can keep the meeting professional, on time, and on topic.

Mediators

Postmortems should have a mediator or someone neutral to keep the meeting going and ensure the topics are addressed. Typical mediators could be the artistic director or the production manager. This person can lead the discussion from an unbiased approach to find solutions. The leader of the conversation makes sure that the responses are limited and monitor that the topics stay on target and do not veer off into a subtext category. One may consider emailing the topics or questions beforehand so that no one feels railroaded at the meeting. An example of a mediator asking questions could be the following:

> **Mediator:** *"Why did department XYZ go over budget?"* If a department or person is aware that this question will be brought up, then perhaps they will not feel attacked and will provide honest answers and not feel so defensive.

> **Answer:** *"The reason the set piece went over budget is because of the current economic climate. The price of materials has quadrupled since we were in preproduction a year ago. And we discussed it with the producer and the choreographer, concluding that this was an essential element to the story and the choreography. So, it was greenlighted."*

HOW NOT TO POSTMORTEM

Artistic Director: Thank you all for being here today. I'm really glad this show is over. *[Buzzer cuts them off. Try again.]*

Artistic Director: Well, that sure did stink. *[Buzzer cuts them off. Try again.]*

Artistic Director: Well, that sure was great. *[Buzzer cuts them off. Try again.]*

Artistic Director: Congratulations on a wonderful show! Unfortunately, we didn't make enough money to pay any of you. *[Buzzer cuts them off.]*

Let's imagine how that might go much better:

Artistic Director: Thank you all for being here today. I have shared an agenda with you all so we can stay on track and make sure everyone gets an opportunity to share. Our meeting norms are the following:

- ❥ Respect the time.
- ❥ Respect each other: Let people finish their thoughts and assume they have the best intentions.
- ❥ Address issues and roles, not individuals—this is not personal.
- ❥ Provide a possible solution for every issue you highlight.
- ❥ I'd like to begin by saying I am so proud of the work everyone has done. I'd like to hear your thoughts on the production process for the purposes of improving our efficiency, effectiveness, financial responsibility, and impact on the community. The results of this meeting will guide our decision-making and preparation for our next production.

At this point, the issue is either resolved or creates another question (or multiple questions) about chain of command, communication, and protocol within the company. When a company is in a good place and has a group who trusts each other and has open communication, a postmortem should be a focused conversation on the weaknesses and strengths of the experience. It is appropriate to celebrate what *was* accomplished as well—do not forget to celebrate the positive. Ask the important questions: How are we going support to keep the successful and positive elements of the production process going forward? How can we support the departments or people who need increased resources to succeed?

And remember that we can make powerful art that touches lives under incredibly challenging circumstances as a team. Evaluation is an important step in the production process. The postmortem is a place for open and constructive communication.

Feedback

A final piece of reflection for the team is giving and accepting constructive feedback from peers or mentors. This is where you need to separate yourself from the work and try to listen to all the feedback; even the suggestions that you may not like or agree with are important to hear and digest. It's equally important to remain impartial and professional when offering constructive feedback to others.

Giving Constructive Feedback

Constructive feedback offers thoughtful, well meaning, and truthful opinions about the work and art of others. This process should include both positive and negative feedback or comments. It is most helpful and digested when done in a friendly manner as opposed to an oppositional or confrontational one. The entire purpose of constructive feedback is to improve the outcome for all participants involved. When working in a collaborative environment such as dance production, this kind of feedback is an invaluable tool.

Remember that constructive feedback should always be focused on the art and not on the person creating the art. This is not the time or place to let personal feelings about someone cloud the feedback session. Constructive feedback is most effective when it is specific, clear, and *actionable*. The clearer and more specific your feedback is, the easier it is

Constructive feedback should be thoughtful, well meaning, and truthful.

for the person receiving to let it in. If the comments are based on actionable things, then the feedback can be thought about and implemented right away.

Providing effective constructive feedback can be thought of as a three-step process. You begin with a compliment, add constructive criticism with suggestions, and end with a positive plan to move forward.

1. Always start off by focusing on the strengths of the work. What were things that you enjoyed or that stuck out as being effective in the art?
2. Next, offer thoughtful criticisms or questions regarding why certain things were done in the work—the things that struck you as not fitting the vision or problematic in some way. What are the areas where improvement can be suggested?
3. The last part of your constructive feedback statement summarizes what was previously stated and suggests ways of moving forward. This approach considers both the positives and the suggestions and provides actionable strategies and ideas.

Receiving Constructive Feedback

Have you ever met anyone who goes into a feedback session with enthusiasm or excitement to hear comments about their work? We are human, after all, and no one likes to hear negative comments. Even when they are not directed at the person but at the work, sometimes it is very hard to separate the person from the work. But you have to try to do so anyway. Constructive feedback is one of the best ways to grow as an artist. The audience will see the work eventually, so it is always best to get feedback both before opening night and soon after closing night. When you receive constructive feedback, try focusing on the practical and actionable elements of the feedback. Come into the session with an open mind and an attitude toward receiving feedback, knowing that it will be both positive and negative. If you can do this, it will contribute greatly to your personal development and will reveal areas of concern that you may have missed because you were so deeply connected to the work.

> *"The process is most fruitful when artists are invested in the future evolution of the art they are showing, or at least in the possibility that they can learn something of value to apply to future projects"* (Lerman and Borstel 2003).

The next time you receive feedback, follow these four steps. If the feedback is given in the correct way, it will make it easier to not take it personally.

1. *Wait for your gut reaction to pass:* Breathe and take a moment to absorb the feedback.
2. *Remember that you are there to grow from the experience:* Constructive feedback is vital to the process.
3. *Listen with an open mind:* Curb the tendency to defend your choices in the work.
4. *Ask pointed and clear questions:* By asking specific questions, you can better understand the feedback that was given.

The postmortem can serve multiple purposes. For the technical staff and administration, this helps them close all the books, reconcile accounts, and check in with all departments. For the creative designers and choreographers, the postmortem is a time to review the communication process and how all the final design elements came together. The goal is for postmortem to be guided and constructive and not a time to vent or complain. Discussions with clear intention of working out any miscommunications and processes will only make the next collaborative process stronger and supportive. For everyone involved, this can be a sensitive process. Honest self-reflection is key, as is the ability to provide constructive feedback.

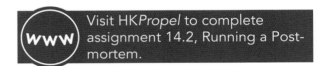

Visit HK*Propel* to complete assignment 14.2, Running a Postmortem.

Now What?

The show is closed, and the postmortem is done. Now what? If this was your first time choreographing and being part of a production, it may take some time to digest everything that just happened. Seeing the inner workings of a production may spark excitement to pursue more training about the different types of jobs involved. Maybe you can't wait to choreograph again, and you see your career unfolding in front of you as you become a sought-after choreographer, artistic director, and maybe even a producer. The opportunities to grow and evolve are endless.

Once you are inspired to continue your career as a creator, the next challenge is to determine how to move forward. As a new choreographer, you must keep creating and experimenting with your art form. You will have many dances that you like, some that you don't, and others that will become your signature works. The first decision is how to continue to create works. If you are still in school, take all the opportunities available to you to choreograph with the technical support the school provides. Beyond those opportunities, you need to start creating your own magic. If you want to start producing your own shows, paying your talent, and even building your own artistic legacy, the next step is to go back to the beginning of this book. The fundamental process doesn't change—just the vision and scope of the dance production.

Glossary

addenda—An additional item added to a contract.

amendments—Changes and deletions to a contract.

amplifier—A device that receives an audio signal and increases that signal into the driving force behind a speaker's output

apron—Any stage space downstage of the plaster line or proscenium.

artistic director—The executive of an arts organization in charge of the direction of the dance or production.

artistic vision—The creative conceptualization of the work you want to create.

assistant choreographer—Works along with the choreographer to assist and contribute to the artistic process.

audience—A group of people who attend, watch, or experience a performance.

audio and video editors—Technicians responsible for assembling the content prepared for the production and creating a product that can be broadcast to a remote audience.

audio frequency—A frequency that corresponds to audible sound waves.

audition—A live or recorded sample performance demonstrating the dancer's skill for an individual or a panel of judges.

backlight—A light source located upstage of scenery or performers, intended to sculpt and separate them from the background. Useful in dance silhouette.

blackout—The complete absence of stage lighting, resulting in a theoretically black environment.

booms (a.k.a. trees)—Vertical pipes (typically), mounted on a weighted base, with lighting instruments hung perpendicular to them, often used as a sidelight position in dance production.

borders—Any horizontal drapes used to mask the battens, lighting, or anything else above the stage.

box office—The place where tickets are sold and distributed.

box office manager—The supervisor dealing with selling tickets for the performance.

budget—Balance of the projected expenses and revenues associated with a project.

cadence meeting—A regularly scheduled production meeting in a round-robin format for departmental updates and establishing new action items.

call back—When a choreographer has narrowed down from a large group to a smaller group but would like to see them again before making a final casting decision.

campaign—A strategic approach to inform and attract an audience and fundraising.

center line—An imaginary line that divides the stage into equal left and right halves.

center stage—The most powerful and important position onstage, existing at the physical center of the performance space, as defined in its context.

choreographer—Composes the sequence of steps and moves for a performance of dance.

collaboration—Working together to create something.

color temperature—A quality of light describing its relative coolness or warmth.

company—A group of dancers and associated collaborators who work together to create a production.

condenser microphone—A microphone that requires power and delivers more accurate signals than its dynamic counterparts do, thus being superior for recording and capturing instrument audio.

contract—A written agreement between two or more parties describing the rights and responsibilities of each party. The contract is a legally binding document and is used for employment, equipment rentals, venues, and any other logistical elements in a production.

co-presentation—A mode of producing in which both the venue and the creator take on risk and share returns from the performance.

copyright—A legal right given to authors to protect the use, publishing, or selling of their work.

cost-out—Specific production meetings dealing with all budget items especially focused on expenses.

costume designer—A person who designs costumes and accessories worn during a performance.

costume shop—The space where costumes are designed, built, and stored for productions.

costume supervisor—Oversees the creation, rental, implementation, and maintenance of costumes.

creative brief—This document outlines the strategy of a creative project. A creative brief contains project details, including general information, your intended concept, thematic environment, structure, lighting and aesthetics, music and sound, costumes, and visual and evocative research.

crossfade—Simultaneously increasing the intensity of one lighting cue while decreasing another, resulting in a dramatic shift of light.

crowdfunding—Raising funds for a project by collecting smaller amounts of money from a larger network of people typically driven by online platforms.

cue-to-cue rehearsal—An early rehearsal in the technical phase of production development wherein the directors, designers, and choreographers work with the stage crew and operators to establish the timing and execution of each cue, generally in sequence, with or without a cast. After the successful execution of a cue, the stage manager asks the staff to set for the following cue, moving past sections of the performance that do not require direct intervention on the part of the running crew.

cyc lights—Lighting instruments specifically purposed for illuminating the cyclorama with a wash of light in a desired color and/or intensity.

cyclorama—A large curtain or wall, typically positioned at the most upstage position of the performance space, providing a neutral surface for creating unique lighting looks or feels, or certain backdrops.

dance captain—Typically a member of the dance ensemble whose main responsibility is to maintain the integrity of the choreography once the show opens.

dance—A form of communication and art that involves improvising, choreographing, comparing and contrasting, refining, interpreting, practicing, rehearsing, and sometimes performing.

dancer—A person who dances or performs through the medium of dance.

deck—Common term referring to the floor of the performance space in a theatre venue.

deductible—An amount that needs to be paid before an insurance company proceeds with paying a claim.

deliverables—Anything and everything a collaborator (generally a designer in this context) is required to submit for payment and approval.

designer run—Also known as a *designer run-through*, this is a type of rehearsal typically accompanied by a comprehensive large-group production meeting following the run or perhaps smaller meetings interspersed between dance numbers, choreographers, or acts.

designer—Individuals who create the visual, physical and auditory environment to support a performance.

deux ex machina—An early Greek scenic element that allowed performers to fly in the air.

downstage—The performing area onstage that is closest to the audience. Early stages were built as a ramp, or "raked" from back to front from the performer's perspective while facing the audience, resulting in performers advancing down the slope of the stage toward the audience, from back (upstage) to front (downstage).

dress rehearsal—The final rehearsals in the performance space with all production elements involved intended to emulate what an actual performance will look, sound, and feel like in every aspect.

dynamic microphone—The microphone of choice for live entertainment due to its reliability and durability, features resulting from its relatively simple technological design and construction.

ellipsoidal reflector spotlight (ERS)—A stage lighting instrument, characterized by its unique and ubiquitous body shape—with its many shutters and accessories for the control and alteration of its light beam—that provides strong directional light (and commonly, the instrument of choice for side lighting in dance production).

employee—A person or company employed for wages or salary.

EQ—Highlights different wavelengths of sound in an output sound mix and can isolate certain sounds (low, mid, and high tones).

evening-length productions—A dance or production lasting at least 40 minutes and focusing on one continuous story for the entire show.

evocative research—A compilation of a range of elements, such as images, video, text, and colors, that help define the general aesthetic, tone, and feeling of a work.

expense—Any service, resource, or component of a production that has a required cost.

fade in—The increase of light onstage, at a specified rate of speed, intended to create different moods and dramatic effects and indicate a transition.

fade out—The diminishing of light onstage, at a specified rate of speed, intended to create different moods and dramatic effects and indicate a transition.

festival—A mixed-bill production where choreographers have submitted to have their works showcased.

fill light—Light focused on the front of the subject that compliments the key light by filling in the shadows created by the key light.

fiscal receiver—Nonprofit umbrella company that allows tax-deductible donations to be given to independent artists.

follow spot—A single beam of light that can move and follow a performer around the stage.

Fresnel—A lighting instrument, characterized by its uniquely designed flat lens—shaped with a series of concentric grooves, ridges, or terraces—that provides a relatively sharper beam of light as compared to other wash type instruments.

front of house—The part of the performance venue that is open to the public, usually the auditorium and foyer.

gain—The "loudness" of sound going into a sound mixer.

Gantt chart—A type of calendar tool that production managers use to show the relationships between production tasks and dependencies between them.

gel—A thin sheet of plastic secured in a frame at the end of a lighting instrument (in the path of the light beam) affecting the color and or distribution (diffusion) of the light beam.

gobo—A thin metal plate or glass disc placed in the path of the light beam in an ERS lighting instrument, or built into an LED/moving instrument, that causes specific images, patterns, or textures to be seen in the field of light created by the associated instrument.

going dark—A verbal warning yelled out by an individual prior to shutting off all the lights in a performance venue. This is critical for alerting anyone present and within earshot that they will experience a sudden and complete blackout, and to prevent avoidable injury or mishap as a result.

grand rights—Music rights obtained when the intention is to host an audience for entertainment and perform a dramatic act with music.

grant—A fundraising process to receive a specific amount of money given by the government or other entity to a deserving organization or person for a specific purpose.

ground row—Lights set on the floor from edge to edge of the cyc curtain.

hair designer—Designs and facilitates any visual appearance of the performers' hair or the use of wigs.

handheld microphone—Any microphone you see people hold in their hands to speak or sing into.

heads—A verbal warning to those onstage that work is happening above their heads, or in the case of emergency, to indicate that something is falling from above.

high-side lights—Lighting effect at an angle closer to 45 degrees from above and that contours the head and shoulders of dancers.

house manager—The supervisor who coordinates the audience experience, box office, and ushers.

house—The portion of a theatre or performance venue from where the audience observes the production.

houselights—The lighting in the audience chamber of a theatre or auditorium.

hue—The literal color of the lighting effect.

independent contractor—A person or business that provides goods or services under a written contract. They are hired for a specific job or event and are not considered a regular employee.

installation—A dance created in a different space that is then installed in a new venue that will need restaging.

iris—An adjustable gate (manual or automated) in an ERS lighting instrument that increases or shrinks the cone of the light beam, essentially making it narrower or wider.

key light—The primary light focused on the front of the subject, establishing a basic look.

lavalier microphone—A microphone that is usually clipped onto a shirt or jacket and is connected to a wireless body pack and transmitted to a receiver.

LED pixel mapping—Digital scenic design using LED wall technology made up of many smaller panels and even smaller pixels (or single point sources of light).

legs—Any vertical drapes to the side of the performance space that create the alleys for travel on and off stage and help mask the wings and backstage space.

letter of agreement—An offer of employment; it includes the terms of employment and an acceptance of the offer in letter format.

liability—Identifies responsibility for bodily injury or property damage claims that result from accidents occurring during a production.

lighting designer—Creates the lighting, atmosphere, and overall visual environment for the production.

makeup designer—Designs and facilitates any visual appearance of any makeup worn by the dancers.

managing director—In charge of the logistical day-to-day operations and focused on the business aspects of the dance company.

market—An intended audience for a production; the group of people it is aimed toward, and the environment in which it sits.

Marley—Vinyl floor covering for dance spaces.

memorandum of understanding (MOU)—An agreement before the contract is finalized; it gets the terms written in a new form for a rewritten contract.

merchandise—Items to be sold at events to promote the business or company and raise additional revenue.

mixed bill—A collection of pieces presented in a singular performance.

multimedia designer—Also called a *visual designer*, this person is responsible for integrating the visuals and video into a scenic or lighting design.

notes—A list of comments about a production created to support clear communication between collaborators. Also a type of production meeting scheduled to communicate notes, clarify them with all involved, and distribute the notes list.

offstage—Any area out of sight of the audience.

onstage—The act of, or location enabling, being in front of or seen by the audience.

open call—An audition open for anyone wishing to try out.

orchestra—The space where the storytelling took place in ancient Greek performances.

panel light—LED technology used to emit a less-controlled beam of light at a lower intensity.

paper tech—When the stage manager goes through a cue-by-cue, a page-by-page walkthrough of the entire show documented in a prompt book to confirm the cues on paper before or between any live rehearsals.

parabolic aluminized reflector (PAR) light—A type of self-contained electric lamp commonly used in theatrical lighting.

periaktoi—A Greek scenic element; a three-sided revolving column portraying three different scenes.

personal ask—Asking people for money to support the production.

plaster line—The imaginary line on the stage floor that creates the bottom "fourth side" of the proscenium opening.

postproduction coordinator—Technicians responsible for assembling the content prepared for the production and creating a product that can be broadcast to a remote audience.

premiere—The first public performance or showing of a work.

premium—An amount of money paid to an insurance company for a policy.

presented—A mode of producing in which an artist is asked to create work specifically for an organization. The organization is responsible for general marketing, ticket sales, crew, and everything in between while the artist is paid a fee to make their art.

press release—A way to get the word out about your performance. These are targeted, concise, and bring attention to your production as a unique and newsworthy performance.

producer—A person who oversees a production from start to finish.

production manager—They coordinate the technical and logistical aspects and facilitate communication of the entire production.

production meeting—An opportunity for primary stakeholders to gather for a status update on the production process, and to delegate new action items across the teams.

production week—The week leading up to a production that includes the key rehearsals in the performance space.

production—Using technical elements, including costumes, lighting, music, physical and virtual space, publicity, and audience engagement, to amplify the unique talents of the performing artists.

projection mapping—The practice of layering a front-projected image onto a surface of any shape.

prompt book—A copy of a script, score, or other order of show amended with the technical notes and cues from which a stage manager "calls" a performance.

prop designer—Creates and designs the necessary props to align with the scenic designer's plan.

prop master—The person in charge of all rentals and purchases and may build the necessary items.

proscenium—A wall or arch in a theatre that separates the performance space from the audience space.

publicity creators—Individuals who design and create materials to provide information about the production, dancers, and upcoming events.

reel—A short video representation of an artist's prior credits.

rehearsal director—Runs rehearsals and classes and creates the dancer schedules. It is their responsibility to make sure the dance and dancers are ready to perform.

rehearsals—The practice of the dance in preparation for a performance.

rep plot (repertory plot)—A standardized lighting system that can be easily adapted to various performance requirements.

repertory—A company that performs choreographed works from a specific choreographer.

repertory dance company—A dance company with several works from various choreographers they can pull from for performances throughout their season.

revenue—Income (money) received by an organization or entity.

rider—A document specifying all the requirements of the production and talent for the venue to satisfactorily prepare for the show.

routing—Assigns the outputs on a sound mixer and establishes through which monitors and other elements any given input will be heard.

running lights—These are also called *working lights*. They are usually a low-intensity blue light that helps performers and stage crews work and move around safely backstage.

scene shop—A specialized workshop intended for building scenery, props, and other components of a production.

scenic designer—Also called a *set designer*, this person creates the physical environment for the production.

scrim—A loosely woven gauze that can appear transparent or solid depending on how it is lit.

season—A series of events or performances scheduled for a company or at a venue over the course of a year.

self-producing—A mode of producing in which an artist creates and produces their own work. The artist takes any risk (financial or otherwise) along with any success.

self-tape—A video audition used for screening applicants, a supplemental audition, or an audition used for selecting a performer for a specific production.

SFX—Sound effects built into a sound mixer that can be added to a sound score.

sidelight—Lighting directed from just offstage that illuminates the dancer at a perpendicular angle to the audience sight line. The contour of the human body is accentuated by sidelights.

site-specific—A performance created for a specific space or environment. These venues are untraditional performance spaces.

site-specific performance—A dance production that occurs outside the conventional theatre space.

skene—From the Greek word for "scene building," this was a space in ancient Greek theatre that the performers used to change masks or makeup.

sky cyc—Lighting hung from above the stage, in front of, or behind the cyc.

sound designer—A collaborative artist who creates audio that accentuates the performance.

sound engineer—A technician who works with audio recordings and editing as well as the technical equipment needed for a performance.

soundboard (a.k.a. console or mixer)—This is the specific console used to run the sound for a production.

source device—Any piece of audio hardware that originates an audio signal.

speakers—The final output device in an audio signal flow that creates the sound heard by an observer.

spike tape—Specialty cloth tape used to mark locations and placement onstage.

stage left—Directional term for a performer onstage described as the performer's left side when facing the audience.

stage manager—They provide practical and organizational support to all the collaborators in the production process. During the performance, the stage manager makes sure the production runs smoothly.

stage monitor speaker—A speaker pointed toward the performers onstage to facilitate their ability to hear the audio during the performance.

stage right—Directional term for a performer onstage described as the performer's right side when facing the audience.

streaming engineer—Technician responsible for setting up all the equipment for the stream and operates the computer or control deck on the day of the stream.

strike—The time after a performance where all scenery, lighting, media, costumes, and other production elements are torn down and taken away to return the stage to its original state.

strip light—A row of small floodlights used for special effects and lighting paths and can create indirect lighting or be used to light the cyc.

SWOT analysis—A strategic planning tool used to assess internal (strengths and weaknesses) and external (opportunities and threats) factors of organizations.

sync rights—Music rights required if planning to stream or broadcast your dance production.

technical (tech) rehearsal—The first full run-through of a piece in a space intended to effectively integrate and cue technical elements for performance and get the performers and crew used to cues and elements at play.

technical director—They are in charge of the production's technical elements, including everything backstage and onstage.

theatre—A building or area designed to support performances.

theatre-in-the-round—A form of staging in which the audience is seated completely around the stage.

theatron—An ancient Greek performance space.

thrust stage—A stage that extends into the audience so that the audience is seated on three sides.

ticket sales—The income from selling access or seats to an event.

tour manager—The coordinator for the production who sets up community engagements and travel logistics and coordinates all production elements as a show goes on the road.

upstage—The performing area onstage that is furthest away from the audience.

visual designer—Also called a *multimedia designer*, this person is responsible for integrating the visuals and video into a scenic lighting design.

volume—The loudness of sound coming out of a sound mixer.

wings—The area adjacent to the left or right of the performance space, just offstage and out of sight of the audience, where performers standby for entrances and to where they make their exits. Scenery, props, lighting, and other production elements are typically stored here, often in a preset position to be moved on or offstage during or between scenes or dance pieces.

workers' compensation—A benefit that covers employees who suffer illness or injury while working for a wage or salary.

Bibliography

Chapter 1

Ambrosio, Nora. 2018. *Learning About Dance, Dance as an Art Form and Entertainment.* 8th ed. Kendall Hunt Publishing.

Beaman, Patricia Leigh. 2018. *World Dance Cultures from Ritual to Spectacle.* Routledge.

Campbell, Tori. 2020 Artistic Collaborations: Martha Graham and Isamu Noguchi, Artland Magazine. https://magazine.artland.com/artistic-collaborations-martha-graham-isamu-noguchi/

Carver, Rita Kogler. 2018. *Stagecraft Fundamentals: A Guide and Reference for Theatrical Production,* 3rd ed. Focal Press.

Das, Joanna Dee. 2017. *Katherine Dunham: Dance and the African Diaspora.* Oxford University Press.

Dils, Ann, and Albright, Ann Cooper, eds. 2001. *Moving History/Dancing Cultures.* Wesleyan University Press.

Emery, Lynne Fauley. 1989. *Black Dance: From 1619 to Today.* Princeton Book Company.

Frederick, Eva. 2019. Dancing Chimpanzees may reveal how Humans started to Boogie. *Science.* doi:10.1126/science.aba6904.

Gillette, J. Michael. 2019. *Designing with Light: An Introduction to Stage Lighting.* 7th ed. Routledge.

Gillette, J. Michael. 2019. *Theatrical Design and Production: An Introduction to Scene Design and Construction, Lighting, Sound, Costume, and Makeup.* 8th ed. McGraw Hill Education.

Guarino, Lindsay, and Oliver, Wendy, eds. 2015. *Jazz Dance: A History of the roots and Branches.* University Press of Florida Reprint Edition.

Hahn, Tomie. 2007. *Sensational Knowledge: Embodying Culture Through Japanese Dance (Music/Culture).* Wesleyan University Press.

Kassing, Gayle. 2007. *History of Dance: An Interactive Arts Approach.* Human Kinetics.

Kenrick, John. 2017. *Musical Theatre: A History.* 2nd ed. Bloomsbury Publishing Plc.

Kourlas, Gia. 2014. *He Can Fly, in a Flash, Right Before Your Eyes.* The New York Times.

Mallare, Marie-Lorraine. 2008. *Behind the Mask: The Jabbawockeez, America.* In Dance.

McDonald, Marianne. 2011. *The Cambridge Companion to Greek and Roman Theatre (Cambridge Companions to Literature).* Illustrated Edition. Cambridge University Press.

Murphy, Jacqueline Shea. 2007. *The People Have Never Stopped Dancing: Native American Modern Dance Histories.* University of Minnesota Press.

Nair, Sreenath. 2014. *The Natyasastra and the Body in Performance: Essays on Indian Theories of Dance and Drama.* McFarland.

Tell, Caroline. 2016. "Hamilton's Costume Designer Talks About Modernizing 18th-Century Style". *Observer.* June 18, 2016. https://observer.com/2016/06/hamiltons-costume-designer-talks-about-modernizing-18th-century-style/.

Wilson, Edwin. 2017. *Living Theatre: A History of Theatre.* 7th ed. W. W. Norton & Company.

Chapter 2

Blakeman, Robyn. 2019. "Team Creative Brief: Creative and Account Teams Speak Out on Best Practices." *Journal of Advertising Education* 23 (1).

Coleman, Basha. 2021. "How to Write a Creative Brief in 11 Simple Steps [Examples + Template]". *HubSpot.* September 20, 2021. https://blog.hubspot.com/marketing/creative-brief.

Dan, Avi. 2013. "The Heart of Effective Advertising is a Powerful Insight." *Forbes.* June 8, 2013. https://forbes.com/sites/avidan/2013/07/08/the-heart-of-effective-advertising-is-a-powerful-insight/?sh=-35f3a68c21d5.

Jones, Peter, and Karen Yates. 1998. "The Pollitt Ingredient." *Campaign.* October 23, 1998. https://link.gale.com/apps/doc/A21245120/ITOF?u=chap_main&sid=-bookmark-ITOF&xid=db6bd2bc.

Komatsu, Sara. 2020. "The Pandemic Has Radically Changed Dance—Maybe for the Better." *The Harvard Crimson.* October 17, 2020. www.thecrimson.com/column/backstage-at-the-ballet/article/2020/10/17/columns-the-pandemic-has-radically-changed-dance.

"Revelations." 2021. Alvin Ailey American Dance Theater. July 21, 2021. www.alvinailey.org/performances/repertory/revelations.

Chapter 3

Chapman, Terry S., Mary L. Lai, and Elmer L. Steinbock. 1983. *Am I Covered for . . .?: A Guide to Insurance for Nonprofit Organizations*. Consortium for Human Services.

Indeed. 2020. "The Fundamentals of Nonprofits." April 3, 2020. www.indeed.com/career-advice/finding-a-job/how-do-non-profits-work.

IRS. 2022. "Exempt Organization Types." Last modified June 15, 2022. www.irs.gov/charities-non-profits/exempt-organization-types.

Indeed. 2021. "Nonprofit vs. Not for Profit." March 29, 2021. www.indeed.com/career-advice/career-development/nonprofit-vs-not-for-profit.

LawDepot. n.d. "Free Performance Contract." Accessed November 2, 2021. www.lawdepot.com/contracts/performance-contract.

Moore, Adam, and Ken Himma. 2018. "Intellectual Property." In *Stanford Encyclopedia of Philosophy*. Stanford University. https://plato.stanford.edu/archives/win2018/entries/intellectual-property.

National Council of Nonprofits. n.d. "Fiscal Sponsorships for Nonprofits." www.councilofnonprofits.org/tools-resources/fiscal-sponsorship-nonprofits.

Teoli, Dac, Terrence Sanvictores, and Jason An. 2021. "SWOT Analysis." *StatPearls*. September 8, 2021. https://ncbi.nlm.nih.gov/books/NBK537302.

ZipRecruiter. n.d. "Q: What Is the Difference Between a Long Term Short Term Full Time and Part Time Position." Accessed November 2, 2021. www.ziprecruiter.com/e/What-Is-the-Difference-Between-a-Long-Term-Short-Term-Full-Time-and-Part-Time-Position.

American for the Arts. n.d. www.americansforthearts.org.

League of Resident Theatres. 2017. "USA Agreement." https://lort.org/assets/documents/2017-22-LORT-USA-Agreement.pdf

Legis Music. n.d. https://legismusic.com.

Reed, Chris. 2021. "The Basics of Insurance for Artist." *Artrepreneur*. April 1, 2021. https://artrepreneur.com/journal/artbusiness/basics-insurance-artists.

Volunteer Lawyers and Accountants for the Arts. n.d. "Sample Performance Agreement." https://vlaa.org/wp-content/uploads/2015/05/Sample-Performance-Agreement.pdf.

ZipRecruiter. 2022. "Dance Choreographer Salary." www.ziprecruiter.com/Salaries/Dance-Choreographer-Salary.

Chapter 4

Arthurs, A., F. Hodsoll, and S. Lavine. 1999. "For-Profit and Not-for-Profit Arts Connections: Existing and Potential." *The Journal of Arts Management, Law, and Society* 29 (2):80–96.

Artwork Archive. n.d. "How to Get Artist Grants Funding." Accessed October 11, 2021. https://www.artworkarchive.com/blog/how-to-get-artist-grants-funding.

Dalla Chiesa, Carolina, and Erwin Dekker. 2021. "Crowdfunding in the Arts: Beyond Match-Making on Platform." *Socio-Economic Review* 19 (4):1265-1290.

Dan, Avi. 2013. "The Heart of Effective Advertising Is a Powerful Insight." *Forbes*, July 8, 2013. www.forbes.com/sites/avidan/2013/07/08/the-heart-of-effective-advertising-is-a-powerful-insight/?sh=35f3a68c21d5.

Di Orio, Laura. 2015. "The Freelance Game: Could You Be a Freelance Dancer?" Dance Informa Magazine. May 06, 2015. https://www.danceinforma.com/2015/05/05/working-as-a-freelance-dancer/.

Fractured Atlas. https://www.fracturedatlas.org/site/blog/case-studies-how-for-profit-arts-companies-build-community

GoFundMe. 2016. "How to Ask for Donations: Tips for Beginner Fundraisers." June 28, 2016. www.gofundme.com/c/blog/ask-for-donations.

Merriam-Webster.com Dictionary. s.v. "freelance." Accessed October 11, 2021. https://www.merriam-webster.com/dictionary/freelance.

Merriam-Webster.com Dictionary. s.v. "nonprofit." Accessed October 11, 2021. https://www.merriam-webster.com/dictionary/nonprofit

National Endowment for the Arts. n.d. "Grants." Accessed October 11, 2021. https://www.arts.gov/grants

O'Keeffee, Kimberly. 2018. "Crowdfunding in Public Art." *Americans for the Arts*. December 2018. https://www.americansforthearts.org/sites/default/files/Crowdfunding%20for%20Public%20Art_Final.pdf.

Prive, Tanya. 2012. "What is Crowdfunding and How Does it Benefit The Economy." *Forbes*. November 27, 2012. https://forbes.com/sites/tanyaprive/2012/11/27/what-is-crowdfunding-and-how-does-it-benefit-the-economy/?sh=7f15bedcbe63.

Renz, Loren. 2003. "An Overview of Revenue Streams for Nonprofit Arts Organizations." Grantmakers in the Arts. Summer 2003. www.giarts.org/article/overview-revenue-streams-nonprofit-arts-organizations.

Sickler, Erin. 2021. "Effective Grant Writing." *Artrepreneur*. October 5, 2021https://abj.artrepreneur.com/effective-grant-writing/.

The New York Times. 1982. "The Life of a Freelance Choreographer." February 28, 1982. https://www.nytimes.com/1982/02/28/arts/the-life-of-a-freelance-choreographer.html.

Thorpe, Devin. 2018. "How to Organize the Perfect Fundraising Gala." *Forbes*. August 29, 2018. www.forbes.com/sites/devinthorpe/2018/08/29/how-to-organize-the-perfect-fundraising-gala/?sh=b0adc6e79dfa.

Chapter 5

Oxford. 2000. *Oxford Advanced Learner's Dictionary of Current English*. Oxford University Press.

Chapter 7

Taylor, Clifton. 2019. *Color and Light: Navigating Color Mixing in the Midst of an LED Revolution, A Handbook for Lighting Designers.* Quite Specific Media, a division of Silman-James Press.

Gillette, J. Michael, and Michael McNamara. 2020. *Designing with Light: An Introduction to Stage Lighting.* 7th Ed. New York, NY: Routledge.

Chapter 10

Alvin Ailey American Dance Theater. 2022. "Alvin Ailey American Dance Theater." Accessed October 06, 2021. www.alvinailey.org.

Burke, Siobhan. 2019. "Dancing in Museums: A Decade of Movement." Art and Education. Accessed October 6, 2021. www.artandeducation.net/classroom/306373/dancing-in-museums-a-decade-of-movement.

Koplowitz, Stephan. 1998. *Babel Index.* British Library: Dance Umbrella.

Koplowitz, Stephan. "Babel Index - site-specific performance for the British Library (1998) Stephan Koplowitz," YouTube video, 18:16, Accessed October 06, 2021, www.youtube.com/watch?v=FlpcMqGvNmc.

Yu, Kathryn. 2018. "25 Immersive Creators and Companies to Watch in NYC." Medium. Accessed October 06, 2021. https://noproscenium.com/25-immersive-creators-and-companies-to-watch-in-nyc-4a054b10fb83.

Chapter 14

Lerman, Liz, and Borstel, John. 2003. Dance Exchange Inc. "Critical Response Process, a method for getting useful feedback on anything, from dance to dessert."

Index

Note: The italicized *f* and *t* following page numbers refer to figures and tables, respectively.

A

AAC files 111
accent lighting 107
accessibility 50-51
active speakers 113
ADA (Americans with Disabilities Act) 50-51
addenda to contracts 42
administrative tasks 134-135
aesthetic 25-26
AIFF (audio interchange file format) 111
Alvin Ailey American Dance Theater 64, 145
amendments to contracts 42
Americans with Disabilities Act (ADA) 50-51
amplifiers 112-114
apron 6*f*, 18*f*, 95*f*, 96
archiving 67
art elements 71, 73, 74, 75
artistic directors 64
artistic vision 14-16, 18-19, 25-27
arts administration 40-47
assistant choreographers 67
audiences
    overview 16-17
    experience of 149-152
    management of 185
audio editors 77
audio interchange file format (AIFF) 111
audio file types 111
audio frequency 114
auditions 84-89

B

backlights 102, 107
backstage crew 186-187
barn doors 103
blackout 108
Blu-ray 111
booms 94, 163*f*
borders 95*f*
boundary microphones (PZM) 112
bow 179
box office managers 78
box offices 184. *See also* front of house
brand 147
breakup 107
budgets
    overview 46-47
    postmortem meetings and 194
    production process and 132-133
    sample production budget 47*f*
build phase 133
bussing 165

C

cadence meetings 133
calendars 128-129, 194-195
call backs 85
campaigns 134. *See also* marketing
center line 96, 96*f*
center stage 94
choreographers 66-67, 197-198
choreography 131-132
co-choreographers 67
collaboration 4
collaborative organizational structures 38-39

color temperature 107, 162
commercial property insurance 45
communication 79-80
companies 39*f*, 40*f*, 43-44, 130*f*, 190
competitions 54-55
concept 24
concert directors 64
condenser microphones 112
consoles 112, 113*f*
construction site 98
constructive feedback 199-200
contracts 42-44, 43*f*
contributed income 52-55
co-presentation 41
copyright 45
cost-out meetings 139
costume inventory 118
costumes. *See also* makeup
    overview 9-11
    artistic vision and 26-27
    costume designers 72-73, 118-121
    design 122
    infrastructure 118-122
    integration 123, 166-168
    postmortem meetings and 195-196
    strikes and 191
costume shops 118
costume studios 119
costume supervisors 73
creation 132
creative briefs 22-27, 22*f*
crew viewing rehearsal 173
crossfades 108
crosslight 107

213

Index

crowdfunding 53
cue-to-cue rehearsals 132, 173-175
cyc lights 102, 104f
cycloramas 102

D

dance, early performances and vision 4-5
dance captains 67
dance collaborators
  assistant choreographers 67
  choreographers 66-67
  dance captains 67
  dancers 65-66
  rehearsal directors 67
  roles of 66f
dance companies 39f, 40f, 43-44, 130f, 190
dance production 65f
dancers 65-66
deck 96
deductibles 44
deliverables 41, 132
dependencies 131
design
  costumes 122
  digital media 116-117
  lighting 105-106
  makeup 122
  production process and 132-134
  scenery and props 99-100
  sound 114
design collaborators
  audio editors 77
  costume designers 72-73
  hair designers 74-75, 121-122
  lighting designers 75-76
  makeup designers 74-75, 121-122
  multimedia designers 76-77
  overview 4
  postproduction coordinators 77
  prop designers 70-71, 100
  set designers 70-77
  sound designers 77
  sound engineers 77
  streaming engineers 77
  structure of 71f

video editors 77
  visual designers 76-77
design elements 6-11, 132
designer runs 132, 140
designers. *See* design collaborators
design meetings 140
design principles 72, 73, 75, 78
deux ex machina 6
digital media
  design 116-117
  evening-length productions and 147
  festival performances and 148
  infrastructure 115-116
  integration 117, 166
  mixed bill productions and 145
directors
  artistic directors 64
  concert directors 64
  managing directors 64
  rehearsal directors 67
  technical directors 70
donations 52-53
downstage 94
drafting phase 132
dress rehearsals 180
dying fabric 166
dynamic microphones 112

E

earned income 51-52
egos 196
ellipsoidal reflector spotlight (ERS) 104-105, 104f
employees 41
end mark 96f
EQ 165
errors and omissions 45
ERS (ellipsoidal reflector spotlight) 104-105, 104f
evening-length productions 146-148
event collaborators
  box office managers 78
  front of house managers 78
  producers 78-79
  publicity creators 78
  tour managers 78-79
event costs 53

events 53-54
evocative research 22, 27
expenses 46

F

fabric dying 166
Facebook 53
fade ins and fade outs 107
feedback 199-200
festival performances 19, 54-55, 148-149, 157-158
fill lights 102
film 19-20
financial structure 35-38
flash and trash 164
flash mobs 149
flooring 97-98, 97f, 156-157
follow spots 102
for-profit organizations 38
freelance artists 39f
Fresnel lights 103, 103f
front of house 184-186
front of house managers 78
funding and fundraising. *See also* marketing
  overview 51-55
  comparisons of 54t
  production process and 134
  revenue and 51f

G

gain 165
Gantt charts 136-139, 136f-138f
gel frames 103
general liability insurance 45
gobos 102, 105, 163
GoFundMe 53
going dark 108
Google Meet 92
grand rights 46
grants 55
ground row 164
group reflection 198

H

hair
  evening-length productions and 147-148
  festival performances and 148-149

hair designers 74-75, 121-122
mixed bill productions and 145-146
strikes and 191
handheld microphones 111
heads 108
high-side lights 163
historical research 21-22
hosted events 54, 54*t*
house 94, 186. *See also* front of house
houselights 104
house managers 78
hue 162

I

improvisation 87, 88
independent artists 35-36
independent choreographers 39*f*
independent contractors 37, 41
indoor venues 157
infrastructure
    costumes 118-122
    digital media 115-116
    lighting 101-105
    makeup 118-122
    scenery and props 98-99
    sound 110
inspiration 15
installation performances 149
insurance 44-45
integration
    costumes 123, 166-168
    design elements 132
    digital media 117, 166
    lighting 106-108, 161-164
    makeup 123
    scenery and props 100-101, 158-160
    sound 114-115, 165-166
intelligent lighting 105, 162
irises 105

J

Jacob's Pillow 64
job postings 86

K

key lights 101-102
kickoffs 139

Kickstarter 53

L

lamps 101
language 79-80
lavalier microphones 112, 112*f*
LED pixel mapping 116
LED technology 102
legs 94
lens flare 103
letter of agreement (LOA) 44
liabilities 44-45
lighting
    artistic vision and 25-26
    design options 107
    effects 163
    evening-length productions and 146-147
    festival performances and 148
    Fresnel lights 103*f*
    high-side lights 163
    houselights 104
    infrastructure 101-105
    integration 106-108, 161-164
    intelligent lighting 105, 162
    key lights 101-102
    mixed bill productions and 144
    overview 7-8, 101-108
    panel lights 103
    parabolic aluminized reflector lights 102, 103*f*
    running lights 104
    sidelights 102, 107, 163
    sky cyc lights 164
    strike and 190
    strip lights 103
    three-point lighting system 102*f*
    wash lights 102-104
lighting designers 75-76
live auditions 87
livestreaming 77
LOA (letter of agreement) 44
load-in phase 133
local arts councils 55

M

makers 98
makeup. *See also* costumes

design 122
evening-length productions and 147-148
festival performances and 148-149
history of 11
infrastructure 118-122
integration 123
makeup designers 74-75, 121-122
mixed bill productions and 145-146
strikes and 191
managing directors 64
marketing. *See also* funding and fundraising
    four Ps of 56-58
    funding 51-55
    marketing plans 58-60
    press releases 59-60
    production process and 132
    publicity 59, 78
marketing plans 60*t*
Marley surfaces 97, 97*f*, 156-157
masks 11
materials 99
McGregor, Wayne 64
mediators 198-199
meetings
    cadence meetings 133
    cost-out meetings 139
    design meetings 140
    notes meetings 132, 140
    paper tech meetings 140, 175
    postmortem meetings 140-141, 194-196
    private meetings 133, 139
    production meetings 80-82, 132, 139-140
    sidebars 133, 139
memorandum of understanding (MOU) 42
merchandise 52
microphones 111-112, 111*f*, 112*f*
milestones 129-131
mixed bill productions 144-146
mixers 112, 113*f*
mood 161
MOU (memorandum of understanding) 42

Index

MP3 files 111

multimedia designers 76-77

multiple perspectives 88

music. *See* sound

music rights 45-46

N

nonprofit organizations 36-37, 55

nontraditional spaces 19

notes meetings 132, 140

O

offstage 94

onstage 94

open call auditions 85

orchestra 5

outdoor venues 157-158. *See also* festival performances

P

PA (public address) speakers 113

panel lights 103

paper tech meetings 140, 175

parabolic aluminized reflector (PAR) lights 102, 103*f*

participatory events 54, 54*t*

passive speakers 113

performance spaces 5-6, 17-21

performers 187-189

periaktoi 6

personal asks 52

personnel 41-42

photography 55-56

physical resources 195-196

place 57

planning 133, 139

plaster line 96, 96*f*

postmortem meetings 140-141, 194-196

postproduction coordinators 77

Potsdam New York Department of Theatre and Dance 99*f*

premieres 149

premiums 44

presented 40

press releases 59-60

price 57

private meetings 133, 139

producers 78-79

product 57

production

    budgets 47*f*

    languages 79-80

    modes of 40-41

    overview 4

    process 131-135

    production process and 132-134

    production schedules 128-129, 194-195

    tasks 135*f*

production collaborators

    audio editors 77

    costume designers 72-73

    hair designers 74-75, 121-122

    lighting designers 75-76

    makeup designers 74-75, 121-122

    multimedia designers 76-77

    postproduction coordinators 77

    production managers 68-69

    set designers 70-77

    sound designers 77

    sound engineers 77

    stage managers 69

    streaming engineers 77

    technical directors 70

    video editors 77

    visual designers 76-77

production leadership teams

    production managers 68-69

    stage managers 69

    structure of 68*f*

    technical directors 70

production management 66*f*, 68-69

production meetings 80-82, 132, 139-140

production riders 69

production scope

    evening-length productions 146-148

    festival performances 148-149

    installation performances 149

    mixed bill productions 144-146

    site-specific performances 149

production week 172-181

profile instruments 102, 104-105

projection mapping 116

projections 107

promotion 57-58

prompt books 140

props. *See also* scenery and sets

    evening-length productions and 147

    festival performances and 148

    mixed bill productions and 145

    moving 179

    overview 98-101

    postmortem meetings and 195-196

    prop designers 70-71, 100

    prop masters 70-71

    strikes and 190

proscenium stages 6*f*, 18, 18*f*, 95*f*

public address (PA) speakers 113

public domain law 46

publicity 59, 78. *See also* marketing

publicity creators 78

PZM (boundary microphone) 112

Q

quarter mark 96*f*

R

raked stages 96

reels 36

reflection 196-198

rehearsals

    crew viewing rehearsal 173

    cue-to-cue rehearsals 132, 173-175

    dress rehearsals 180

    overview 89-92

    rehearsal directors 67

    technical rehearsals 129, 176-180

repertory dance companies 39*f*, 40*f*, 43-44, 130*f*, 190

rep plots (repertory plots) 105

research 21-22, 27

revelation of form 161

revenue 46

riders 69

routing 165

running lights 104

S

scenery and sets. *See also* props

    evening-length productions and 147

festival performances and 148

infrastructure 98-99

integration 100-101, 158-160

mixed bill productions and 145

overview 6-7, 98-101

postmortem meetings and 195-196

scene shops 98, 99*f*

strikes and 190

scenic (set) designers 70-77

schedules

    production schedules 128-129, 194-195

    10-of-12 hour schedule 173-175

    time management and 89-90, 135-136, 173

scrims 95

seasons 150

selective focus 161

self-evaluation 196-198

self-managed events 54, 54*t*

self-producing 40

self-tape auditions 88

sets. *See* scenery and sets

SFX 165

showtime 186-187

Shure SM58 microphones 111*f*

sidebars 133, 139

sidelights 102, 107, 163

site-specific performances 19, 149

skene 5

sky cyc lights 164

snoots 103

social media 53, 56, 89

sound

    amplifiers 112-114

    artistic vision and 26

    design 114

    evening-length productions and 147

    festival performances and 148

    history of 8-9

    infrastructure 110

    integration 114-115, 165-166

    mixed bill productions and 145

    soundboards 112

    source devices 110-112

    speakers 112-114

    strike and 190

soundboards 112, 113*f*

sound designers 77

sound engineers 77

source devices 110-112

speakers 112-114

special 107

spike tape 96, 96*f*

spot 107

sprung floor 97*f*

stage left and stage right 94

stage managers 69

stage monitor speakers 113

stages

    considerations 156-158

    flooring 97-98

    overview 94-98

    proscenium stages 6*f*, 18, 18*f*, 95*f*

    raked stages 96

    thrust stages 18, 18*f*

starving artists 38

streaming 20

streaming engineers 77

strikes 132, 134, 189-191

strip lights 103

structure of a piece 25

SWOT analysis 30-35, 31*f*, 35*f*

sync rights 46

T

tax-deductible donations 52

taxes 36

teams 17

technical directors 70

technical production equipment 195-196

technical rehearsals 129, 176-180

technical riders 69

technique classes 87, 88

10-of-12 hour schedule 173-175

theatre-in-the-round 18, 18*f*

theatres

    artistic vision and 18-19

    defined 5

    styles of 18*f*

theatron 5

thematic environment 24-25

three-point lighting system 102*f*

thrust stages 18, 18*f*

ticket sales 51-52, 184

time management 89-90, 135-136, 173

top hats 103

tour managers 78-79

trees 94, 163*f*

trust 81

U

union rules 90

upstage 94

V

venues 50-51

video auditions 88

video editors 77

visibility 55-60, 161

visual designers 76-77

visual research 27

volume 110, 165

W

warm-up guidelines 178

wash 107

wash lights 102-104

WAV (waveform audio file format) 111

wings 94

workers' compensation 45

Z

Zoom 92

About the Authors

Robin Kish, MS, MFA, is an associate professor of dance at Chapman University in Orange, California, and has over 20 years experience in dance kinesiology. She earned a master of science degree in kinesiology and a master of fine arts degree in dance, allowing her to combine the fields of dance and science in her research and teaching. She mentors student choreography projects and co-teaches the Chapman University dance department's senior seminar course. She has coauthored *The Embodied Dancer: A Guide to Optimal Performance* and the second edition of *Dancing Longer, Dancing Stronger*. Robin has created unique educational content for the National Dance Education Organization's Online Professional Development Institute and the Performing Arts Medicine Association. She has been asked to contribute to 4Dancers.org, Safe in Dance International, Bridge Dance Project, and CLI. A former modern dancer and a product of the private studio and competition environment, she is passionate about bringing dancer wellness and safe teaching practices to the industry.

Wilson Mendieta, MFA, is an assistant professor of dance at Chapman University with a diverse background in theatre, dance, musical theatre, film, and television. Prior to arriving at Chapman, he served as director of the musical theater program at the University of Washington, where he also earned a master of fine arts degree in dance and a nonprofit management certificate from the Evans School of Public Affairs. A bachelor's degree in acting with a minor in dance from Montclair State University prepared Wilson for work in television and radio commercials, concert dance companies, and Broadway and off-Broadway musicals. His choreographic work has been seen throughout the United States, including at the Kennedy Center, and he has been invited to festivals in Venezuela, Colombia, and Australia. He has been invited to present at several international conferences on the topic of sustained careers for performing arts students. Wilson has served as a panelist for several arts funding organizations, including the National Endowment for the Arts.

Jennifer Backhaus, MFA, is founder and artistic director of Backhausdance, Orange County's award-winning contemporary dance company. In addition to being the energetic and creative force spearheading the development and growth of Backhausdance, she is a full-time dance faculty member at Chapman University. Jennifer holds a bachelor's degree in communications and dance from Chapman University and received her master of fine arts degree in choreography from Hollins University. From the inception of Backhausdance in 2003, Jennifer has been committed to choreographing and producing contemporary concert dance with a professional company while simultaneously designing and implementing an extensive dance education and performance program for all ages. She created and now teaches the dance production course at Chapman University. As an award-winning and in-demand choreographer, Jennifer's works have been presented by Musco Center for the Arts, Brigham Young University, Segerstrom Center for the Arts, McCallum Theatre, Los Angeles Ballet, Old Town Temecula Theatre, and The Joyce Theatre.

About the Authors

Marc Jordan Ameel, MAED, is a technical producer for global corporate events. He has worked extensively as a performing arts production manager and technical director, having experience in professional, academic, and nonprofit organizations. He holds a master's degree in adult education and distance learning from the University of Phoenix, a California teaching credential with an emphasis in educational technology, and a bachelor's degree in theatre from Arizona State University.

Samantha Waugh, BFA, is a professional dance artist and educator located in southern California. Originally from Austin, Texas, she received her bachelor's degree in dance performance from Chapman University in 2018. Passionate about arts education, Sammi has taught and created curriculum for private studios, community centers, and elementary schools across southern California. As a professional dancer, Sammi performs with Orange County's Backhausdance, both on the stage and in schools through their educational outreach programs. She has performed in many project-based festivals around the Los Angeles area and has presented her own choreographic and movement research works. In addition to assisting with the development of Backhausdance's education programs, she currently serves as director of the early childhood music and dance program at OC Music and Dance in Irvine, California.

Kerri Canedy, MFA, is a visiting assistant professor in the department of theatre and dance at the State University of New York at Potsdam. She holds a bachelor's degree in dance from California State University at Fullerton and a master of fine arts degree in dance from Smith College. She has danced, choreographed, and taught dance professionally all across the country. She has been the artistic director and production manager of 20 large-scale dance concerts and has been choreographer and assistant director for numerous theater and opera productions.

Todd Canedy, MFA, is an associate professor of design for the theatre and dance department at the State University of New York at Potsdam. Canedy previously taught and directed at Bowling Green State University, Southwestern Oklahoma State University, and Lawrence Academy in Groton, Massachusetts. He earned a bachelor's degree in communications with an emphasis on technical theatre from Chapman University and a master of fine arts degree in scenic design from California State University at Fullerton. He has worked all over the country in the theatre and dance industry. He has been working in theatre professionally for more than 30 years. While his main focus is set design, his artistic talents also include costume design, technical direction, lighting design, makeup, and scenic painting.